MW00776115

# The Politics of Technology in Africa

As more Africans get online, Information and Communication Technologies (ICTs) are increasingly hailed for their transformative potential. Yet, the fascination for the possibilities of promoting more inclusive forms of development in the information age have obfuscated the reality of the complex negotiations among political and economic actors who are seeking to use technology in their competition for power. Building on over ten years of research in Ethiopia, Iginio Gagliardone investigates the relationship between politics, development, and technological adoption in Africa's second-most populous country and its largest recipient of development aid. The emphasis the book places on the 'technopolitics' of ICTs and on their ability to embody and enact political goals, offers a strong, and empirically grounded, counter-argument to prevalent approaches to the study of technology and development, that can be applied to other cases in Africa and beyond.

IGINIO GAGLIARDONE teaches Media and Communication at the University of the Witwatersrand in South Africa, and is Associate Research Fellow in New Media and Human Rights at the University of Oxford, UK. He holds a PhD from the London School of Economics and has spent years living and working in Africa, including for UNESCO. His research focuses on the relationship between new media, political change, and human development, and on the emergence of distinctive models of the information society in the Global South. He has extensively published in communication, development studies, and African studies journals, and his work has been translated into Arabic, Chinese, French, and Italian.

# The Politics of Technology in Africa

## Communication, Development, and Nation-Building in Ethiopia

Iginio Gagliardone

University of the Witwatersrand / University of Oxford

# CAMBRIDGE
## UNIVERSITY PRESS

University Printing House, Cambridge CB2 8BS, United Kingdom

Cambridge University Press is part of the University of Cambridge.

It furthers the University's mission by disseminating knowledge in the pursuit of education, learning and research at the highest international levels of excellence.

www.cambridge.org
Information on this title: www.cambridge.org/9781107177857

First published 2016

*A catalog record for this publication is available from the British Library*

*Library of Congress Cataloging in Publication data*
Names: Gagliardone, Iginio, author.
Title: The politics of technology in Africa : communication, development, and nation-building in Ethiopia / Iginio Gagliardone.
Description: New York : Cambridge University Press, 2016. | Includes bibliographical references.
Identifiers: LCCN 2016021107 | ISBN 9781107177857 (hardback)
Subjects: LCSH: Telecommunication–Political aspects–Ethiopia. | Telecommunication–Government policy–Ethiopia. | Information technology–Political aspects–Ethiopia. | Information technology–Government policy–Ethiopia. | Ethiopia–Politics and government–1974-1991. | Ethiopia–Politics and government–1991–
Classification: LCC HE8479.Z5 G34 2016 | DDC 384.30963–dc23 LC record available at https://lccn.loc.gov/2016021107

ISBN 978-1-107-17785-7 Hardback

*To Nicole*

# Contents

# Acknowledgments

I have always been fascinated by how technology evolves and, throughout its evolution, opens new opportunities for us to understand the individuals, groups, and societies who designed and made use of it.

When I first stumbled upon one of Schoolnet's plasma TV screens in a secondary school in Addis Ababa, I could not resist but start asking questions about how that apparently costly and complex system came about, who designed it, and what else it was connected to. At the time – it was March 2005 – I did not know this book would have emerged from that first encounter, but I am still deeply fascinated by how much technology – if properly asked – can tell us about how a society thinks of itself and its future.

Along this ten-year journey I have hugely benefited from the time, advice, and wisdom of numerous people. Firstly, I want to thank the many individuals who generously agreed to sit with me and patiently explain why they did what they did, what influenced them, and what they envisioned through their activity. Especially in its initial phases, this book required collecting and trying to piece together many pieces of a puzzle only a few people were trying to solve. This meant I often had to come back to the same individuals and ask more, test with them whether an apparently promising connection was pointing in the right direction, or other avenues should be pursued instead. Some of these individuals are named throughout the book, and their words are reported as often as possible, also to offer the reader a glimpse of our meetings and conversations. Others asked to remain anonymous, but I am deeply thankful for their generosity and willingness to share their views and information with me, often in trying circumstances.

This book is also the result of many revisions and transformations and I am indebted to the people who contributed to shaping it, in one form or another. I am grateful to Robin Mansell, who offered continuous and precious feedback when this book was still a PhD thesis in the making. I also want to thank the many colleagues and readers who accessed various sections and versions of the book and provided precious comments: Christopher Clapham, Monroe Price, Emanuele Fantini, Matti Pohjonen, Sharath Srinivasan, Marco DiNunzio. I was very fortunate to be able to regularly visit Ethiopia until the very last stages of writing and to engage in numerous conversations with colleagues at Addis Ababa University and other research institutions in Ethiopia. I am particularly grateful to Zenebe Beyene and Abdissa Zerai, with whom I had the pleasure to collaborate on numerous research projects and develop a rich intellectual partnership.

Finally, I want to thank Nicole Stremlau, my partner and fellow researcher. Without her support, ideas, and encouragement, this book would probably not exist.

# 1 Introduction

On 8 November 2006, the Ethiopian Telecommunication Corporation and the Chinese telecom giant ZTE signed the largest agreement in the history of telecommunications in Africa. Backed by the China Development Bank, ZTE offered a loan of $1.5 billion to overhaul and expand Ethiopia's telecommunication system. Six years later, another $1.6 billion was entrusted to ZTE and Huawei, one of China's most successful multinational corporations, to continue the expansion, bringing Chinese government support for Ethiopia's Information and Communication Technology (ICT) sector to over $3 billion.

Despite the unprecedented investments, however, Ethiopia has continued to score at the bottom of regional and global rankings in terms of access to ICTs. In 2014, less than 3% of the population was regularly using the Internet and only 31% had a mobile phone. In neighbouring Kenya, the same figures were 43% and 74% respectively (ITU, 2015). While Chinese support has somehow contributed to expanding access (in 2006, when the contract with ZTE was signed mobile connectivity was at 1.1% of the population, making Ethiopia the country with the least access to mobiles in Africa), the quality of the service provided to customers has remained appalling, so bad in fact that even tightly controlled official government media in Ethiopia have been allowed to criticize technical glitches and incompetence.

And yet, the Ethiopian government has developed some of the most ambitious projects in Africa employing ICTs to support development and improve service delivery, even in the most remote parts of the country. Woredanet and Schoolnet, the two projects that are at the core of this book, have employed satellite connectivity and the same protocol the Internet is based upon, to expand the reach and capacity of the state over Ethiopia's vast territory. Woredanet, which stands for 'network of district (woreda) administrations' has been used to improve and straighten communication between the centre and the peripheries, enabling ministers and cadres in Addis Ababa to videoconference with regional woreda offices and instruct them on what they should be doing

1

and how. Schoolnet has used a similar architecture to ensure that every secondary school student in the country, in urban and in rural areas, has access to education of the same quality, even if this had to come in the form of pre-recorded classes broadcast through plasma TV screens.

In a country well known to the world for its food insecurity, the state has profoundly innovated how food demand and supply are matched, creating the first commodity exchange in Africa. The Ethiopian Commodity Exchange (ECX) has used ICTs to link the trading floor in Addis Ababa with grading centres, warehouses, and display sites all around the country, as well as to allow inventories to be updated in real time, payments to be made the day after purchase, and information to be provided to different audiences through the web, the radio, and mobile phones.

This commitment to investing in new technologies for development, however, has been matched by an equally strong resistance towards uses of ICTs that could challenge central power and destabilize the country. In 2005, Ethiopian protesters challenging the results of the parliamentary elections made use of new and traditional media in ways that closely resemble those that would later be reported during the 'Arab Spring', when new media received significant attention as tools for circulating slogans and coordinating protests. Similar to their peers in Tunisia and Egypt in 2011 (Wilson & Dunn, 2011), Ethiopian protesters often resorted to 'media relays', communicating information through a medium other than the one on which they had received that information from, often with the aim of reaching those who had little or no access to the newest communication technologies. Before and after the 2005 elections, commentaries and political manifestos published online were printed and turned into leaflets. Mobile phones, especially SMS, were used to mobilize people in real time and disseminate calls for action posted in web forums. Despite these types of uses of the media attracting very little international attention, they caused very harsh responses within the country. Ethiopia is now the nation in Africa that most pervasively filters the Internet and surveils communications. Most opposition websites are not accessible in Ethiopia and the use of proxies and anonymizers have been made increasingly difficult (Opennet Initiative, 2007). Companies headquartered in China, Italy, and the United Kingdom have offered equipment and expertise to the Ethiopian government to surveil communication and even spy on opposition leaders living abroad (Human Rights Watch, 2014). In April 2014, six bloggers were arrested with the accusation of 'plan[ning] to destabilize the country using social media'.

Explaining the adoption, evolution, and re-shaping of ICTs in Ethiopia therefore presents a challenging puzzle. Ethiopia has very low levels of

Internet penetration and yet some of the most severe measures in Africa to contain its destabilizing potential. It has charted new avenues of collaboration with emerging donors, especially with China, but also continues to be Africa's largest recipient of development aid from traditional, Western donors. It has championed uses of ICTs that have later appeared elsewhere in Africa, including videoconferencing for government communication in Rwanda, and ICT-enabled commodities exchanges across the continent, and yet it is considered backward when it comes to innovation and ICTs.

This book offers some solutions to this puzzle and, by examining the case of Ethiopia, sheds light on some of the complexities that have characterized the evolution of ICTs in Africa. How, and to what extent, have the visions championed by international organizations, technology entrepreneurs, and philanthropists – that ICTs could transform development processes and be a force for progress – found realization in Africa? Why have some of the discourses characterizing 'ICT for development' policy and practice been embraced while others have been actively resisted? And, more broadly, how can the innovations that have emerged in Africa, making original uses of ICTs to address local challenges, be studied and understood in their own terms?

Answers to these questions will be provided not only by engaging with the empirical material collected in Ethiopia, but also by emphasizing the role of politics in shaping technology and development. In development circles, ICTs have too often been treated as neutral tools that can optimally contribute to a set of pre-defined indicators, including supporting economic growth, enlarging the educated population, or democratizing institutions. This book challenges the assumptions that ICTs are simply passively received in African countries and act as a force for development. It suggests instead that ICTs should be analysed as sites of multiple conflicts, and understood for their ability to embed values and visions, which can be accepted or contested, and can serve to quietly, but not less effectively, enact political plans.

## Development and Politics

The optimism that emerged in the 1990s that ICTs would redefine politics has been partially eroded by the realization that traditional forms of politics are still able to shape or re-shape technology, even in countries with limited technical capabilities. The reasons for this change in attitude are both conceptual and historical. Despite having been proclaimed dead on multiple occasions, techno-determinism has consistently proven its ability to come back to life every time a new technology recognized as a game changer appears. Techno-determinists tend to shape the terms of early debates, until their faith that social problems can find technical solutions is challenged by the much slower pace at which technologically enhanced change actually occurs and by the ways in which old systems and logics adapt and thrive in new scenarios.[1]

The historical roots of this shift have been well summarized by Milton Mueller. As he has pointed out, 'the explosion of ideas, services, and expression associated with the Internet's growth in the mid-1990s happened because states weren't prepared for it and because states weren't in charge' (Mueller, 2010: 185). Since then, however, states seem to have learned their lessons and have been fighting hard to assert their control in the digital era.

While the 1990s were dominated by the 'digital divide' rhetoric, framing the new global challenge as a matter of access to the same technologies that were driving the digital revolution in parts of the Western world, the 2010s are characterized by the astonishing diversity of ways in which different countries have blended old and new technologies.

This unique combination of ICTs, politics, and culture is not new. It rather represents one of the latest incarnations in a long series of technological innovations that, despite being celebrated for their revolutionary potential, have been reshaped to fit in sociopolitical networks that are different from those of their origin, becoming both the objects and the subjects of change. Just as the configuration of electric grids in nineteenth-century Europe depended less on technical constraints than on political ideologies (Hughes, 1983), and the design of nuclear reactors in post-war France was determined by the tensions between Cold War politics and energy efficiency (Hecht, 1998), so have ICTs in the new millennium been caught up in multiple conflicts between competing conceptions of the role of technology in society.

Most studies that have examined these conflicts in developing countries, as this book does, have relied on categories and dichotomies of global relevance, such as authoritarianism vs. democracy, corruption vs. transparency, or closure vs. openness to chart this diversity. Indices ranking countries according to their e-readiness and Internet freedom

---

[1] Ithiel De Sola Pool (1983), Alvin Toffler (1980), and Nicholas Negroponte (1995), for example, have been instrumental in shaping the imagery of the information revolution before empirical evidence could offer an indication of the actual impact of ICTs. For a more critical account of techno-determinism see, for example, Hindman (2008) and Morozov (2012).

have proliferated.[2] This approach has allowed comparisons to be made across nations and regions (Groshek, 2009; Howard, 2010), and the mapping of new trends, including correlations between diffusion of ICTs and political behaviours (Bratton, 2013; Nisbet, Stoycheff, & Pearce, 2012). Privileging these typologies, however, has also meant overlooking what is unique in the interactions between specific political cultures and new communication technologies: for example, how a government's conception of citizenship or of the nation may influence the adoption and adaptation of ICTs; or how 'democratic' change may occur through processes and institutions that are different from those characterizing Western democracies but express other conceptions of governmentality.

This book advances a different set of tools to study why ICTs are being re-shaped across the globe and focuses on national politics and discourses, those arousing people's passions and informing national debates, to explain the adoption and adaptation of technology. This does not mean suggesting other dimensions or approaches should be dismissed as irrelevant. As the Ethiopian case makes clear, the authoritarian nature of the country's government can explain why it has been able to realize its vision of ICTs and marginalize alternative ones, but, alone, can say little of the specific shape ICTs have taken at the national level.

## Ethiopia as a Laboratory

Contemporary Ethiopia offers challenging puzzles not just to those studying technology adoption and adaptation, but to any researcher interested in understanding the relationship between development and politics. Since the Ethiopian People's Revolutionary Democratic Front (EPRDF) took power in 1991, after almost two decades of civil war, the country has embarked on a series of ambitious experiments at the economic, political, and institutional levels that have produced dramatically divergent views on the failures and successes of the new regime.

Similar to post-genocide Rwanda (Fisher, 2015; Hintjens, 2014), it has become increasingly common to come across articles, reports, and commentaries on Ethiopia that seem to be referring not to the same, but to two different countries. One is a closed, authoritarian state, governed through fear by an ethnic minority. The other Ethiopia is a

---

[2] See for example Freedom House's *Freedom on the Net* Index (https://freedomhouse.org/issues/internet-freedom) or the World Economic Forum's Networked Readiness Index (www.weforum.org/reports/global-information-technology-report-2014). Last accessed 21 December 2014.

developmental state that has achieved sustained 'double digit' growth and has significantly improved access to basic services.[3]

The discourses on 'ethnic federalism', 'revolutionary democracy', and 'developmental state', which are discussed at length throughout the book, have been one of the sources of this polarization. They each define a different aspect of the EPRDF's complex state- and nation-building strategy, informing Ethiopia's institutional set-up, mode of government, and economic policy. But they all share a similar origin as locally driven attempts to adapt development strategies derived from other countries considered similar to Ethiopia, displaying a tendency towards emulation that has characterized many Ethiopian regimes in the past (Clapham, 2006). Framed by the EPRDF as non-negotiable principles informing its complex plan of state transformation, they have produced strong resistance at the national level, and scepticism among international observers.

Different from other governments in Africa, whose policies have more amply swayed to follow the trends that have characterized the international development agenda, the EPRDF-led government has aggressively protected its independence in defining core aspects of its political and development strategy. This does not mean Ethiopian leaders have been deaf towards all donors' demands and international pressures. The Ethiopian government has shown, for example, significant commitment towards the United Nations' Millennium Development Goals, and has been praised for its progress in attaining most of them by or before the agreed deadline (UNDP, 2015). What the EPRDF has sought to achieve is a delicate balance between loyalty to the principles that have shaped the guerrilla war that eventually led it to power, many of which are rooted in Marxist-Leninist doctrine, and adaptation to pressures deriving from its status of one of the largest recipients of development aid in the world.

This effort has produced a distinctive development trajectory, but has also led to dramatic contradictions. The evolution of the EPRDF's strategy towards the media is a striking example. When the EPRDF first

---

[3] While in the case of Rwanda, polarized views have dominated both policy and scholarly debates (Fisher, 2015; Hintjens, 2014), in Ethiopia this divergence has affected more the former than the latter. Exchanges like those that followed the death of Prime Minister Meles Zenawi suggest competing views do exist among scholars also (de Waal, 2013a, 2013b; Lefort, 2013), but a middle ground has emerged among those who have been writing about Ethiopia, or at least a willingness to engage with the many contradictions that have characterized the project pursued by the EPRDF. Many authors that have sought to build this common terrain are mentioned throughout the book, belonging to different generations, from Christopher Clapham, to Sarah Vaughan, Paulos Chanie, and Jean-Nicholas Bach.

came to power it committed what could retrospectively be identified as the 'original sin' in the contemporary history of communication in Ethiopia: it opened the space for debate but refused to engage with the very debates it had allowed to bloom.

Responding to international pressures and to the determination to signal, nationally and internationally, its difference from previous regimes, the EPRDF initiated a significant liberalization of the press. This process, however, created opportunities for individuals who used to work for the previous regimes or belonged to other political movements the EPRDF had excluded from power, to attack the new leaders and advance alternative political agendas. Although the criticism took on an increasingly adversarial tone, the EPRDF leadership stuck to its policy, ignoring dissenting voices and labelling them as 'anti-peace' and 'anti-constitution'.[4] This polarization and unwillingness to seeking engagement would later poison also the debates emerging on the Internet, leading 'old politics' to capture 'new media'.

## A History of the Future

ICT for development scholars and practitioners are generally interested not only in the current applications of ICTs but also their future potential. They tend to begin with an assessment of a set of challenges and consider how technology can offer a possible solution (but in some not too exceptional cases it can also work the other way around, and technology becomes a solution in search of a problem). Or they may start from a normative standpoint – e.g. the need for an unrestricted flow of information – and envision how technology may help enforcing it. This tendency has had the advantage of offering citizens, both in developed and in developing countries, new ways of imagining the future. It has similarly had the disadvantage of overlooking the friction created by existing imbalances of power and the influence of the communication ecology in which new artefacts become immersed.

To keep past, present, and future together, this book combines insights from three scholarly traditions that take into account both how experiences with previous technologies influence the adoption or rejection of later ones and how new technologies enable individuals and groups to envision and shape their world. First, it is grounded in the work of historians of technology who have examined technologies of national relevance and scale and the systems of relations in which technology is

---

[4] See, for example, *The Ethiopian Herald*, 'Editorial', 6 June 1991, p. 7.

immersed. The concepts of *large technical systems, technopolitics,* and *technopolitical regimes* are incorporated in the study of ICTs to counterbalance the lack of attention paid by ICT for development studies to the systemic nature of new technologies; to their being a component, often the most visible, of larger networks of national and international institutions, corporations, laws, political parties, and information carriers, which are strongly influenced by existing imbalances in the distribution of power and resources. These notions help to take the dialectical understanding of the relationship between technology and organizations developed by information system theorists (Orlikowski, 1992; Suchman, 1994) to a level that analyses interactions among technology, governments, and other political actors who are attempting to influence technology adoption and adaptation nationally and internationally.

A second building block in the analysis of the relationship between technology, politics, and development is constituted by the studies of networks carried out by scholars of international relations. Miles Kahler (2009), Margaret Keck and Kathryn Sikkink (1998), and Milton Mueller (2010), among others, have explored how ideas diffuse at the international level and how they are embraced or resisted by national actors. Examining the discourses embedded in new technologies and how groups or institutions advocate their selection is an essential step in understanding why and how ICTs are accepted, rejected, or reshaped. Looking at these discourses shows how technology is a means not only to do new things or do things differently, but also to promote new forms of imagination.

Finally, the African studies literature provides the instruments to take into adequate consideration the dynamics that characterize political competition and processes of state and nation building on the continent. The literature on contemporary Ethiopia constitutes a cornerstone for the analysis of how a political project became embedded into technical artefacts (Aalen, 2002; Assefa & Tegegne, 2007; Gudina, 2003; Ottaway, 2003; Pausewang et al., 2002; Stremlau, 2008; Tegegne, 1998; Turton, 2006; Young, 1997), but other studies on the role and behaviour of the state in Africa help explain the relationship with donors, the international community and other stakeholders competing for power, and for the hegemony of their ideas. The concept of extraversion elaborated by Jean Francois Bayart (2009; 2000) is adopted to understand how the Ethiopian government has been able to exploit the contradictions characterizing the development agenda to support its own political ambitions. Similarly, the literature on developmental states in Africa (Booth & Golooba-Mutebi, 2012; De Waal, 2012; Kelsall, 2013; Leftwich, 1995; Mkandawire, 2001) offers a critical framework to understand how Ethiopia, but also other countries on the continent, Rwanda in particular, have progressively elaborated a state-centric vision of the information society.

Benefiting from debates in different disciplines, this book also aims to reach different audiences. ICT for development scholars are the primary target but, by using lenses developed by Africanists, historians, and International Relations (IR) scholars, this book aims to engage them on a new terrain, where there are fewer concerns about what technology can do for development, and more attention is paid to understanding the conflictual process through which ICTs are already shaped and re-shaped by a variety of actors in developing countries. The analysis of technologies of international relevance can also offer new insights to IR scholars concerned with understanding the interactions between international and local norms and ideas. The focus in this area has largely been on the reasons that motivate a successful or unsuccessful socialization of local actors to new ideas, but fewer questions have been asked about how these ideas can be reworked in practice. Looking at how discourses are embedded into technical artefacts allows a better understanding of which aspects of these artefacts are magnified, which are marginalized, and how they integrate with existing ones in more or less coherent ways. Historians of technology, for their part, have provided powerful tools to study what at different times have been called *new* technologies (Wu, 2010), but, despite some exceptions, their research has often been limited to processes of innovation rather than the transfer of technology. Studying the relationship between international and national actors when implementing a 'new technology' can open new scenarios to understand which forces are at play when a technology is inserted into contexts that are profoundly different from those of its origin. Africanists, apart from few exceptions (Hyden, Leslie, & Ogundimu, 2002; Nyamnjoh, 2005; Stremlau, 2012), have kept their distance from ICTs, and when they have included them in their analysis they have tended to treat ICTs as something to be understood through frameworks that are different from those that have been successfully adopted to explain the politics of the continent.

## Exploring Technical Artefacts and Technological Visions

This book has taken shape over almost ten years. My first visits to secondary schools where Schoolnet had been installed date back to the early months of 2005. The conversations with the Ethiopian bloggers who have been seeking to use the Internet to create a space for engagement in an otherwise very polarized environment have continued until the very last draft of this book. Overall, more than one hundred interviews were carried out with the politicians and technocrats who envisioned and realized Woredanet and Schoolnet as well as with journalists, opposition leaders, and members of national and international NGOs and of international organizations who practiced and advocated uses of ICTs that tried to oppose, patch, or complement those advanced by the government of Ethiopia. Over time new actors started to appear in the complex ecosystem created by ICTs in Ethiopia. From Chinese engineers working on the ZTE and Huawei expansion projects, to experts of cybersecurity trying to detect the techniques used by the Ethiopian government to spy on Ethiopians in the country and abroad, and disenchanted technocrats who had grown progressively tired of the centralized approach towards developing Ethiopia's information society. I sought to include all their voices in the narration of the evolution of ICTs in Ethiopia; but I also had to leave some of them anonymous, given the sensitivity of some subjects.

I conducted numerous field visits to Woredanet and Schoolnet sites in the regions of Tigray, Amhara, Oromiya, and the Southern Nations Nationalities and People (SNNPR) to understand how the two systems operated in practice and how their users perceived them. This evidence was complemented by the collection of archival material in the form of policies, project documents, newspapers articles, and blog entries.

The most challenging and fascinating component of the research has been reconstructing how certain visions of technology's potential and its risks influenced technology adoption and adaptation. This was achieved through a process of iterative comparison between concepts emerging from interviews and other textual material (e.g. field notes, project documents), and observations of how technical artefacts actually took shape. This going 'back and forth' between the technical and the discursive not only allowed capturing the conflicts emerging throughout the process of technological appropriation, how technology could incorporate specific political plans despite the frequent claims of its neutrality, but also forced political actors to reconsider their visions and ambitions.

## Plan of the Book

The book is divided into eight chapters. The next chapter introduces the concepts of technopolitics and technopolitical regimes, and explains how they can offer innovative lenses to understand the relationship between development, technology, and politics. Chapters 3 and 4 examine the discourses that influenced the appropriation and adaptation of ICTs in Ethiopia. Chapter 3 analyses the discourses advanced by the international organizations that played the most important role in 'bringing' ICTs to Ethiopia and the reactions they produced among various local actors. In addition to illustrating how the same technologies could produce a variety of interpretations, the chapter also roots these interpretations in long-term paths of technology adoption that characterized how rulers in Ethiopia approached the telephone, the radio, and the first computers. It concludes by indicating how local actors, other than the state, were marginalized in their attempts to influence the trajectory of ICTs in the country, leaving the government as the major player in making ICTs what they later became in Ethiopia. Chapter 4 examines more specifically the discourses advanced by the Ethiopian government that have influenced the development of ICTs in the country. Similar to the previous chapter, it does not concentrate exclusively on the present, but engages in a longer term analysis of how these discourses originated, dating back from when the current leaders were fighting against the military dictatorship of the Derg which ruled Ethiopia between 1974 and 1991, and evolved, interacting with new challenges and new opportunities.

Chapters 5 and 6 turn to more technical aspects. Chapter 5 investigates how a developmental and a sovereign technopolitical regime emerged in Ethiopia. It analyses the design and functioning of Woredanet and Schoolnet, explaining how specific features characterizing the two systems were not simply motivated by technical issues, but were the enactments of political goals through the use of technology. It also explains how the shaping of telecommunications in Ethiopia and the resistance towards the liberalization of the sector and towards potentially destabilizing uses of ICTs was rooted in the discourses on ethnic federalism, revolutionary democracy, and the developmental state analysed in the previous chapters. Chapter 6 analyses the technopolitical regimes that actors other than the state tried to develop in order to oppose, complement, or patch the national regimes. These attempts, and some of artefacts and practices they originated, indicate how political conflicts can be fought through technology.

Chapter 7 analyses the most recent evolutions of technopolitics in Ethiopia, including the repercussions of the unprecedented support provided by China to telecommunications in Ethiopia and of the increasing securitization of development, which has characterized the approach of Western donors, especially in the aftermath of the terrorist attacks of September 11, 2001.

Chapter 8 concludes by reflecting on how the concepts of technopolitics and technopolitical regimes can be applied to other cases of technological re-shaping, in developing and developed countries. It uses the trajectory of ICTs in Ethiopia to chart broader changes that have affected communication, politics, and development in Africa, from the ability of states to regain control over ICTs and asserting sovereignty in the information space to the shifting balance between human rights and development.

# 2 Technopolitics, Communication Technologies, and Development

*The emphasis on policy issues as technical issues [has led to] a narrowing of acceptable topics for public debate. This amounts to the "depoliticizing" of public life, such that much political debate becomes merely a war among competing experts, or an exercise in the manipulation of symbols, a wholly theatrical celebration of rival images and icons, all rather than a collective and substantive deliberation about a common societal direction.*

*(Pippin, 1995, p. 44)*

Literature on the politics of technology abounds, and yet the popular discourse on new technologies tends to overlook this aspect and privilege describing the functions technology can serve, as if there was consensus on what technology should be for, and it was just issues of efficiency that need being discussed among experts.[1]

Studying ICTs as components of technopolitical regimes, on the contrary, means taking into consideration how technology can become an instrument of politics, and how political ambitions interact with technological opportunities and constraints and evolve as a result of this interaction. It forces the researcher to 'plunge' into the technical artefact (Callon, 2009) and question technological determinism, while avoiding the excesses of social constructivism, which lead to explaining technology simply through analysing a society and its politics.

A technopolitical regime is both the medium and the outcome of a negotiation between a specific technology, a cultural and political context, and the actors that animate it and compete for power. It 'consists of a configuration of heterogeneous elements, combining mainly technical materialities, discourses, texts, rules, procedures, plans [...] – the list is open – which are rendered mutually interdependent and support

---

[1] For an overview of the subject on the politics of technology, from large technical systems (LTS) to ICTs see for example Bijker, Hughes, & Pinch (1987), Feenberg (1991, 1999), Hecht (2001), Hughes (1983), Joerges (1988), Mansell & Silverstone (1996), Pippin (1995), Weinberger (2001), Winner (1980), Wu (2010).

one another' (Callon, 2009, p. xiii). A technopolitical regime is not a construct 'discovered' by an observer, but is rather the result of layers of decisions made by actors tied to denser or looser networks, and employing technology to achieve political goals in ways that politics alone would not allow.

The emergence of a technopolitical regime is not a linear process. It is the result of conflicts between conceptions of technology and society, actors competing to assert power, and technological artefacts resisting or allowing change to flow through them. As Joseph Schumpeter (1954) first explained, and Tim Wu more recently reminded us, 'innovation involves a continuous state of unrest, is no benignly gradual process, but a merciless cycle of destruction and birth' (Wu, 2010, p. 27). Referring to these assemblages of technology, discourses, and actors as regimes is meant to capture this conflictual nature. In Hecht's definition, regime indicates the contested nature of power, the ideologies guiding the actors who drive them, and conveys the idea of a regimen, a prescription not just about technologies, policies, and practices, but also about broader visions of the sociopolitical order (Hecht, 1998, p. 18).

The term technopolitical regime was first introduced by Gabrielle Hecht to examine the relationship between nuclear power and national identity in France (Hecht, 1998, 2001) and here I extend it to the study of ICTs at a macro level, as technologies of national relevance and scale. Given the unique nature of ICTs, the temptation to coin a new term such as informational or info-political regime has been strong, but has ultimately been discarded. A focus on information alone would risk downplaying the important technical component of these assemblages. Even more importantly, applying a concept grounded in the history of technology tradition to the study of ICT and development may encourage researchers to take a longer view in the analysis of 'new technologies', counterbalancing the lack historical depth that has characterized Information and Communication Technology for Development (ICT4D) as a discipline.

When studying technopolitical regimes based on ICTs, however, one element does need special attention. These regimes produce a particular type of outcome: information and meaning. As Robin Mansell and Roger Silverstone pointed out, echoing Giddens (1984), in the technological realm ICTs are unique as 'they are characterized by their double articulation: they are both machines and media' (Mansell & Silverstone, 1996, p. 9). Technopolitical regimes built around ICTs are not just invested with meaning, as discourses filter in and shape technologies (as well as being shaped by technologies). Nor do they simply produce meaning by virtue of the place they occupy in a specific narrative they contribute to maintaining (as shown by the role of nuclear plants in the French project of grandeur described by Hecht or by the many references to ICTs as 'liberation technologies' in the process of democratization of politics and individual empowerment). They are 'the means (the media) whereby public and private meanings are mutually negotiated' (Silverstone et al. in Mansell & Silverstone, 1996, p. 28). The content that is, or can be, conveyed through a specific regime is its constitutive component.

To sum up, a technopolitical regime can be considered as constituted of three coexisting and interrelated components, which can each be studied as networks of similar elements: a network of technologies, a network of discourses, and a network of actors. A technopolitical regime connects in actuality nodes in each of these networks that are potentially connected with other technologies, discourses, and actors. It can be thought of as a network of networks. Once the links among these nodes are strengthened in ways that make each node part of a more cohesive whole (a technopolitical regime), these nodes start to influence one another, or, more precisely, their more frequent and significant interactions are more likely to influence all nodes that are part of a technopolitical regime.

## Networks of Technologies

Thomas Hughes (Hughes, 1983) was the first to clearly illustrate how the 'same' technology can take on different shapes in different locations. He described this phenomenon by borrowing the concept of style from art historians, emphasizing the possibility of variations of the same technology across cultural and political environments. In the case of electrification, for example, he explained how the distribution of power plants in London and Berlin differed for no particular technical reasons, but responded to differences in the political and regulatory regimes of each country; conservative Britain, where particularistic interests prevailed over the ability of central power to regulate the market, and socially democratic Germany where the state took a greater role as a champion of electrification (Hughes, 1983).

Even within the same country, different regimes may emerge and compete for the definition of a technology's standards and uses. In the case of Hecht's research on France's nuclear programme between the 1950s and the 1970s, for example, she identified the emergence of two regimes, one nationalist and one nationalized, focussed on a different set of goals, grounded in different institutions, and pursuing a different kind of politics (Hecht, 1998). The 'same' technology was captured by competing actors and discourses, profoundly affecting the way it was used and the shape it took.

The number and nature of technopolitical regimes cannot be defined a priori, although it is possible to reconstruct their features and purposes through investigating the distribution of power in a given national context, the discourses permeating it, and the actors advancing these interests. As will be fully explained later, a technopolitical regime is both the expression of how power is distributed in a particular national context as well as an instrument for the exercise of power.

Historians of technology have identified in the problem-solving capacity of a technopolitical regime what distinguishes it from less coherent assemblages of technology and politics. As Hughes described, referring to large technical systems (LTS), a concept that pre-dates the notion of technopolitical regime and was similarly employed to refer to the interconnectedness between the technical, the social, and the political, 'technological systems solve problems or fulfil goals using whatever means are available and appropriate; the problems have to do mostly with reordering the physical world in ways considered useful or desirable, at least by those designing or employing a technological system' (Hughes, 1987, p. 53). This does not mean they do it successfully. Technopolitical regimes, as well as LTS, often develop in messier and more complex ways than originally expected; they have negative externalities, and are difficult to control and coordinate. Quite ironically, as pointed out by Joerges, 'retrospective studies of LTS show that they never develop according to the designs and projections of dominant actors: LTS evolve behind the backs of the system builders' (Joerges, 1988, p. 26). However, because of their scale and scope, they tend to evolve even against the odds of their complexity, in ways smaller artefacts might not do. Railway systems or grids of nuclear plants would be much more difficult to dispose of than smaller technical objects, and would tend to be patched or rethought, rather than abandoned if problems arose.[2]

## Networks of Discourses

The disciplines that have examined the relationship between technologies and societies, from the sociology to the history of technology, from information systems to media studies, have tended to approach technologies both in terms of their material and discursive components.

---

[2] Another way of looking at LTS/technopolitical regimes has been to consider them as mega-projects, which can be considered as large-scale investments attracting significant public attention because of substantial impacts on communities, environment, and budgets. For the literature on mega-projects see for example Bruzelius, Flyvbjerg, & Rothengatter (2002) and Flyvbjerg, Bruzelius, & Rothengatter (2003).

This discursive element of technology can be appreciated in two different, but interrelated and co-present, ways.

First, discourses are what invest the material world with meaning (Laclau & Mouffe, 1985)., meanings are attached to artefacts as descriptions, manuals, and texts, telling users about the appropriate ways of operating a specific technical object. In many cases a technology, when it is marketed or when it is proposed, as has initially been the case for ICTs in developing countries, is not even visible. Only the potentials and expected uses described by the advocates of its application are. As Pinch, Ahmore, and Mulkay have pointed out, 'technologies are often made available through texts, and the meaning given to a technology through such texts can vary from context to context (and/or audience to audience) [. . .] It is only by close attention to the different discursive contexts in which these definitions are offered and an examination of the rhetoric of technology that we can begin to understand the full richness of its multifaceted and interpretative nature' (Pinch, Ashmore, & Mulkay, 1992, p. 242). For the same technology, a multiplicity of possible discourses exists, and the formulation of these discourses is not the exclusive right of inventors or advocates. A new technology can be inserted into a different discursive realm that may develop different interpretations of its nature and use. Discourses are always in competition, looking for a closure that should make a certain meaning prevalent and others hardly possible. This is the reason why some actors can interpret the same technology, the Internet for example, as liberating, while others interpret it as a threat. It is by investigating different discursive realms that these competing readings can be assessed.

A second, more defining, aspect of the discursive nature of technologies rests on the fact that they are not simply material elements, as a stone or a tree are, that need to be invested with discourses to acquire meaning. Because of their very nature as products of human activity, technologies also embed discourses that are enabling and constraining at the same time. Langdon Winner (1980) and numerous authors in the Actor Network Theory (ANT) tradition (see, for example, Latour, 1992, 2005; Law & Hassard, 1999) have illustrated how certain prescriptions can be inserted into objects and work as well, if not better, than norms or warnings. Similarly, with the notion of technopolitics Gabrielle Hecht emphasized how technologies could represent a particular way to perform politics, allowing actors to reach goals that would not be attainable otherwise. As she explained:

I use the term [technopolitics] to refer to the strategic practice of designing or using technology to constitute, embody, or enact political goals. Here I define technology broadly to include artifacts as well as nonphysical, systematic means of making or doing things. [...] Calling these hybrids "politically constructed technologies" is correct; however, it is not sufficient, because technologists intended them as tools in political negotiations. At the same time, these technologies are not, in and of themselves, technopolitics. Rather, the practice of using them in political processes and/or toward political aims constitutes technopolitics. Why not just call that practice "politics"? The answer lies in the material reality of the technologies. These technologies cannot be reduced to politics. The effectiveness of technologies as objects designed to accomplish real material purposes matters – among many other reasons – because the material effectiveness of technologies can affect their political effectiveness, (Hecht, 2001, pp. 256–257)

In the study of technopolitical regimes, and especially of regimes emerging from the diffusion of technologies of global relevance and scale, this duality of technology is taken into account by framing technologies and discourses as two complementary and co-present elements through which societies may change and may aim at changing other societies. In the following chapters discourses will thus be considered both as concepts competing for hegemony, in the Gramscian sense of an internalized set of assumptions which progressively define the common sense (De Waal, 2012; Gramsci, 1975; Laclau & Mouffe, 1985; Mkandawire, 2001), and as they interact and become embedded into technological artefacts.

### Networks of Actors

Technologies and discourses do not emerge and spread by themselves but need actors to create, assert, and spread them. Discourses may resonate with one another to varying degrees, or clash and antagonize one another. Likewise, technologies may encounter acceptance or resistance. The particular fit a technology finds in a country is not simply 'there' as the result of a static combination between given technologies and given discourses. It has to be constructed by international or local actors or, more often, by both.

The growing scholarship on networks in comparative politics and in international relations has largely interpreted networks as coalitions of actors coming together, in more or less organized ways, to support a specific issue or set of issues. Martha Finnemore's (1996) research on science bureaucracies and Peter Haas' (1992) analysis of epistemic communities both illustrate how discourses are supported by groups or institutions – 'active teachers' in Finnemore's terminology – advocating their selection. Margaret Keck and Kathryn Sikkink's (1998) seminal work on transnational advocacy networks has shed light on the conditions under which coalitions of civil society organizations succeed in placing new issues on national and international agendas.

At the domestic level, numerous studies have explored which factors favour or limit the diffusion of new ideas, policies, and norms (Checkel, 1997, 2001; Green, 2002; Kahler, 2009; Keck & Sikkink, 1998; Klotz, 2002; Risse-Kappen, 1994). These works stress how the actual forms that new discourses take on at the local level depend on the relationships and power distribution among competing actors, as well as on the historical trajectory and political culture of a nation. To become effective, discourses (though the same argument can be extended to technologies) need to find agents that endorse them and have the power to enact them on the ground. Or, following a different path, an actor may choose to ride over a discourse (or a technology) that is gaining national or international attention to increase its visibility or power over other actors. In most cases it is not simply one actor – a ministry, a company, or an NGO – that has the power or capacity to perform this task alone, and winning coalitions need to be formed.

In the case of ICTs this process is further complicated by their material component. The fit needs to be found both at the discursive and at the material level. It can be an impossibility to unlock and reshape a particular technology considered to be both useful and harmful by an authoritarian government that prevents its acceptance, until the development of a greater capacity to control it opens the door to its reception. In a country like China, for example, the increase in the number of Internet users has coincided with an increase in the capacity of the central government to prevent specific uses while favouring others (Yang, 2013; Zhao, 2008). It can be argued that in the absence of such a technical capacity, a similar diffusion might not have happened, or perhaps not at the same pace.

Coalitions of actors, similar to assemblages of technological artefacts, are not all the same or equal, and the modes in which they are designed (or lack a conscious design and administration) along with how the nodes that compose them relate to one another, are indicative of different types of groupings. Milton Mueller (2010) has explored this difference in ways that are particularly useful for the analysis of technopolitical regimes. In his study on the global politics of the Internet, he distinguished between network organizations, which are 'bounded and consciously arranged' and whose 'actors [...] design the relationship among a bounded set of individuals or organizations to pursue a common objective'; and associative clusters, 'de facto clusters' that have 'no single point of administration [and] may have different and even conflicting objectives but may nevertheless engage in sustained interaction' (Mueller, 2010, p. 42). Similar to analyses in the technological realm, one of the criteria to identify and separate a cohesive network (be it a technopolitical regime or a network organization) from the myriad of connections its nodes create outside of it, is the consciousness of its design being purposefully created to solve a specific problem. As indicated above when discussing networks of technologies, this characteristic alone does not imply success, as more loosely connected networks may be more successful in reaching a given goal, but it can have implications on how a network endures, capitalizes on its successes, and achieves momentum.

## The Space of Power

In *Networks of Power*, his major work on electrification, Thomas Hughes explained how 'one of the primary characteristics of a system builder is the ability to construct or to force unity from diversity, centralization in the face of pluralism, and coherence from chaos. This construction often involves the destruction of alternative systems' (Hughes, 1987, p. 52). Different technopolitical regimes can coexist and continue to compete for extended periods of time, or the battle for the control of a particular technology can, on the contrary, end with the destruction or marginalization of alternative ones.

Power, both as embedded in artefacts and as exercised by social actors, is ultimately what leads a particular technopolitical regime to eventually fail and another to thrive in a given context. Technical artefacts constantly interact with the political and social forces that surround them and bear with them the results of this relationship. As Allen and Hecht elaborate, the title of Hughes's book, *Networks of Power* has a double meaning:

Electricity drives machines, light bulbs, and tramways, but at the same time its constant flux in networks reflects and makes tangible the political life of nation-states. Thus electrical networks are "charged" with corruption in Chicago, with localism in London, and with centralized social democracy in Berlin. (Allen & Hecht, 2001, p. 2)

Technical artefacts do not simply adapt, but also act as vehicles for exercising power. As Allen and Hecht continue:

Social choices shape technological development. But the resulting physical, financial, and institutional durability of systems means that, once developed, they – and the values they uphold – cannot be changed easily. As material manifestations of human choices, systems acquire momentum. In so doing they embody, reinforce, and enact social and political power. Thus, human power rides upon the history of things. (Allen & Hecht, 2001, pp. 2–3)

Power thus has to be understood as a force flowing through the social and the technical, establishing and performing authority by making specific meanings more widely accepted than others and certain assemblages more likely than alternative ones. Power is not eminently social or technical, but it is only through its performance that its role and nature can be understood as constitutive or constraining, constructive or destructive.

A technopolitical regime is not the benign result of any combination of technologies, discourses, and actors. It is the space occupied by the powerful. It requires a legitimate space from which it can operate and capitalize on its growth. Borrowing terminology from French historian and philosopher Michel De Certeau (1984), it can be said that while ICTs can be used both strategically and tactically, a technopolitical regime is the result of the former rather than the latter mode of operation. In De Certeau's definition, strategies demand locations of power, define what is proper and legitimate, set norms and sanctions, and aim to remain conclusive. They are able to circumscribe a place that can be used as a basis to generate relations with an exterior that is distinct from it (e.g. a competitor or a client), and to measure, include, and control foreign forces and objects. On the contrary, tactics are courses of actions that lack power and are employed to achieve short-term aims. They play with resources and norms owned by an adversary and, as they occur within its 'field of vision', they can be observed and sanctioned by it.

De Certeau developed these concepts to explore the possibilities of individuals and groups subverting an order that overwhelms them. Referring to the relationship between Spanish colonizers and the colonized, for example, he illustrated how the latter were able to use 'laws, practices, and representations that were imposed on them by force or by fascination to ends other than those of their conquerors; they made something else out of them; they subverted them from within – not by rejecting them or by transforming them (though that occurred as well), but by many different ways of using them in the service of rules, customs or convictions foreign to the colonization which they could not escape' (De Certeau, 1984, p. 32). His analysis can be extended to other relations that involve an imbalance of power, like those involving a weak actor (who has to resort to tactics, at least temporarily) and a strong one (who has the opportunity to develop a strategy), be it an individual interfacing with his own government, or a government with a more powerful international order. The censorship of a blog by a government is a tactic when it is a temporary measure in the face of an imminent threat and can be sanctioned by a higher order as illegal. It can also become a strategy when it is grounded in a norm that circumscribes a space as legitimate and recognized by that higher order (e.g. when the censoring is justified by the need to prevent ethnic violence and endures over time). Similarly, the use of the Internet to challenge a regime and denounce its wrongdoings is a tactic when the regime remains in control, even if it is forced to make concessions. But it too can become a strategy, if for example it forces that regime to institutionalize the practice of publishing all public acts online and create a proper space where citizens can legitimately obtain and demand information. Being able to distinguish a practice as a tactic or a strategy is important in understanding where power lies and where it may shift. In the particular case of technopolitical regimes, it is essential to understand whether or not an assemblage of technologies, discourses, and actors have the potential to endure and acquire momentum, or to lose impetus and eventually fade.

## Technopolitics, ICTs, and Development

Despite the claims of the transformative potentials of ICTs, and the multiple conflicts that technologically driven change produces, the concepts of technopolitics and technopolitical regimes have not yet been applied to study the relationship between ICTs and development. The following chapters represent a first attempt to making the connection, explaining how power has been exercised in Ethiopia through the use of technology, and how a certain vision of the state and of the nation have found concrete expression in specific assemblages of technologies, discourses, and actors, while preventing the emergence of alternative technopolitical regimes.

Examining how Ethiopia became the site of multiple conflicts over the appropriation and application of ICTs also offers the opportunity to explore how these conflicts reflected broader tensions that have emerged at the international level. After an initial phase in which the Internet has eroded national boundaries and offered connected citizens the possibility to communicate irrespective of their nationality and physical location, have now states managed to regain control over the national information space? What are the forces that have led to this outcome, and how have they interacted? How new entrants in the ICT4D space, from a more outward-looking China to global corporations such as Facebook whose power and influence have been equated to those of states (MacKinnon, 2012), have related to existing ones, and in which direction they have contributed to move the ICT4D agenda?

# 3    Avoiding Politics
## International and Local Discourses on ICTs

> *Greater production is the key to prosperity and peace, and the key to greater production is a wider and more vigorous application of modern scientific and technical knowledge.*                    *(Harry Truman, 1949)*
>
> *In the service of national development the mass media are agents of social change. [. . .] The mass media can create a climate for development.*
> *(Wilbur Schramm, 1964)*
>
> *Information and Communication Technologies (ICTs) have an immense impact on virtually all aspects of our lives. The rapid progress of these technologies opens completely new opportunities to attain higher levels of development.*                    *(World Summit on the Information Society, 2003)*

Since the coining of the term 'development', technology has been framed as one of the main forces that should lead to 'the improvement and growth of underdeveloped areas' (Truman, 1949), and communication technologies have occupied a special place as part of this endeavour. With each era came new innovations, and with each new innovation came the expectation that it could eventually help attain the results previous technologies had been unable to achieve.

The evolution of these efforts and of the debates on the opportunities and mistakes of applying ICTs to development have been comprehensively mapped in important works (Heeks, 2002; Sparks, 2007) and it is not my plan to retrace it here. What this chapter seeks to highlight, however, is a common thread that has characterized the history of ICTs for development: the de-politicization of conceptions of technology. This refers to the tendency, inaugurated by modernization theorists in the 1950s but still noticeable in many ICT for development projects today, to treat development challenges as technical problems in need of a technical solution (e.g. better training, more outlets, greater access, etc.) or to hail ICTs as neutral tools that can be employed to address other social issues (e.g. improve accountability, extend education, etc.).

Ethiopia is a good example of the modes, implications, and failures of de-politicizing technology, of how, despite these attempts to frame ICTs as docile allies in the fight for a supposedly consensual idea of development, they have been appropriated and resisted by different actors to pursue competing agendas. This chapter tells the story of how technologies and the discourses that came to be associated with them at the international level triggered radically different responses among different stakeholders in Ethiopia. It begins by examining the attempts pursued by international organizations to socialize national actors to the narrative of ICTs as drivers of beneficial processes of modernization, democratization, and globalization. Secondly, it analyses how discourses on the use of ICTs for development adopted at the international level have related to pre-existing experiences of technological adoption in Ethiopia. It then moves to identify and explain the responses of the government, the local civil society, the private sector, and the diaspora to the international framing of ICTs, indicating who prevailed and who was marginalized in their attempts to influence the applications of ICTs in Ethiopia.

## Global Discourses Go Local

The wave of discourses on ICTs for development that characterized the 1990s, triggered by the diffusion of the Internet in Western societies, was sustained by a variety of international organizations, epistemic communities, and NGOs. Similarly to what has been illustrated in other studies on the diffusion of ideas, norms, and policies (Checkel 2001; Finnemore 1993, 1996; Risse-Kappen 1994, 1995; Strang & Meyer 1993), these institutions sought to theorize and explain the advantages of the changes they were advocating and familiare national actors with new ideas. Some of them, such as the World Bank, attempted to articulate policies that could maintain a certain level of coherence across nations and continents, while others chose to pay greater attention to local contexts, focussing on individual countries and regions (Thompson, 2004). In each national context, among international organizations, NGOs, and transnational corporations, unique networks progressively emerged to support the new ICT agenda, seeking allies that could become local advocates in the application of ICTs to development.

In the case of Ethiopia, it was mainly through a few large initiatives and organizations that the new interest in ICTs reached the country and its elites. Different organizations played different roles at different times. Initially it was the United Nations Economic Commission for Africa (UNECA) that emerged as the most significant 'active teacher' (Finnemore, 1993) introducing national actors to these new ideas, artefacts, and norms, mediating the massive discursive production characterizing the new wave of ICTs for development. As recalled by members of the Ethiopian government, civil society, and academia, whose testimonies are reported in the following sections, the events organized by the UNECA and the documents the UNECA produced represented for many the first occasion to learn about the role ICTs can play in national development, from health, to governance, to education. At a later stage, however, as the resistance of the Ethiopian government towards the type of ICT agenda advocated globally and nationally became clearer, the World Bank and the United Nations Development Programme (UNDP) also began to play a significant role, focussing not only on policy change, but also employing their resources to directly implement ICT projects aimed at shaping Ethiopia's information society. These later attempts will be explored in Chapter 5, while the following sections trace the initial steps in the socialization of ICTs in Ethiopia.

### The UNECA and the African Information Society Initiative

The UNECA, headquartered in Addis Ababa, was created in 1954 to support socio-economic development in Africa. By the mid-1990s it had already accumulated substantial experience in promoting ICTs for development. In 1986, with the support of UNESCO, UNDP, and the International Development Research Centre (IDRC), the UNECA launched the Pan African Development Information System (PADIS), a centralized database that facilitated the sharing of information on African development related issues. It was within the context of PADIS that the first electronic connectivity was provided to twenty-four African countries through FidoNet, to enable local and Africa-based international agencies access to the new database.[1]

Ten years later, with resolution 795, 'Building Africa's Information Highway', the UNECA's role in promoting ICTs in Africa was taken to a new level.[2] The UN organization started framing ICTs not just as a tool to share information relevant to the continent, but as an opportunity for all countries to build an African information society, leapfrogging other stages of development and steering the economy towards the exploitation

---

[1] FidoNet is a computer network that was used predominantly in the late 1980s and early 1990s to host bulletin board systems (BBS) used to exchange messages and chat among users and to download software and files.

[2] The resolution was passed at the end of the African Symposium on Telematics for Development, organized by UNECA together with UNESCO, International Telecommunication Union (ITU), IDRC and Bellanet. It took place in April 1995 in Addis Ababa.

of knowledge and information. The African Information Society Initiative (AISI) was the document that embodied this vision and stipulated the policies and standards needed for African governments to achieve it, such as the creation of National Information and Communication Infrastructure (NICI) policies, the establishment of specialized agencies in charge of ICTs, and the development of partnerships with the private sector.

AISI became a dominant node that brought together existing institutions and inspired the creation of new ones. Financial support for the implementation of AISI was guaranteed through the Partnership for ICTs in Africa (PICTA), a forum of donors and executing agencies including the World Bank, UNDP, and the World Trade Organization.[3] This alignment with the policies advanced by similar institutions represented a profound shift for the UNECA. As Nulens and Van Audenhove illustrate, 'the UNECA, with its rather harsh critique on the international economic system of the 1980s evolved towards a more mainstream view with regard to ICTs and development' (Nulens & Van Audenhove, 1999, p. 468). A training centre was set up in Addis Ababa, especially targeting politicians and technocrats, in order to make them aware of the potential of ICTs.[4] To ensure that key decision makers in Africa were aware of the existence of AISI and of the discourses it was advancing, the first African Development Forum (ADF), a continent-wide gathering of African leaders organized by the UNECA, placed the document at its core. In 1999, the ADF had already addressed the 'challenge to Africa of globalization and the information age' (this was

---

[3] PICTA included representatives from: Agence de la Francophonie (ACCT), Bellanet International Secretariat, Carnegie Corporation, COMNET-IT Foundation, United Nations Economic Commission for Africa (UNECA), Food and Agriculture Organisation (FAO), Global Information Infrastructure Commission (GIIC), International Development Research Centre of Canada (IDRC), ITU, Rockefeller Foundation, Swedish International Development Cooperation Agency (SIDA), US Department of State, the United States Agency for International Development (USAID), UNDP, UNESCO, WK Kellogg Foundation, The World Bank, and the World Trade Organisation (WTO).

[4] The presence of the UNECA headquarters in Addis Ababa placed Ethiopia in a privileged position to be included in most of the activities for the implementation of the AISI objectives. Ethiopia was involved in most, if not all, the activities organized to facilitate the use of ICTs for development (UNECA, 2008). It was one of the first thirteen African countries to be initially assisted in the development of a National Information and Communication Infrastructure plan. Between 2000 and 2004 it was part of a group of six countries that were surveyed by the SCAN-ICT initiative to identify a set of indicators to assess the progress of the information society on the continent. Ethiopia has benefitted the most from the trainings organized by the UNECA for various stakeholders to encourage their participation in the information society. Over the years Ethiopian representatives took part in workshops and conferences targeting groups from parliamentarians to on-line journalists, and from medical doctors to small entrepreneurs.

the subtitle of the conference), and it ended by proposing acceptance of AISI as the response to the uncertainties and opportunities brought about by ICTs. Some of the issues proposed during the forum, however, were contested by African leaders, who regarded some of the discourses employed to frame the initiative and ICTs as alien to their own agendas.

Although the AISI framework was designed to serve as a reference point for many African governments, its language appeared disconnected from the sociopolitical reality that characterized the continent in the 1990s. Its regional scope did not distinguish it significantly from other documents with a global focus and, apart from generic references to poverty, poor governance, and the shortage of basic services, it lacked references to the politics of the continent. It reflected the tendency of most international organizations to avoid mixing the technical with the political so as to appear neutral.

In the decade in which the AISI framework took shape, Africa was blighted by an average of 7.5 civil wars per year, a very small reduction from the previous one which was considered the most violent in history (Elbadawi & Sambanis, 2000; Nkurunziza, 2008). After the fall of the Berlin Wall and the dissolution of the USSR, which had been supporting numerous governments on the continent, many African nations had to find new models of governance and experiment with new political arrangements. Some states became fragile democracies, while violent competition for power turned others into battlefields. A vocal diaspora often formed an oppositional force, trying to build alternatives to incumbent governments. In this context, failing to acknowledge that new technologies could be interpreted through the lenses of politics, conflict, and power, proved to be a severe shortcoming. This had profound consequences for how the AISI framework would be received in many African countries, including Ethiopia, where the government was dealing with an ambitious internal agenda that partially conflicted with the principles advanced by international organizations.

A closer look at the AISI document shows how references to the politics of the continent were carefully avoided, privileging more general references to how ICTs could act as *modernizing*, *globalizing*, and *democratizing* agents.[5]

---

[5] The full document can be accessed at www.uneca.org/cfm1996/pages/africas-information-society-initiative-action-framework-build-africas-information-and and a review of the accomplishment of AISI after ten years can be accessed at www.uneca.org/publications/african-information-society-initiative-aisi-decades-perspective. For a critique of the document see Nulens & Van Audenhove (1999).

ICTs were framed as both *modern*, meaning the product of a greater technical prowess, and *modernizing*, allowing nations that had been lagging behind to catch up to those perceived as more developed. The document was filled with references to the novelty of new technologies and how they could be employed to unleash 'new forces'. The information society was labelled as belonging to a new 'age', inaugurated by a 'revolution', thus interrupting continuity with the past and with previous failures in bringing development to poor nations. The men and women who would be 'fostered' by the information society were described as belonging to a 'new generation' who would know how to use ICT for development. At the same time, however, the potentially disruptive consequences each 'revolution' brings with it were absent from the text or were tamed by references to how ICTs will 'support' or 'accelerate' socio-economic development across the region.

Similarly, the references to the flow of information and free markets were used to describe ICTs both as an expression of a *globalized* world and as a *globalizing* agent. The rhetoric that had prevailed during the debate on a 'New Information and Communication Order' (NWICO) in the 1970s and 1980s seemed to have been resurrected. According to the document a 'continuous flow of information' within the society had to be facilitated, while still ensuring that Africa would be linked 'with the rest of the world by improving the flow of new technologies in both directions'. Without any regulation in place and in countries lacking a skilled IT workforce and with minimal information literacy, however, the African 'information highways' that the AISI process was expected to encourage and their 'off-ramps' in the villages were more likely to lead to a flood of information in small localities rather than villagers seizing the opportunity to produce valuable information and goods for the global economy. In addition, although it was claimed that ICTs should benefit every sector, it was 'business' that was asked to 'exhibit strong leadership capable of forging the build up of the information society'. Similarly, 'free markets' were described as a core component of an African information society, which, in accordance with the free flow rhetoric, should be increasingly linked to the global economy, allowing goods to circulate without protectionism.

Finally, AISI's discourse on the processes of *democratization* that ICTs should facilitate was largely reliant on idealized principles of liberal democracy. Apart from general mentions of 'democratic and human rights (freedom of speech and freedom of cultural and religious expression)', the document pointed at individuals, at 'every man and woman', as the key beneficiaries of the new opportunities and freedoms afforded by ICTs. There were no references to the collective and communal rights that had been placed at the core of other documents aimed at setting continental standards, such as the African Charter on Human and Peoples' Rights and which were similarly influencing governments like Ethiopia's in their state- and nation-building efforts.[6]

After its proclamation, the AISI became the inspiring document for a variety of initiatives spanning across the continent, of which the creation of National Information and Communication Infrastructure (NICI) policies and the national plans charting the development of ICTs in individual countries were the most significant (Hafkin, 2002). The greatest successes in defining national policies were obtained in countries such as Ghana, Mozambique, Tanzania, and Uganda (Hafkin, 2002). These countries subscribed to the new policies at an early stage, while the relationship with the Ethiopian government was often unproductive, despite the UNECA being headquartered in Addis Ababa. The next section explains why this was the case, examining the interaction among the competing meanings attributed to ICTs by different agents who had a stake in the development of ICTs in Ethiopia. It focusses primarily on the government response, while the following sections explore how other actors, including civil society organizations, the private sector, and the Ethiopian diaspora, interpreted the potential of ICTs differently.

### Re-interpreting ICTs: Modernization, Globalization, and Democratization in the Ethiopian Context

In Ethiopia the new wave of discourses on ICTs initially produced conflicting responses. The first division that emerged was between individuals connected to the government, both politicians and technocrats, on the one side, and members of the local civil society, the private sector, and the diaspora on the other. The latter group appropriated most of the images and recipes proposed by international organizations. As explained later, however, many of their attempts to influence the generation of a local approach to ICTs ended in frustration. The local civil society grew progressively disengaged, local entrepreneurs continued to

---

[6] It is also important to note that the AISI document used highly technocratic language and mimics scientific jargon offering disputed claims as objective knowledge (McKenna & Graham, 2000). The document, for example, employs circular arguments, collapsing causes and effects of particular phenomena. It inextricably connects information society and ICTs as mutually dependent and reinforcing, suggesting, for example, that there can be no information society without ICTs, but it is only a fully developed information society that can make proper use of ICTs. This technocratic language is also coupled with its normativity. The measures the AISI proposes are based on development 'imperatives', on 'priorities' that will have to be strictly followed to align the continent with the frantic rhythm that characterizes the 'information age'.

be excluded from shaping ICT policies and projects, and many Ethiopians living abroad developed a mostly adversarial use of new technologies, in order to challenge the government at home.

A second important split can be identified within the government camp. Most technocrats and some progressive members of the government welcomed ICTs as potentially useful tools. As the dean of the Graduate College of Telecommunication and Information Technology, the most important institution in the country for the training of the Ethiopian IT workforce, pointed out, the result of the first wave of training and conferences organized at the UNECA was that 'the attitude towards ICTs was very positive. Not only positive. People were thinking that computers could do miracles, that they were the panacea to solve every problem'.[7] Similarly, a technocrat at the Ethiopian ICT Development Agency (EICTDA), the institution created by the government in 2003 to centralize all ICT-related activities, who was a young graduate in computer science in the late 1990s, recalled, 'at the time my expectations were great. I thought that everything was going to come immediately, to change and reform our country in a few years. [...] But also in general, there were such big expectations about what technology could do'.[8] However, in contrast to other cases, including post-war France narrated by Hecht (1998), where technocrats constituted a powerful and influential class able to advance its own political plans, technocrats in Ethiopia were largely an appendix of the central government. It was mostly the understanding of ICTs developed by the EPRDF's cadres that drove their application in the local context. At least during the initial phase, the most influential members of the party appeared to focus on the potentially harmful uses of ICTs rather than their development potential, highlighting their concerns about security.

This reaction is illustrated by the words of a UNECA officer commenting on the Ethiopian resistance to implement the strategies advocated by his organization. He focussed in particular on the requests made to the Ethiopian government to liberalize the telecommunication market, a measure that had been opposed since the AISI was created. As he pointed out in his reply, the Ethiopian leaders saw their strategy as even more legitimate after having witnessed how a more open ICT regime as it emerged in other countries on the continent could lead to challenging political power.

---

[7] Interview: Nega Alemaheiu, Dean, Graduate School of Information and Communication Technology, Addis Ababa, 14 March 2008.
[8] Interview: Civil Servant, Ethiopian ICT Development Agency (EICTDA), Addis Ababa, 21 May 2008.

We discussed a lot with the Ethiopian government but they said "Not now". They are very intelligent, they understand very well the situation, all of the cases, all the best practices we present them, but their political strategy is different. Now they can use Kenya as a justification.[9] And say "You see? We told you that this technology can be used for violence in Africa. There are people ready to use technology to destabilize". So they are afraid, it is a strategy, they want to move slowly, to be given time for implementing technology in a way that is not dangerous for them. When I speak to them they tell me "We understand very well what you are telling us but we do not want to use that now". It is not a question of knowledge, it is a question of political strategy.[10]

These conflicting responses were the result of the different meanings various individuals and groups attributed to ICTs. These meanings were connected to competing political plans, but they were also dependent on how key concepts used to describe and interpret ICTs, such as modernization, democratization, and globalization, had been framed in Ethiopia's past.

### Modernizing Ethiopia

Modernization in Ethiopia has been pursued for a long time as a strategy for the state to maintain its independence, compete with other nations, and strengthen control over its territory (Clapham, 2006; McVety, 2012; Zewde, 2002). Since the late nineteenth century the modernization of infrastructure, the military, and other key areas of society became vitally necessary to resist the colonial ambitions of countries like Italy and Great Britain. Rulers of Ethiopia adopted various approaches to develop the country's resources, but in most cases they followed what Christopher Clapham has termed a 'politics of emulation' (Clapham, 2006). The leaders looked to other countries, such as Japan or the then USSR, with which they believed Ethiopia shared a common past or a common spirit, in order to elaborate strategies that could guide Ethiopia into the modern world.[11] Through this

---

[9] The reference here is to the unrest in Kenya which stemmed from the elections held in 2007, and to the use of blogs, radios, and mobile phones to incite violence across different ethnic groups within the country. For a detailed illustration see, for example, the BBC World Service Trust policy briefing *The Kenyan 2007 elections and their aftermath: the role of media and communication* (Abdi & Deane, 2008), or *The role of the media in the upcoming Somaliland elections: Lessons from Kenya* (Stremlau, Blanchard, & Abdi Gabobe, 2009)

[10] Interview: International Civil Servant, United Nations Economic Commission for Africa (UNECA), Addis Ababa, 13 March 2008.

[11] According to Clapham (2006) and Zewde (2002), the Ethiopian rulers saw the imperial past of Japan to be very similar to Ethiopia. The government was fascinated by how a nation that managed to maintain its ties with tradition could modernize so quickly and

process of identification and because of the significance the appropriation of the new tools held for the extension and consolidation of the borders of the state, modernization became an essential aspect of the country's political culture. In contrast to impositions by colonial powers forcing other African countries to follow their models, as well as subsequent attempts by UN agencies and NGOs to influence international and national policy agendas through insistent advocacy activities, for most of the nineteenth- and twentieth-century Ethiopian rulers actively browsed the international arena seeking solutions to their own challenges. Even when they apparently adhered to some of the principles of the development agenda articulated since the end of the Second World War, they sought to use their alliances and newly available resources largely as tools to extend their own control and power, rather than to substantially transform their models according to external standards and templates (McVety, 2012).

ICTs occupied a special place in Ethiopia's modernization process from an early stage. Ethiopia was the first state in Africa to have a public telecommunication operator (ITU, 2002). In 1897 Emperor Menelik II inaugurated the first telephone line, connecting the capital Addis Ababa with the city of Harar, annexed to his expanding empire only a few years earlier. The new technology was adopted and employed as a key resource for maintaining control over the new territories, enabling the emperor to obtain information as well as to impart orders to the rulers of the annexed province.[12]

During conversations with both older and younger interviewees, this event was often mentioned as an example of Ethiopia's potential. It was an initial referent in a longer chain of episodes where modernization, in its different manifestations, was framed as an element that had been actively sought to help exploit the country's dormant capital. This discourse continued to apply to more recent technological advances as well. As the Dean of the Civil Service College of Addis Ababa, the institution mandated to train Ethiopian civil servants, noted:

they assumed that the same destiny awaited Ethiopia. Similarly, Russia was seen as comparable to Ethiopia due to the orthodox faith, and during the Marxist-inspired military dictatorship of the Derg, Marxist-Leninism became the inspiring ideology of the state. Other countries have also inspired emulation. The EPRDF leadership, for example, looks to South Asia as a model of the developmental state which constitutes a possible trajectory for Ethiopian development.

[12] The telecommunication infrastructure later expanded to reach other major towns and, apart from a line built in cooperation with the Italians to connect Addis Ababa and Asmara, the priority continued to be given to the territories that had been recently conquered, in the South and the West – Sidamo, Nekemte, Gambella.

I remember a book about Japan, "How did Japan modernize?"[13] People were fascinated by it. The educated people learned that modernization was key in development and now with ICTs they are trying to reach as many people as possible to make this plan real.[14]

As in other authoritarian polities, the idea of modernization that emerged in Ethiopia across different political regimes was that of a force that could be channelled to support development plans defined at the local level and augment the outputs of ongoing processes (Scott, 1998). Similarly to the telephone in imperial times, the use of ICTs such as computers – from mainframes to PCs – was framed in this context, interpreting them as tools that could embrace and enhance projects already defined at the centre. At the beginning, computer use involved only academic institutions, a few ministries, and state-owned companies, as these were the only entities with enough resources and experience to operate what were still complicated machines.[15] At a later stage, the use of PCs for basic office automation was slowly introduced and civil servants were trained to use word processors and spreadsheets. In both phases, computers were used mostly to improve the efficiency of the state apparatus, extending and enhancing its control over the country.

Differently from the era in which the first telephone line was laid down, however, in the 1970s foreign countries and international organizations had begun to play a greater role in encouraging specific uses of technology. Following the example of the USSR Academy of Sciences, in 1975 the Derg set up the Ethiopian Science and Technology Commission (ESTC), and twelve years later, advised by UNESCO, created a National Computer Centre as part of the Commission, 'to promote the development of computer knowledge and services in Ethiopia; to provide consultancy and maintenance services; to provide training courses' (Kebede, 1994). Those who worked for the Centre described it as the

---

[13] The book, which transliterated from Amharic is *Japan endet seletenech*, was published in the early 1950s by Kebede Michael, an intellectual who worked under Haile Selassie as Director General for the Ministry of Education and Deputy Director for the Ministry of Foreign Affairs. The book was written in Amharic and never translated into another language.

[14] Interview: Haile Michael Aberra, Ethiopian Civil Service College, Addis Ababa, 4 June 2008.

[15] Ethiopian Airlines was the first organization to introduce modern management information systems in 1961 with the purchase of an IBM class 421. They were closely followed by the Ethiopian Electric Light and Power Authority in 1962, and a few years later by the Central Statistical Office, in 1964, and by the Ministry of Finance, in 1968 (Kebede, 1994). The first appliances to be used in those offices were mainly cash registers and mechanical accounting machines and it was only a few years later that electronic data processing systems (such as IBM 360/20 or HP 3000) started being employed in government institutions.

place where the first ideas about the relationship between IT – Information Technology – and development started circulating. According to a former member of the National Computer Centre, 'the centre was where a number of Ethiopians were first introduced to IT and to the role IT can have for growth and development. Since the beginning IT was strictly connected to the idea of development, in particular increasing the efficiency in certain sectors'.[16]

### Globalization is a Double-Edge Sword

In contrast to modernization, globalization occupies a more problematic place in the history of Ethiopia. The government led by the EPRDF has accepted it as an unavoidable challenge, something to negotiate and balance, to slow down so as to allow the country to cope with new influences coming from the outside. This attitude is well summarized by Bereket Simon, one of the most influential, and discussed, leaders of the EPRDF.

We studied globalization and we understood that it is a double edge sword. It creates opportunities and it also creates challenges. [. . .] At the end we concluded that we cannot be out of this globalized world. In the case of technology this means that on the one hand, if you have money you can buy the latest technology, and you can implement it here. But on the other hand when you implement it you also import the challenges that you have to avoid. And if you are not ready you will lose. One thing is sure: you cannot stand still.[17]

The use of broadcasting to weaken the control of the government over its citizens was probably the earliest case in which the EPRDF could experiment with the challenging potential of technology referred to by Bereket. Interestingly, the first actor to exploit this potential was the movement from which the EPRDF later originated, the Tigreyan People's Liberation Front (TPLF), which fought for the rights of the people of Tigray in northern Ethiopia, before extending its struggle to a national scale. To support their war effort the TPLF set up its own clandestine radio station, known as *Voice of Woyane*, allocating substantial resources to it to win the hearts and minds of the Ethiopian people.[18]

---

[16] Interview: Abebe Checkol, Consultant and Former Head of Information Services for the British Council, Addis Ababa, 26 February 2008.

[17] Interview: Bereket Simon, Advisor to the Prime Minister and former minister of Information, Addis Ababa, 24 June 2008.

[18] The guerrillas' clandestine radio station started broadcasting in 1979 and successfully broadcast for the next twelve years on an almost daily basis. It was initially used by two insurgency groups, the TPLF and the EPLF, however, after a series of ideological battles between the two fronts, the TPLF started its own radio station in 1985.

Debretsion Gebremichael, who later served as the Director of EICTDA and then as the Minister of Information and Communication Technology, was in charge of radio maintenance at the time of the struggle. As he explained: 'Our role was teaching about the struggle and trying to convince the people about our principles. [...] You had really to convert people, to make them think in a different way. And unless you communicate well and deeply you cannot get to the point of converting people'.[19] The TPLF's radio was not the only voice advocating a competing idea of the nation over the Ethiopian airwaves. In 1982 *Voice of America* (*VOA*) inaugurated its Amharic service with the intent of fighting Soviet influence in Ethiopia (Alexandre, 1989; Nelson, 1997). The strategy was grounded in Cold War politics, but the initial aim was soon hijacked by a more local agenda. In 1986 the *VOA* management appointed as Editor in Chief of the Amharic service a former supporter of the Ethiopian People's Revolutionary Party (EPRP) which, similar to the TPLF, was fighting against the Derg, but was also firmly opposed to the ethnic based front.[20] Under his direction, *VOA*, in addition to its mandate of challenging state propaganda, also began attacking the TPLF, commencing a war over the airwaves that continued even after Mengistu's defeat (Sheckler, 1999).[21]

By the time they came to power the EPRDF's leaders had thus developed substantial experience with the multiple and conflicting uses that could be made of broadcasting. Through *Voice of Woyane* they had learnt how effective it is to counterbalance propaganda in an autocratic state, where the ownership of the media is only in the hands of the government. However, because of *VOA*, they also understood that the airways can be appropriated easily by opposing forces and that some ICTs can make borders too porous to block dissenting voices coming from a vocal diaspora and other actors.

---

[19] Interview: Debretsion Gebremichael, Director of EICTDA, Addis Ababa, 10 June 2008.
[20] The EPRP was established in Ethiopia in 1972 with the aim of removing the imperial regime and transforming the country into a popular democratic republic. It took an active part in the revolution that lead to the overthrow of Haile Selassie, but, when the transition process became dominated by the military, members of the party, members of the EPRP were marginalized and later persecuted. EPRP refusal of ethnic politics and accusations to the EPLF and TPLF of dismembering the country, led to open confrontations also with the two ethnic based groups, and to the eventual defeat of the party, whose members either left Ethiopia and continued their political activities in exile or joined other political organizations (Gudina, 2003; Young, 1997)
[21] As a sign of the tension between the government of Ethiopia and VOA, the government started jamming the signal of its Amharic service, as accused by VOA itself as well as by the Committee to Protect Journalists. Information about the jamming of VOA as well as of Deutsche Welle (DW) can be found at www1.voanews.com/english/news/africa/a-13–2008-01–16-voa42.html, last accessed 14 April 2010 and www.cpj.org/2009/02/attacks-on-the-press-in-2008-ethiopia.php, last accessed 14 April 2010.

A similar suspicion towards opening the country too much to external influences can be seen in the economic domain. A powerful expression of this attitude was the speech Prime Minister Meles Zenawi delivered at the African Development Forum (ADF), the event organized by the UNECA to make the entire continent aware of the AISI. The Ethiopian Prime Minister used his privileged position not to endorse the idea that ICTs and globalization would help Africa, but to question it.

The choice Africa has is not whether it should be part of the global economy or not. It is already part of it. [...] But being part of the global economy does not necessarily mean that one has become a productive part of the process and in a position to draw benefits from it. If present conditions remain unaltered and the trend we see were to continue, then being more enmeshed within the globalized economy would only mean that by force of circumstances, Africa would be made to stay on the margins of the global economy, not as an integral part of the process, but as a part which, having been excluded from benefiting from the process in a bona fide manner, would have to fall back on other options likely to be opened up by those engaged in extra-legal business activities. (Zenawi, 1999)

The analysis of how globalization was affecting African countries did not simply lead Meles to refute its logic, but was seized upon as an opportunity to articulate a complex alternative vision of the role the state can play in promoting development in a globalized world. As he continued:

The path to development that has so far been encouraged by international financial institutions and more or less accepted willingly by governments in Africa, has been far from being effective. Their economic prescriptions have proved to be narrowly focused on liberalization and on macro-economic stability. The orthodoxy has thus been devoid of comprehensive vision, which is so essential for ensuring durable and sustained economic growth and development goals which can be achieved only through structural transformation. [...] One of the basic features of this model is in effect the sidelining of the transformative role of the state. African countries are not assisted in finding ways of enhancing the capacity of the state and in addressing its weakness for carrying out its transformative function with some degree of effectiveness. Instead the policy prescriptions encouraged by international financial institutions has had the effect of weakening the state and of ensuring its emasculation. A radical change in policy prescriptions with respect to the state is thus a condition for any meaningful growth and development in our continent. (Zenawi, 1999)

Many Ethiopians I interviewed over the course of this research who attended the event recalled Meles' speech as both inspiring and foundational for the policies that would follow, including in the ICT sector. The Prime Minister, while demonstrating his understanding of globalization and recognizing the possibility of resisting it as naïve, openly challenged the claim that the integration it implied would benefit African countries. This framing of the effects of globalization stood in sharp contrast with those advanced by the AISI and other initiatives, which suggested that the lack of understanding on the part of African countries was the cause of their being excluded from the benefits brought by globalization and ICTs.

### Liberal Democracy and Revolutionary Democracy

The speech delivered by Meles at the ADF pointed to broad disagreements on some of the principles that should inform the economics and politics of African countries. This divergence between discourses articulated nationally and internationally, however, was not always clearly spelled out. Some key concepts, such as *democracy*, could appear to be consensually embraced at both levels, while concealing fundamental conflicts beneath the surface. Sarah Vaughan and Kjetil Tronvoll, among other influential scholars of Ethiopian politics, have made numerous attempts to warn the international community on this point. In a publication commissioned by the Swedish International Development Agency (SIDA) to introduce key aspects of the local politics to development practitioners, for example, they explained that:

A point of primary importance is that donors and the EPRDF have not meant the same thing by "democracy". The ruling party has its own understanding of democracy, which differs significantly from the type favoured, and ascendant, in the West; the institutions it has created accordingly function differently. Its conception of democracy is not the liberal bourgeois variety based on individual participation, a diversity of interests and views, and plural representation. [. . .] What the Front calls "popular democracy" [or revolutionary democracy] is based on communal collective participation, and representation based on consensus. (Vaughan & Tronvoll, 2003, pp. 116–117)

Even if donor agencies and local institutions may profess an apparently similar commitment to democratization, the processes they support are rooted in different traditions. In one case they aim at fostering individual rights such as private property, personal initiative and at having a variety of views competing in the public arena. In the other, public participation is structured within the framework of a privileged relation between a vanguard party and the masses, while the cultures, traditions, and rights of representation of each ethnic group are publicly recognized as building blocks of the nation.

As will be further discussed in the next chapter, revolutionary democracy emerged at the time of the struggle and contributed to shape both the theory and practice of EPRDF rule. Its definition continued to evolve after 1991, as part of a strategic response to changing geo political circumstances; but also as a reaction to events that threatened the continuity of the control of the EPRDF over the nation, including elections in 2005, when the opposition made gains that went far beyond what the EPRDF expected. With substantial input from Meles Zenawi, both as a key contributor of party booklets that dictated the new line for all party members, and as public author seeking to articulate his vision for international audiences, as in papers like 'State and markets: neoliberal limitations and the case for a developmental state' (Zenawi, 2012), the concept morphed and became increasingly aligned to ideas of the developmental state. In the realm of state-society relations the idea of the developmental state championed by Meles presupposed a developmentally oriented vanguard committed to lead by example and minimize the weaknesses that had characterized other African states, including corruption and clientele. The relationship between the vanguard party and the masses, initially articulated with specific reference to the peasants, was progressively extended also to include the urban classes, which during the 2005 elections emerged as the greatest challenge to the hegemony of the EPRDF (Bach, 2011; Di Nunzio, 2014). In the economic domain it presupposed the primacy of the state, and the party, in directing and shaping the economy and the relationship between different productive forces, including through more or less explicit party ownership of key assets (De Waal, 2012; Vaughan & Gebremichael, 2011). In the ICT sector this meant preventing the private sector from taking a leading role as advocated at the international level, preferring strong state interventionism. Similarly, while the transformative power of ICTs was recognized, ICTs were channelled to ensure they could use by state actors to attain specific policy goals.

This discussion of the local meanings attributed to *modernization, globalization,* and *democratization* offers an initial base to understand why and to which extent the discourses advanced by the AISI and other international initiatives were selectively adopted by the Ethiopian government. As illustrated in the next section, in some cases the discourses articulated locally and internationally emerged as congruent and compatible, while in others the discourse proposed by international organizations and NGOs were resisted or partially rejected. In this initial phase, the Ethiopian government adopted a prevalently tactical approach towards ICTs, resisting and delaying policies and projects proposed by international organizations and NGOs, and ensuring that no other actors could seize ICTs in ways that could threaten its control over the country.

## The Ethiopian Government's Response

Of all the discourses on ICTs for development articulated by the AISI and other organizations seeking to socialize national actors to the new agenda, the potential for ICTs to modernize Ethiopia and support its government's plans emerged as the most appealing to the country's ruling elite. Substantial resources were invested, first to understand how these new technologies could be put to work for the country's benefit, and later to implement the plan that emerged from this deliberation. ICTs were often referred to as 'shortcuts' or 'accelerators'. Debretsion Gebremichael – who was, as mentioned earlier, was in charge of the set up and maintenance of the clandestine radio the TPLF used in the bush and later became Ethiopia's first Minister of Communication and Information Technology in 2010 – explained this point:

This is why we are focusing on strengthening the government. ICTs are just an instrument to get the government working well. This is the purpose of the struggle. If we want to transform the country we have to transform the government first. In this process ICTs have the role to speed up and to facilitate. ICTs can accelerate our development.[22]

The potential impacts of ICTs were channelled to serve specific priorities, while sectors that could have benefitted from them, but were not considered instrumental for the transformation of the country envisioned by the EPRDF, were marginalized. As the first computers were used to simply enhance the capacity of pre-existing institutions or to increase the efficiency of particular sectors, now more advanced technologies were being reshaped to fit into a similar model; to expand, but not threaten, the capacity of the state to operate. The modernization paradigm, which had been criticized in the past for its Western bias, nonetheless seemed able to exercise a strong appeal.

On the contrary, the global nature and the globalizing power of ICTs encountered active resistance in Ethiopia. This did not lead to a purely ideological refusal, but motivated careful analyses by political and intellectual elites. As illustrated by the words of Meles Zenawi and Bereket Simon cited earlier, at the turn of the millennium, there was a sense of urgency among EPRDF cadres to understand the possible consequences of a process Ethiopia had to accept, but which could also threaten its stability. This resistance to globalization was articulated in various ways. The idea of a free flow of information was opposed because of the challenges it could present to the leadership in controlling the adversarial

---

[22] Interview: Debretsion Gebremichael, Director of EICTDA, Addis Ababa, 10 June 2008.

voices coming from abroad. The power of ICTs to threaten governments had already been experienced during the struggle and it could similarly materialize, as it eventually did, in new platforms from which to attack the idea of the nation advanced by the EPRDF. More generally there was widespread scepticism that an unrestrained circulation of information would benefit the population as a whole. As the Dean of the Graduate College of Information and Communication Technology noted:

If you have little local content and you build information superhighways the result is that only the external content will come. And people will be exposed to it. People who speak the local languages should be put in the position to access their own content. To be capable of reading and using the Internet with the mediation of their culture. It can be really dangerous to have these people exposed to too much external information. They would not know how to process it.[23]

Similarly, the idea of liberalizing the ICT market and letting the private sector lead the creation of an information society was strongly opposed. The government repeatedly resisted pressures from international organizations, affirmed its sovereignty, and fought hard to maintain a monopoly over telecommunications. In stark contrast to the benign image attributed to market forces by the AISI, these forces were interpreted as mostly hostile by the Ethiopian government and its allies. Amare Anslau, the CEO of the Ethiopian Telecommunication Corporation (ETC), for example, explained the refusal to liberalize by arguing, 'We have to grow first. Only when we will be strong enough, and we will have the capacity, we will liberalize. Things have to be done gradually. And when we will be ready we could go to the fight'.[24]

Finally, the democratizing potential of ICTs was apparently embraced with enthusiasm. The ICT policy, for example, placed democracy and good governance at its very core. According to the document, the ICT vision for Ethiopia was:

To improve the social and economic wellbeing of the peoples of Ethiopia through the exploitation of the opportunities created by ICT for achieving rapid and sustainable socio-economic development, and for sustaining a robust democratic system and good governance. (EICTDA, 2006, p. 9)[25]

---

[23] Interview: Nega Alemaheiu, Dean, Graduate School of Information and Communication Technology, Addis Ababa, 14 March 2008.
[24] Interview: Amare Amsalu, CEO, Ethiopian Telecommunications Corporation, Addis Ababa, 27 June 2008.
[25] The ICT policy was drafted and amended numerous times between 2003 and 2006 (and the redrafting process has continued until 2009). The quote reported here has been kept in all versions between 2003 and 2006.

Similarly, the politicians and technocrats I interviewed often referred to democratization as one of the pillars of projects such as Woredanet and Schoolnet. For example, Bereket Simon, commenting on the benefits brought by Schoolnet, claimed that because of the new system, 'now we will have a new generation that has been trained in the principles of democracy in secondary education and they will know how to contribute to the development of the country'.[26] However, as illustrated in the previous section and as further explained in the following chapter, the meanings attached to the term democracy by the EPRDF's leaders were, and remain, significantly different from those implied in the mainstream discourses on ICTs for development. The training Bereket refers to is civic education where, among other things, some of the discourses the EPRDF placed at the centre of its idea of the nation were taught to students. In general 'sustaining a good democratic system and good governance' through the use of ICTs for the Ethiopian government meant creating a functioning state and increasing its capacity to provide services to the population, but also dominating the political space, marginalizing competing ideas of the nation. Employing ICTs for democratization did not signify empowering individuals to contribute various ideas and participate in the public debate on how the country should be run, but reinforcing the nation-state so that it could best realize the principles of revolutionary democracy embraced by the EPRDF. This conceptualization of democracy and its successful implementation on the ground implied a centralized application of the new resources and the marginalization of possible competing uses.

## The Marginalization of Non-State Actors in the Development of an Approach to ICTs

Civil society, the private sector, and the diasporic communities in the United States and in Europe responded more positively to the discourse on ICTs articulated at the international level. This reaction was the result, in part, of the strategy adopted by international organizations attempting to involve non-state actors in their activities, and of the perception by these actors of ICTs as a window of opportunity to increase their influence and initiate a gradual change in Ethiopia. However, the country's highly centralized power structure made most of the ideas and projects developed in these areas of little relevance for the actual re-shaping of technology at the local level. Many pioneering

---

[26] Interview: Bereket Simon, Advisor to the Prime Minister and former Minister of Information, Addis Ababa, 24 June 2008.

activities, especially those in line with the international discourse and taking the local context into lesser account, were blocked or marginalized by the government, forcing some of their promoters into adversarial positions and progressively alienating them from active participation in the development of ICT policies and plans.

### International Alignments: Importing New Solutions to Old Problems

Diverging from the EPRDF's cadres, most members of Ethiopian civil society and the private sector did not only perceive the modernizing role of ICTs to be positive, but also accepted some aspects of their global nature as potentially beneficial for Ethiopia. The local ICT firms, for example, even if small and poorly resourced, strongly advocated liberalization of the market. As Bogaled Demissew, head of the Ethiopian Information Technology Professional Association (EITPA) remembered: 'EITPA has been always advocating for liberalization. It was the main actor in promoting this agenda [...] But also the World Bank put a lot of pressure. We organized many events together. We showed to the government that if there is competition the state is also going to get more revenues. But it did not work. They just had a different agenda'.[27] Given the interest IT professionals have in expanding the telecommunication and service sector, their reactions are not surprising, but other initiatives promoted by non-state actors were not so closely connected to the advantages its members could have derived from their implementation. They depended more on the interest in the social and political transformation ICTs could bring and on a general acceptance of the discourses promoted at the international level.

The first debate over the significance of the Internet for Ethiopia, for example, benefitted from the active participation of representatives from NGOs and professional bodies, who were trying to strike a balance between the hype coming from the West and the initial scepticism and conservatism shown by the EPRDF. Initiated in 1995 by Dawit Yohannes, the speaker of the House of People's Representatives, and known as Bringing Internet to Ethiopia (BITE), this debate was aimed at producing concrete recommendations on how policy makers could handle the new technology effectively. Dawit Bekele, one of the most active advocates for an open and inclusive use of ICTs, described his own involvement in BITE:

---

[27] Interview: Bogaled Demissew, Former Head of the Ethiopian Information Technology Professional Association, Addis Ababa, 8 March 2008.

At the time nobody knew about the Internet. From Ethiopia we did not even have access to the Internet, so we could not have access to relevant information for the BITE commission. But we made a series of recommendations anyways. [...] We had realized that the government would have not accepted a privately owned Internet provider, so we proposed to have a flexible system under ETC.[28]

The system Dawit refers to was a public network service provider, a 'not-for-profit service organization with the main objective of serving the public and developing services' (Furzey, 1995), independent from any actor in particular and accessible to all. The Ethiopian government rejected the idea and decided instead to place service provision under its direct control.[29] This was only the first of a series of frustrations civil society faced in its attempt to import tools and discourses emerging at the international level.

A few years later, in 1997, Abebe Checkol, the Head of Information Services for the British Council in Addis Ababa, initiated a process that would have led to the creation of the first telecentre in Ethiopia. In the late 1990s telecentres were one of the most popular solutions proposed by international organizations to bring connectivity to remote areas. As Abebe himself remembered, 'the ITU and IDRC were organizing a lot of conferences at the UNECA, in particular on telecentres. It is there that I picked up the idea to start one of them in Ethiopia, using a public library in Wolisso, in Oromiya'.[30] With the support of the British Council, and after having obtained approval from the regional and local information bureau as well as training a number of local IT experts for the daily running of the centre, Abebe inaugurated it on the 26 February 2000. Unfortunately, as he recalled, 'the government closed it after a few days. We opened on a Saturday and on Monday it was closed. They said it was against the Ethiopian Telecom Law, but the main reason why they closed the centre is because they were scared'. It took a lot of lobbying through international organizations such as the Commonwealth Tele-communication Organization, the UNECA, and the UNDP to have the telecentre reopened a year later.[31]

---

[28] Interview: Dawit Bekele, Professor at Addis Ababa University and Africa Focal Point for the Internet Society ISOC, Addis Ababa, 3 March 2008.

[29] Dawit stressed the risks connected with being too proactive by noting that 'the guy who made the recommendations, the chair of the technical committee was marginalized since then. It was bad judgment. The government did not really know what the Internet was and it did not want to listen. They did not like the Internet' (Interview: ibid.).

[30] Interview: Abebe Checkol, Consultant and Former Head of Information Services for the British Council, Addis Ababa, 2 February 2008.

[31] The next telecentre was established in 2005 in Harar, sponsored by UNESCO. In 2007 the World Bank initiated an ambitious programme that would lead to the creation of numerous telecentres across Ethiopia. This programme is illustrated in greater detail in Chapter 5.

These experiences illustrate how the efforts made by actors other than the government to develop a more dynamic information environment were strongly opposed at the central level. As previously argued, this reaction was motivated by the need to slow down the pace of transformation in order to exert more control over it and by the desire to occupy the new political space that was created by ICTs in ways that would primarily benefit the government and its national project. As the next section illustrates, the incidents which occurred during this period, far from increasing the chances for civil society to be involved in the change ICTs were supposed to bring, led to further polarization between state and non-state actors, making ICTs yet another contentious issue in the Ethiopian society.

### Disillusionment and Disengagement

After initial attempts to shape local ICT policies and plans, NGOs, academics, and pressure groups continued to take part in initiatives aimed at contributing to the local development of new technologies. New projects were initiated to localize software in Amharic, a group for the promotion of Free and Open Source Software was established and many civil society organizations participated in a forum created to draft a comprehensive ICT policy for Ethiopia. However, none of these activities offered individuals and groups outside the government the opportunity to have a real influence in shaping the future of ICTs in Ethiopia, leaving many at the margins and forcing others to be co-opted and enter government ranks. These failures, especially when combined with the expectations that the discourses about the transformative power of ICTs had created, left many with a strong sense of disillusionment. This feeling is captured by Dawit Bekele, who, after his initial experience with BITE, initiated many other ICT projects in the country, which left him, however, profoundly pessimistic about the possibility of creating an inclusive information society in Ethiopia.

We understood that the government works alone. Everybody tried to work with the government, NGOs, academia, etc. But they have not been effective. The UNECA was instrumental in activating the civil society but was not enough.[32]

Similarly, Abebe Checkol, after his enormous efforts to start the first Ethiopian telecentre, later began to doubt the real value of the model he embraced and promoted in his country.

---

[32] Interview: Dawit Bekele, Professor at Addis Ababa University and Africa Focal Point for the Internet Society ISOC, Addis Ababa, 3 January 2012.

The problem with telecentres is sustainability. These centres were not really demanded by the community. They were more the result of international advocacy.[33]

The hype created by the discourses on ICTs articulated in the 1990s did not only frustrate the hopes of members of civil society because of their exclusion from an active role in influencing the ICT sector. The unprecedented scenarios envisaged for developing countries also created optimism among government officers who were later faced with a different reality. Earlier in this chapter the words of two technocrats were reported to illustrate the initial faith in ICTs shared in some government circles. Reflecting on the stages that followed those early days they recognized that 'after a while we realized that technology cannot do miracles'[34] and that 'everything happened at a much slower pace [...] During our meetings the politicians were saying "We invested so much money in it, and see what we have. There is nothing compared to what could have been done!"'[35]

These observations help show some of the drawbacks of technocratic discourses on ICTs proposed by the UNECA and other international organizations in the 1990s and 2000s. Presenting mere possibilities as facts resulted in the creation of expectations that could not be fulfilled in practice. The anticipation that the local and international civil society could be drivers of change did not take account of the power structure in Ethiopia and their inability to affect important decisions in the shaping of ICTs eventually fostered disillusionment.


### The Response of the Diaspora: Failing to Engage and Waving Conflict

Ethiopians residing outside the country reacted differently to the government's refusal to engage other forces in the development of a more consensual path to ICTs. In contrast to their compatriots in Ethiopia, they did not have to engage with the local authorities to develop their own projects and they were seemingly free from the control exercised by the government over what it considered to be improper or adversarial uses of the new technologies. As a result, some Ethiopians living abroad

---

[33] Interview: Abebe Checkol, Consultant and Former Head of Information Services for the British Council, Addis Ababa, 26 February 2008.
[34] Interview: Nega Alemaheiu, Dean, Graduate School of Information and Communication Technology, Addis Ababa, 14 March 2008.
[35] Interview: Civil Servant, Ethiopian ICT Development Agency (EICTDA), Addis Ababa, 21 May 2008.

could make bolder attempts to influence the path of ICTs in the country, relying on the success or reputation they gained abroad. In other cases, members of the diaspora started to employ technologies such as the Internet precisely in the ways that were opposed at home, to challenge the government and its political ambitions.

The most notable example of an Ethiopian citizen abroad trying to influence the development of ICTs in the country was Noah Samara, the founder of the first satellite radio network, World Space Radio. Noah had started the company with the ambition of offering clear and consistent information across Africa, fighting HIV/AIDS, providing education in remote areas and supporting a variety of programmes in health and agriculture. He successfully exploited the interest surrounding digital technologies at the end of the millennium and welcomed the opportunity to operate in his home country to create what he called 'information affluence', a term he used during the speech he delivered at the African Development Forum inaugurated by Meles Zenawi in 1999 (Samara, 1999). As will be explained in greater detail when analysing the genesis and development of Woredanet and Schoolnet, his role was important in explaining to Ethiopian leaders how different uses of ICTs were possible, combining satellite communication, Internet Protocols, and various systems for the reception of information. This could have represented the initial step in a longer term collaboration between World Space Radio and the government of Ethiopia, offering the private sector a leading role as advocated by the UNECA. However, the EPRDF, in line with the approach followed with local civil society and the private sector, preferred to continue alone, minimizing the possibilities for skilled Ethiopians in the diaspora to contribute to shaping the future of ICTs in the country.

If Noah Samara saw in ICTs a chance to extend his business interests and fulfil his ambition to bring information affluence to Africa, many Ethiopians abroad interpreted ICTs to be less of a business opportunity, but rather as a new channel, or a safe platform, to wage political attacks on the government at home. The reasons why a medium such as the Internet was employed in this manner can be found in the recent history of the Ethiopian diaspora in the United States and Europe. As illustrated in the next chapter, since the 1970s the country had been entangled in multiple conflicts resulting in significant waves of migration (Terrazas, 2007). A large majority of migrants were professionals and intellectuals who escaped political persecution (Abye, 2004) and many refugees also belonged to political groups opposed to the EPRDF. Throughout the 1970s and 1980s they were members of parties such as the Ethiopian

People Revolutionary Party (EPRP) and the All-Ethiopia Socialist Movement (better known with its Amharic acronym MEISON which stands for *Mela Ethiopia Sosialist Niqinaqē*). These groups were also opposed to the Derg regime but supported a nationalist agenda equally hostile to ethnic politics. More recently, others that fled abroad were former Derg supporters who were defeated in 1991 along with other ethnic based movements critical of the monopolizing strategy of EPRDF (Lyons, 2007). This composition turned many new opportunities to reconnect the diaspora with the homeland into a significant obstacle for the EPRDF's nation building and development plan, and for the capacity to assert it without facing substantial political confrontations.

When the Internet started to become a space to discuss Ethiopian politics, the debates took on increasingly polarized tones, similar to those that had developed in the press. In the early 1990s, numerous newspapers were launched in Ethiopia by individuals who used to work for previous regimes or belonged to other political movements the EPRDF had excluded from power. Owners and editors of these new publications interpreted the relatively free media environment the EPRDF had allowed to flourish as a mark of discontinuity with the Derg as an opportunity to attack the new regime and advance their alternative political agendas (Stremlau, 2011). A few years later, online platforms such as the *Ethiopian Review*, *Nazret*, and *Ethiomedia*, all launched by Ethiopians living in the diaspora, adopted a similar language and style, hosting articles that could have easily appeared in the newspapers printed in Addis Ababa. In fact, from the very beginning it became common to find cross-references between online and printed outlets. The new media, rather than being seized as an opportunity for a new generation of leaders and advocates to test innovative ideas, as would have been the case in neighbouring Kenya for example, were instead initially captured by 'old politics', going back to grievances rooted in the 1960s and 1970s when a powerful student movement challenged first the Emperor and later the Derg.[36] While some middle ground emerged, both online and offline, the discussions they promoted

---

[36] In the case of Kenya new media were seized at an early stage by activists and civil society groups to develop ways to check those in power. A famous example is Mzalendo, a platform launched by Kenyan activist Ory Okollo to check on the activities and performance of Kenyan MPs. Kenya also hosts one of the most active communities of bloggers in Africa, which has productively engaged with public authorities to promote reforms in governance and other sectors. The latest example is the launch of the 'Open Data Initiative', through which government data for example on spending on health and education are published online and made available to the public.

tended to remain in the background and were unable to galvanize or mobilize passions and political energy in the same way as the poles of the debate.[37]

As explained in the next chapter, despite criticisms of the EPRDF, which took on increasingly adversarial tones both online and offline, the party leadership stuck to its policy, ignoring dissenting voices and labelling them as 'anti-peace' and 'anti-constitution'. This stemmed from a belief that those writing for the private press and for online media were not part of the EPRDF's constituency in any case, so there was little need, at least initially, to expend political capital either repressing or engaging them. Over time, however, the trading of accusations and the inability of opposing factions to command each other's attention progressively poisoned the debate.

## Conclusion

New technologies have the potential to transform societies not only in relation to their characteristics, but also to the types of actors that succeed in appropriating and (re)shaping them at different points in history. By investigating how the same artefacts were interpreted differently by different stakeholders, and by providing some initial indication of whether or not each stakeholder was able to turn their aspirations into reality, this chapter has begun to illustrate how ICTs are practically influenced by wider networks of discourses and actors.

More specifically, it explained how the discourse promoted by the UNECA, which had emerged as the most important 'active teacher' in the country, produced conflicting responses in Ethiopia, supporting great expectations among the most progressive elements of society, but even greater concerns within the government ranks. The process of appropriation of the new technologies was dominated by the EPRDF, frustrating the attempts by other actors to influence the adaptation of ICTs in the country. The ways in which the EPRDF reacted to the new discourses on ICTs was influenced by how previous communication technologies, including the telephone, the radio, and computers were introduced in the country, illustrating how the longer term paths of

[37] The Reporter, a newspaper started by Amare Aregawi, a former TPLF member and editor in chief of TPLF's clandestine radio during the guerrilla, was started to provide a form of constructive criticism to the EPRDF. Papers such as Meznania were representative of a younger generation trying to move the debate to the centre. Similarly moderate online spaces were those of created by bloggers such as Dagmawi or Enset.

technological adoption may influence the interpretation of newer technologies, despite the claims of their unique attributes.

While this chapter has illustrated how the same technology and the same discourses were charged with different meanings – how the term democracy, for example, was describing different realities for international organizations and for the Ethiopian government – the next chapter focusses more closely on the specific discourses articulated by the EPRDF and explores how these came to influence the re-interpretation, re-definition, and re-shaping of ICTs in the country. As international organizations and NGOs were promoting a new wave of activities on ICTs, the government of Ethiopia was engaged in a difficult process of state and nation building and needed to ensure that ICTs would support rather than threaten this complex project.

# 4    A Quest for Hegemony
## The Use of ICTs in Support of the Ethiopian National Project

*Do not harass the peasantry, let them stay there,*

*Do not harass the exploited, let them stay there,*

*Disaster will be seen when things are upset.*
              *[Anonymous, Gedeb Giorgis, East Gojjam, Amhara Regional State]*

*Having measured out and measured out, they redistributed the land,*

*To anyone, who can plough and live, be it a Muslim or an Amhara.*
              *[Anonymous, Dejj Mariam, East Gojjam, Amhara Regional State]*[1]

Ethiopia has a long history of oral poetry composed by peasants to support their struggles against the oppressors or articulate grievances in times of hardship (Finnegan, 1970; Gelaye, 1999; Levine, 1965; Tareke, 1991). The verses above were composed by two poets in the Amhara region and offer competing perspectives on the coming to power of the EPRDF and on one of the reforms it introduced after it took control of the country, redistributing land among peasants. Taken together, they are indicative of the deep divide encountered after almost two decades of civil war. The distribution of the land to the peasants, however, was only one of the initial instruments the EPRDF employed to re-found the state and the nation on a new basis, and was accompanied by new reforms the government progressively added for its project to gain roots both at the centre and at the periphery of the state.

After initial indifference, over time ICTs also became a building block of this strategy, and their development came to be influenced by the two core discourses that have charted the path the EPRDF took to rule over Ethiopia. First, a discourse on the nation-state, which reframed the Ethiopian nation as a patchwork of different ethnic groups, each with an inalienable right to self-determination, rather than a unitary state.

---

[1] Oral poems recited by peasants of East Gojjam as quoted in (Gelaye, 1999).

Second, a discourse on democracy that was similarly grounded in the ideological background of the EPRDF and its Marxist-Leninist past, favouring group rights and consensus, in antagonism to liberal conceptions of democracy and advancing a culture of communication that emphasized a direct connection between the leadership and the masses. As indicated at the end of this chapter and later in Chapters 5 and 7, after the war with Eritrea and the split within the EPRDF that threatened the leadership of Meles Zenawi in 2001, and the elections in 2005, which challenged the hegemonic position of the EPRDF as a whole, these two discourses progressively started to be integrated into the discourse of Ethiopia as a developmental state; an idea which could be more easily communicated to both internal and external audiences and offer a more credible alternative to the models promoted by Western donors.

This chapter analyses these discourses from their origins during the struggle in the bush to their subsequent influence on the re-interpretation and re-shaping of ICTs, picking up where Chapter 3 left off and delving more deeply into the EPRDF's relationship with technology. The relevance of considering this extensive period of time comes from the recognition that many key decisions and projects related to ICTs were grounded in a relatively distant past. As illustrated in the next sections and further in Chapter 5, even if technologies were new and were described internationally as radically innovative, focussing on events surrounding their recent introduction seemed to have little explanatory power. A more revealing story emerged from considering how the political thinking of the current leadership had evolved and continued to influence more recent courses of action, eventually leading to the creation of two complementary technopolitical regimes in the country.

## Ethnic Federalism and the Re-foundation of the Nation-State

I have to balance otherwise I cannot create good citizens. Technology is used to build the nation, for the people at the centre and at the peripheries. But this is true in general. For example when we build a university in Addis Ababa we make sure that another one is being built in the regions at the same time.[2]

Since coming to power in 1991, the EPRDF has struggled to unite Ethiopian citizens around its idea of the nation (Tronvoll, 2000).

---

[2] Interview: Amare Amsalu, CEO, Ethiopian Telecommunication Corporation, Addis Ababa, 27 June 2008.

As Amare Amsalu the CEO of the Ethiopian Telecommunication Corporation (ETC) between 2006 and 2010, suggests, technology has emerged as just one of several instruments that have been developed over time to achieve this goal, incorporating the discourses at the core of the government's national plan.

Ethnic federalism emerged as the centrepiece of this project and ethnicity became both a means and an end to re-invent the nation. It served as an operational principle for the redistribution of resources to those recognized as separate ethnic groups. But the provision of material benefits along ethnic lines was also aimed at convincing people on the ground that it was in their interest to be recognized as ethnically diverse. Building a university in each of the regional states, as reported by Amare, can thus be interpreted not just as a response to a generic redistributive principle, but also as a way to show citizens that their rights were being realized primarily as members of a distinctive ethnic group. Projects like Schoolnet and Woredanet were designed to further enforce these principles on the ground. As a technocrat who had been working on Woredanet illustrated, 'Woredanet is to complete the decentralization process. The success of the government will have to be measured against this goal. [...] This issue is both managerial and political'.[3]

The discourse on ethnic federalism emerged during the civil war against the Derg, the military dictatorship that had ruled Ethiopia since 1974. For almost two decades the precursor to the EPRDF, the TPLF, fought for the rights of ethnic groups within the larger Ethiopian state. Its agenda was grounded in the historic marginalization of the region of Tigray, in northern Ethiopia, whose people first revolted against the central government in 1942–43. The insurrection, known as Woyane, was crushed with the support of the British army, but survived in the mind of Tigreyans as a key referent in the struggle of oppressed ethnicities. Following its formation in 1975, the TPLF joined forces with another ethnically based liberation movement, the Eritrean People's Liberation Front (EPLF). Together, the two groups came to represent the strongest, and eventually decisive, threat to the Derg.[4]

[3] Interview: Civil Servant, EICTDA, Addis Ababa, 21 May 2008.
[4] The TPLF and the EPLF were not the only ethnic based movements fighting against the Derg regime. The other most important ones were the Oromo Liberation Front (OLF) and the Ogaden National Liberation Front (ONLF). However, the TPLF and the EPLF emerged as the most successful movements, whose activity was decisive in overthrowing Mengistu's regime. In an initial phase the OLF and the ONLF were invited to take part in the transitional federal government created after the Derg defeat, but they left soon after and the Ethiopian government now labels them as terrorist organizations.

The struggles of the EPLF and the TPLF were a response from the northern peripheries of Ethiopia to a dominating and assimilating centre. However, even if strongly related, the insurgencies fought to attain different objectives. The EPLF had a secessionist agenda, with the independence of Eritrea as its final goal. The TPLF had a more ambitious and complex programme. The movement started in the name of the Tigrayan peasantry, but soon began to locate its activities in the wider context of the rights of all *nations, nationalities, and peoples*, as it termed the ethnic groups composing Ethiopia. Its ultimate aim was not just Tigrayan self-rule, but control of the country.[5] In accordance with this objective, before entering Addis Ababa, the TPLF leadership decided to create a new party, including fighters from ethnic groups other than Tigrayan. In 1990 the Ethiopian People's Revolutionary Democratic Front (EPRDF) was born as a coalition of ethnic-based movements: the TPLF, the Ethiopian Peoples' Democratic Movement (EPDM), composed mainly by ethnic Amhara, and the Oromo People's Democratic Organization (OPDO), founded to represent the Oromo, the largest ethnic group in the country. However, neither EPDM nor OPDO were the expression of a large popular movement, but were rather ad hoc parties created by the TPLF to demonstrate its commitment towards a larger constituency (Young, 1997).[6]

The EPRDF captured Addis Ababa on 28 May 1991, marking the end of the civil war and the beginning of the quest to transform a military success into a broader consensus on the future of the nation. A new discourse was articulated in support of this agenda and to legitimate what could otherwise have been seen as the rule of a minority, representing only 5.8 per cent of all Ethiopian citizens[7]: Ethiopia was not a unitary nation but a federation of ethnicities which, at least on paper, were all entitled to the same rights to self-determination that mobilized the people of Tigray. By connecting the Tigrayan minority to other oppressed groups and offering them, at least in principle, the opportunity to participate in the re-founding of the nation, the EPRDF was reframing its de facto capture of the state as a victory for all

---

[5] At the beginning of the struggle the TPLF leaders were also advocating the secession of Tigray from Ethiopia, but soon abandoned this agenda (Young, 1997).

[6] EPDM was created by a group of disbanded members of the Ethiopian People's Revolutionary Party (EPRP), whose fight against the Derg was based on a class, rather than ethnic, basis. After having been defeated by the TPLF, some of the members of EPRP created the new party with the support of TPLF. OPDO's members in contrast were mainly Oromo soldiers which had been fighting for the Derg and were later captured by the TPLF's forces (Young, 1997).

[7] Central Statistical Agency of Ethiopia, 1994.

marginalized groups. As is shown in the next sections, achieving this objective proved to be more complicated than expected.

### Ethnic Federalism, and Its Discontents

Ethnic federalism, in theory, gives all major ethnic groups the right to promote their language, culture, and history, to elect their local government and to equitable representation in the federal government. It was this ideology which underpinned the drafting of the Transitional Period Charter in 1991, where the right of Ethiopian nations, nationalities, and peoples to self-determination was affirmed for the first time, as well as of the Ethiopian constitution, which came into force on 21 August 1995, extending the right of self-governance up to a right to secede.[8]

Because of its uniqueness as well as its contradictory character, ethnic federalism has been one of the most researched areas in the history of modern Ethiopia. Major recent works in comparative politics and international relations have addressed it as a whole (Aalen, 2002, 2006; Assefa & Tegegne, 2007; Gudina, 2003; Mengisteab, 1997; Pausewang, Tronvoll, & Aalen, 2002; Tegegne, 1998; Turton, 2006; Vaughan, 2003) or dealt with specific components of it (Ottaway, 2003; Stremlau, 2011; Young, 1997)

As with all attempts to generalize a particularistic view across a national polity, the EPRDF's vision emerged antagonistically with competing versions and entailed a struggle over the interpretation of Ethiopian history. Of the many challenges faced by the EPRDF in attaining its goal, two were probably the most complex to overcome.

First, ethnic federalism stood in sharp contrast to the nation-building project promoted by previous Ethiopian regimes, which was characterized by the imposition of the culture of one specific ethnic group, the Shewan-Amhara, over all others. This process was initiated in the second half of the nineteenth century by emperors Tewodros II and Menelik II who respectively ended a long period of competition between feudal princes and annexed the regions in the South to the Abyssinian empire, creating Ethiopia as we know it today.[9] During his fifty-year-long reign, Emperor Haile Selassie further consolidated the 'Amharization' of Ethiopia, also extending it to Eritrea, which was annexed after the defeat of

---

[8] According to Article 39, first paragraph, of the Ethiopian constitution, 'Every Nation, Nationality and People in Ethiopia has an unconditional right to self-determination, including the right to secession'.

[9] Between Tewdros and Menelik another emperor, Yohannes IV, reigned over Ethiopia, but he spent most of his reign protecting the empire from foreign incursions.

the Italians in World War II.[10] This process did not stop with the deposition of Haile Selassie and the end of the feudal system supporting his empire. The Derg regime in theory refused to distinguish between different ethnicities, but in practice continued to impose the culture of Amhara over the rest of the nation (Clapham, 1990). Amharic was chosen as the national language, the use of vernacular idioms was prohibited and Amhara urban elites were favoured as representatives of the government across Ethiopia.

For more than a century the mission of the central authority had thus been the creation of a unified nation based upon a set of values that should bring together all Ethiopians. In 1991, this project was reversed, and the foundation of the nation was recalibrated to focus on the multiple ethnic groups and distinctive cultures composing it. The language used to advance and justify this competing discourse demonstrated a marked contrast with that which had been employed previously, as is well illustrated in the newspapers of the time. The two excerpts below are from editorials published by *The Ethiopian Herald*, the state controlled English daily. The first piece is taken from the newspaper before the end of the civil war, when it was in the hands of the Derg, and the second is from after the war, when it was controlled by the EPRDF. They represent occurrences of diametrically opposed, but repetitive discourses. It can be argued that for months before and after the transition two basic editorials were being written, one praising unity, the other praising diversity, with only slight variations.

The Derg attempted to rally the population around its long-term motto, *unity*, in particular, against TPLF and EPLF, defined as anti-unity and anti-peace movements.

Ethiopians throughout the length and breadth of the country have continued to voice their concern over the danger posed against the nation's *unity* and sovereign integrity. The outrage of the people is mounting. Ethiopians everywhere are expressing their readiness to be deployed to the war front and thereby pay any and every sacrifice to safeguard the long-standing freedom and *unity* of the country. The Ethiopian people are very well aware that in *unity* lies our strength. They are equally aware that *unity* is the reliable guarantee for the attainment of socio-economic progress. Accordingly, all stand for *unity*. They bitterly oppose all forces that are bent on undermining the *unity* of the nation. To this end, the people are prepared to pay any sacrifice the struggle calls for. Ensuring national *unity* and security is the driving force behind the people's mounting concern and firm commitment. *The Ethiopian Herald, Editorial, Friday 5 April 1991 (emphasis added).*

[10] Haile Selassie ruled over Ethiopia between 1916 and 1974, first with the title of regent and later as emperor. His reign was interrupted between 1936 and 1941 by the Italian occupation, during which he found refuge in Bath in the United Kingdom.

The second editorial tries to reverse this discourse, illustrating that the foundation of a new Ethiopia resides, instead, in its *nations and nationalities*.

Ethiopia is a country of many *nations and nationalities*. Not only have the various *nationalities* and oppressed people of this country been neglected for too long but deliberate efforts have been exerted to cause them to live completely forgotten and neglected and to remain in a dismal state of backwardness. [...] By convening a national conference for the peaceful and democratic transition aimed at resolving the complex national tasks, the EPRDF has given particular emphasis for the resolution of these problems. The problems of *nations and nationalities* have thus come out for serious discussions on a priority basis. This is the first major accomplishment of its kind in the history of Ethiopia. Through this forum, convened by the EPRDF at which representatives of different minority *nationalities* were represented, it was possible to hear the various political outlooks particularly in connection with the burning issue of *nations and nationalities*. On the basis of the draft proposals submitted by the EPRDF regarding this major *national* problem, participants have held frank and open exchange of views and adopted unanimously a resolution on ways ensuring the democratic rights of oppressed *nationalities and nations*. *The Ethiopian Herald, Editorial, Friday 5 July 1991 (emphasis added).*

The two pieces almost mirror each other, obsessively reiterating the terms at the core of two competing discourses of the nation, and attaching opposite meanings to similar concepts. In the first editorial, unity is linked to socio-economic progress: 'They are equally aware that unity is the reliable guarantee for the attainment of socio-economic progress'. While in the second editorial it is framed as oppression and becomes a cause of backwardness: 'deliberate efforts have been exerted to cause them to live completely forgotten and neglected and to remain in a dismal state of backwardness'. Similarly, the two pieces indicate different sets of values associated with what animates Ethiopian citizens. In the first editorial, unity is presented as being a cause people would die for: 'Ethiopians everywhere are expressing their readiness to be deployed to the war front and thereby pay any and every sacrifice to safeguard the long-standing freedom and unity of the country'. While in the second article the issue of nations and nationalities is said to be the one addressed when people were given the chance to speak out for the first time: 'The problems of nations and nationalities have thus came out for serious discussions on a priority basis'.

This debate did not end with the victory of the EPRDF, but continued, first in newspapers such as *Tobiya*, which was founded by journalists who had worked for the state owned press under the Derg regime, and subsequently through blogs and websites dominated by opposition parties and the diaspora.[11] An excerpt from an editorial in *Tobiya* can be illustrative of this point:

The attempt by the fascist Italians to divide the people and the country was not successful, but now it is getting rooted thanks to the current regime. The people of the country are being divided along ethnic line … The 1991 Charter follows and adheres to the secessionist ideology of a few Eritreans. It seems that the Charter was prepared to facilitate the secession of Eritrea from Ethiopia … The attempt to view unity as a marriage is very simplistic and incorrect. The people of Ethiopia are connected by history, nature, culture and psychological make-up … We also think that no group should be allowed to disintegrate the country. In the new Ethiopia, the unique and terrifying term is "unity". The charter is not in favor of unity. It also seems that the constitution fears the same term. It rather pronounces and emphasises the phrase "self-determination up to secession" … The regime supports the division and disintegration of the country and we think this is the first national government to do such a thing in the world. *Tobiya, Editorial, 24 February 1994*[12]

Over the years the two poles of the debate remained almost the same: unity, which the EPRDF was accused of having destroyed by allowing the secession of Eritrea and imposing a new divisive nation-building agenda, and ethnic federalism, equated to positive change by the government, which the opposition parties have been accused of opposing as forces of conservatism and enemies of development. As will be shown when analysing online debates, this polarizing rhetoric also came to influence newer media, with some of the most popular blogs attacking the EPRDF's ethnic federalist agenda, and the government trying to censor critical articles and posts while at the same time trying to occupy new online spaces with its own narrative.

A second problematic aspect of the ethnic federalist discourse, and a reason for the resistance it initially provoked, is connected to how it attempted to construct ethnicities from above, extending the experience developed by the TPLF among the peasantry in Tigray to other ethnic groups in Ethiopia. As the vast literature on nationalism and nation building has variously illustrated (Anderson, 1983; C. S. Clapham, 1996; Deutsch, 1953; Featherstone, 1990; Gellner, 2006; Hecht, 1998; Ignatieff, 2010; Kymlicka, 2001; Smith, 1995; Smith & Smith, 2003), as concepts like ethnicity and nation are constructed, their meanings are

---

[11] A second threat to the ethnic federalist discourse did not come from the forces that used to control the state under the Derg or Haile Selassie, but from other movements which, like the TPLF, had been opposed to those regimes. Although the TPLF emerged as the most successful among the groups opposing the state it was far from being the only one.

[12] As quoted in (Stremlau, 2008, p 90).

also contested by competing political projects. However, in different locations and at different points in time the extent to which a particular discourse is challenged varies. At the time of the civil war against the Derg, for example, a variety of factors made the Tigrayan identity more stable and less contested than others in Ethiopia (Young, 1997). Tigrayans had powerful common referents: the glorious Aksumite empire,[13] the Woyane revolution in the 1940s, and the struggle itself, which was uniting the population further against central authority. The vernacular language, Tigrinya, had been used for centuries and, like Amharic, had a written script. For sixteen centuries orthodox Christianity had been professed by almost the entire Tigrayan population. However, these factors were far from being present across other groups within Ethiopia, and, more importantly, were not necessarily understood by other ethnic groups as a reason to revolt against the centre and request official recognition of their ethnic diversity.

The EPRDF's programme was based on a map of the social composition of Ethiopia imposed from above, and like other 'top-down' nation building projects, encountered a great deal of hostility on the ground. As Ahmed Hassen, a member of parliament responsible for information and communication, recalled, 'at the beginning of the new government the idea of a federal Ethiopia was opposed from everywhere. We felt highly misunderstood'.[14] A concrete illustration of this reaction is offered by Vaughan's research in the southern region of Simien Omo, where the government tried to amalgamate different ethnic groups into more manageable units (Vaughan, 2006). As part of this operation a new language was created from a variety of dialects spoken in the area intended for use in administration, for educating children in primary schools and for providing new glue to unite the different groups living in the region. However, far from being perceived as a manifestation of ethnic rights, this act led to strong resistance and sparked violence among the population. The first textbooks written in the newly created idiom were publicly burned during protests that resulted in several deaths and imprisonments (Vaughan, 2006).

---

[13] The Aksumite Empire represents the foundation of the modern state of Ethiopia. Between the third and seventh century Aksumite emperors controlled most of northern Ethiopia, Eritrea, part of Southern Sudan, and Yemen. It entertained trading relations with most of the Arab world, but also with India and Rome. King Ezana II was the first to convert to Christianity in 324 AD, making Aksum the first centre of Christianity in the continent. It is also claimed that the rests of the Arch of covenant are preserved in a church in Aksum. For more information about the history of the Ethiopian empire see Collins and Burns (2007)

[14] Interview: Ahmed Hassen, Deputy Chairman of the Information & Culture Affairs Commission, Addis Ababa, 13 June 2008.

It is difficult to reconstruct the degree to which such reactions surprised the new leaders or were anticipated, but since ethnicity alone could not mobilize all people of Ethiopia to the extent it did in Tigray and in Eritrea, a variety of different strategies had to be adopted to implement the EPRDF's ethnic federalist agenda throughout the country.

### Ethnic Federalism in Practice: Building the State to Build the Nation

To translate the ethnic federalist discourse into more concrete forms and, at the same time, to increase its control over the territory, the government started developing institutions that embodied the principles of ethnic federation. As key components of the new order, these institutions had to fulfil two main requirements: first, they had to be based on ethnicity, incorporating quotas to equally represent different groups in society; second, they had to be efficient, or at least more efficient than those Ethiopian citizens had known in the past. The two principles were presented as being strictly interconnected and mutually reinforcing, with ethnicity providing the ideational framework for the creation of the new administrative infrastructure on the ground. Efficiency and an equal redistribution of resources among the identified groups were meant to substantiate this and reinforce a belief among the population that an ethnic federation was the most appropriate form of government.

These processes can be interpreted as further examples of how nations are created as imagined communities (Anderson, 1983). It was through the invention of new symbolic referents that a different idea of the nation was proposed and negotiated, in the attempt to reach some form of consensus among the Ethiopian population. Ideational referents, however, need to be grounded in a material reality in order to function among communities at large. Some of these material referents may already exist and can be invested with new meanings that are functional in a nation-building process. One example could be the case of a location becoming a destination for pilgrimage. Others need to be constructed, such as a series of reactors, as explained by Hecht in her research on the ambitious French nuclear programme, to signify the country's new radiance after World War II. In the case of Ethiopia, it was systems like Woredanet and Schoolnet, together with numerous other physical substantiations of EPRDF's national project that came to play this role. They were designed to simultaneously embody the principles of the ethnic federalist state, represent it on the ground, and improve its image. Debretsion Gebremichael illustrates this point:

Ethnic federalism is a key component. In Woredanet you can see the federal system reproduced at the technical level. You have the federal, the regional and the woreda. The system is organized in a way that you can make sure the message is delivered to the lowest levels of the government.[15]

To establish the ethnic federalist discourse at the political and social levels, the country was divided into nine regional states,[16] each intended to represent 'a group of people who have or share a large measure of a common culture or similar customs, mutual intelligibility of language, belief in a common or related identity, a common psychological make-up, and who inhabit an identifiable, predominantly contiguous territory'.[17] The states were split into *woreda*, units of approximately 100,000 people, governed by administrations modelled on *baito*, the councils created by the TPLF in Tigray during the war. The woredas were in turn divided into village councils called *kebele* representing grassroots units of government.[18] In 1992, elections were held to provide the new institutions with a popular mandate and to signal to the population that a new order was being created. The EPRDF had founded a number of ethnically based parties that could compete in each of the regions, but the only two genuine opposition parties, the Oromo Liberation Front (OLF) and the All Amhara People's Organization (AAPO) withdrew due to harassment and intimidation.[19] Subsequent elections, for the constitutional assembly in 1994 and for the regional and federal governments in 1995, were similarly uncontested. This was not novel for the Ethiopian population, who had never been called to vote in free and fair elections. The electoral contests were rather a means of providing the new leaders with a symbolic mandate that, even if it did not emerge from genuine competition, could be used in support of their national

---

[15] Interview: Debretsion GebreMichael, Director of EICTDA, Addis Ababa, 10 June 2008.

[16] The cities of Addis Ababa and Dire Dawa were also granted administrative status.

[17] The Constitution of the Federal Democratic Republic of Ethiopia, art. 39, paragraph 5.

[18] The *kebeles* were originally created by the Derg as peasant associations and largely maintained a similar structure under the EPRDF.

[19] The four member parties of the EPRDF were the Oromo People's Democratic Organisation (OPDO), the Amhara National Democratic Movement (ANDM), the Southern Ethiopian People's Democratic Front (SEPDF) and the Tigray People's Liberation Front (TPLF). The affiliates were the Afar People's Democratic Organization (APDO) in Afar region, the Somali People's Democratic Front (SPDF) in Somali, the Gambella People's Democratic Front (GPDF) in Gambella, the Benishangul-Gumuz Peoples Democratic Unity Front (BGPDUF) in Benishangul-Gumuz, and the Harari National League (HNL) in Harari. They are officially independent but have been created by the EPRDF and have strong links with it.

discourse and to justify continued reforms in the country, especially among the rural population.[20]

The political remapping of the country along ethnic lines was accompanied by a similarly ambitious reform of the civil service, also in apparent resonance with the donor-driven agenda that emphasized decentralization as a strategy for guaranteeing better governance.[21] Many administrators I interviewed at different levels of the government apparatus had become obsessed with keywords such as efficiency, good governance, empowerment, and service delivery. The meaning of these terms seemed, however, to be increasingly distorted at lower levels of the administration. It was common to see manuals of Business Process Re-engineering (BPR) on the desks of the General Managers of many government agencies, which had been selected by the party leaders as one of the many techniques employed to reform the civil service.[22]

The most important reform, especially in relation to the influence it would have had on Woredanet and Schoolnet, was the *National Capacity Building Programme* (NCBP), which started in 2001. It was a multi-sector intergovernmental programme, involving a variety of activities, the most

[20] As indicated by von Bogdandy, Häußler, Hanschmann, & Utz (2005), processes of state and nation building are closely related and successful reforms of the state can be undertaken only if the ruling elite has a certain degree of legitimacy. This relation can be found in their definition of state and nation building, focusing in particular on post-conflict situations of the kind experienced in Ethiopia after 1991. 'State-building means the establishment, re-establishment, and strengthening of a public structure in a given territory capable of delivering public goods. Essential to state-building is the creation of sovereign capacities of which the fundamental one is the successful and generally undisputed claim to a "monopoly of the legitimate use of physical force"' (583–584). 'Nation-building is the most common form of a process of collective identity formation with a view to legitimizing public power within a given territory. This is an essentially indigenous process which often not only projects a meaningful future but also draws on existing traditions, institutions, and customs, redefining them as national characteristics in order to support the nation's claim to sovereignty and uniqueness. A successful nation-building process produces a cultural projection of the nation containing a certain set of assumptions, values and beliefs which can function as the legitimizing foundation of a state structure.' (586).

[21] The World Bank, for example, described the operation in a background paper: 'Following the fall of the Derg regime in the early 1990s, the EPRDF-coalition Government embarked on a long term strategy of "state transformation" characterized by bold attempts to implement multiple reforms in parallel; the massive scale-up of institutional development efforts across tiers of government; and the deliberate expansion of the scope of public sector capacity building initiatives' (World Bank, 2004, 5).

[22] BPR is an interesting example of how a tool that emerged from a neoliberal approach to public sector reform (New Public Management) was problematically adopted by a government supporting socialist principles to reform its civil service. For details of BPR and for a comprehensive illustration of the decentralization process and civil service reform see the Special SIDA Study written by Vaughan and Tronvoll (2003), or the book edited by Tegegne (1998).

relevant being the creation of the Super-Ministry of Capacity Building and the reinforcement of the woreda as the fundamental building block of the Ethiopian state machinery. Prior to 2001 the decentralization process had not produced the expected results and the NCBP was intended to improve performance by devolving authority to lower levels of the administration, the woredas, while at the same time linking them tightly to a newly created institution. NCBP also emerged in response to the power struggle within the EPRDF that followed the war with Eritrea between 1998 and 2000, which eventually ended with the reaffirmation of Meles Zenawi at the helm of the party and the purge, arrest or marginalization of his opponents (Vaughan, 2011). NCBP thus emerged as an institutional response to the split that had almost destroyed the EPRDF and was aimed at transferring functions that had previously been the purview of the party to the state apparatus. The programme was initially piloted in four regions (Oromia, Amhara, Tigray, and Southern Nations Nationalities and People Regions) and was later expanded under the name of the Public Sector Capacity Building Programme (PSCAP).

Woredanet and Schoolnet were set to play an important role in this wave of state transformation, supporting some key aspects of the reforms. The link between investment in technology and the decentralization process was evident to the engineers and technocrats that were asked to formulate solutions to the challenges presented by the NCBP and PSCAP reforms. The testimony below is from one of the technocrats who had been involved in the design and implementation of Woredanet from the very beginning:

The Minister of Capacity Building was asking and demanding and we had to come up with solutions to what he was asking. There was frustration after frustration. All the decisions were political decisions, to decentralize, to follow the project of decentralization, to create a sense of collectiveness among different communities and the centre.[23]

This explanation suggests how the decentralization project influenced the design of Woredanet, and how the newly created Ministry of Capacity Building exercised a prominent role in the initial phases in which it took shape. It also illustrates how the political nature of technology is often appreciated and portrayed as an explanation for technical decisions by technical personnel. The interview from which the quote above is taken was one of my first and, just as Hecht has reported her surprise at the explicit references to politics in technocrats' answers to her questions, I too was not expecting to receive such straightforward accounts of issues

---

[23] Interview: Civil Servant, EICTDA, Addis Ababa, 13 March 2008.

that I considered problematic in terms of using technology to enact specific political needs. As the interviewee continued,

Another request was to diffuse information up to date to the periphery and to know what was going on in there. A minister cannot wait for too long. Now the Prime Minister can speak to the rural areas, all at the same time. All the costs for his transportation, his security, are not there anymore. [. . .] The Prime Minister can use the system every time he wants, while for the other nodes, they should fill a form.[24]

The tendency to underline the political nature of systems like Woreda-net and Schoolnet was confirmed in many interviews with technocrats and other non-political personnel. As a computer scientist working at Addis Ababa University explained:

China is now the model. To be effective and deliver is a way for them to stay in control. The government thinks that if they do a good job with the economy and provide good services the people should keep quiet and let politics take its course.[25]

The above examples are initial illustrations of how Woredanet and Schoolnet emerged as technopolitical regimes, as the embodiment of a political plan that could be enforced with the support of technology. Their scope, however, was not simply supportive of a decentralized state. The combination of the foundational discourse of the nation advanced by the EPRDF and the kind of state-building project this 'dictated' in practice, created a more intricate distribution of forces that the new systems had to 'fix'.

### A Contradictory Project: Controlled Decentralization

This is the paradox the current government created: it is a minority government and it needs to justify with an ideology like ethnic federalism its staying in power. They need to decentralize to support their ideology but also to exert a central control to make sure they can stay in power.[26] (Bahru Zewde, Historian)

Bahru Zewde is one of Ethiopia's renowned historians, and his words indicate the contradictions the EPRDF became embroiled in as a result of its complex nation- and state-building projects. While ethnic federalism was likely the only possible compromise that could legitimate the EPRDF's control over the country, in order to bring this about, it had

---

[24] Interview: ibid.
[25] Interview: Computer scientist, Addis Ababa University, 20 March 2008.
[26] Interview: Bahru Zewde, Historian, Addis Ababa, 7 July 2008.

to strengthen centrifugal forces; forces which had the potential to threaten the capacity to maintain the control and authority sought by new leaders.

Different strategies have been devised to resolve this paradox, many of which have been illustrated in previous studies. From the creation of a de facto single party system, based on ethnically rooted parties able to win majorities in both local and parliamentary elections (Aalen, 2002; Emmenegger, Keno, & Hagmann, 2011; Pausewang et al., 2002); to the establishment of a relation of dependency between local administrations, which have been practically denied the right of collecting taxes and define their priority spending, and the central government, which has been entitled to centralize and then reallocate resources (Assefa & Tegegne, 2007; Chanie, 2007, 2009; Habtu, 2003); to more specific measures, such as the use of the federal security forces to control unstable peripheral zones (Vaughan & Tronvoll, 2003) and the provision of a wide range of training and courses to universalize the philosophy of the EPRDF (Chanie, 2009; Vaughan, 2011).

Woredanet and Schoolnet represent one of the latest incarnations of the desire for controlled decentralization. Since power was further devolved to woreda level, a new mechanism was required to ensure that, whilst granted greater responsibilities and increased capacity to operate, the units did not fall outside of the control of the state. The system, although bidirectional in principle, has been used mostly to consolidate the EPRDF's influence in the periphery, ensuring that the powers to which local administrators were entitled were exercised within a framework decided at the central level. An EICTDA technocrat elaborated on this:

Woredanet is used mainly to connect people with the centre for administration purposes, to govern the entire community and provide services. By using technology, information is not lost when it is transferred. This is at the base of everything. Let me give you an example. If you are in a school where the professor teaches by saying something to a student and asking him to pass the message to the next student, and so forth, the last student will have information that is completely different from the one communicated at the beginning. Woredanet prevents this from happening.[27]

Making sure that all receive the same message and can act accordingly contrasts with the principles that should inspire a decentralized state, where those working in the localities are able to make decisions autonomously on the basis of their knowledge of the local context. However, this had been one of the major requirements in designing Woredanet,

---

[27] Interview: Civil Servant, EICTDA, 5 May 2008.

a project aimed at intensifying the presence of the centre in the periphery and empowering local administrations without the risk that they could fall outside of the orbit of the central leadership.

Beyond government circles, this characteristic of the system was heavily criticized for magnifying the need to control the local administrative structures rather than enhancing their capacity. Yemane Kidane, a former guerrilla fighter and government official who left the government in 2001 as a result of the split within the EPRDF described earlier, argued that this excessive attempt to control could jeopardize the whole state building project.

Through Woredanet there can be a commitment to building their [the local cadres] capacity and probably they are doing it. But the problem is that the people at the centre do not allow people at the woreda level to make their own mistakes. There is this obsession with control and command. So the people in the woredas even if more trained and skilled [...] they are not allowed to learn from trial and error. They will always wait for instructions and will be afraid of taking responsibility.[28]

Merera Gudina, Professor of political science at Addis Ababa University and Deputy Chairman of the United Ethiopian Democratic Forces (UEDF), a moderate opposition party, expressed an even more critical stance.

The rhetoric is about decentralization, the empowerment of the people. But when you look at it in practice very little is happening in this direction. The government strategy is to control, not to empower. So Woredanet is to transfer their message from the centre to the periphery. It is used to control and indoctrinate. Maybe they say it is for public service delivery but I saw very little results so far. Good governance is just a way to cover all this with nice words.[29]

Projects such as Woredanet emerged as the latest incarnation of a complex, and partially contradictory, nation-building and state-building project. These projects embodied the ideologies that sustained the guerrilla struggle in the bush, and at the same time were aimed at enforcing some key components of those ideologies on the ground. As such they could not but emerge in competition with alternative political plans advanced by other key actors in Ethiopia, operating domestically and from abroad. To succeed, the EPRDF had to marginalize not only the oppositional discourses, but also the actors articulating them. The next

---

[28] Interview: Yemane Kidane, Former Member of EPRDF and Officer in the Ministry of Foreign Affairs. Director, Centre for Policy Research and Dialogue, Addis Ababa, 5 June 2008.
[29] Interview: Merera Gudina, Professor, Addis Ababa University and Chair of the United Ethiopian Democratic Forces, Addis Ababa, 3 June 2008.

section illustrates how this was achieved in practice and how it has resulted in the polarization of the Ethiopian society where citizens are framed as either beneficiaries or as enemies of the EPRDF's national plan.

## Revolutionary Democracy and Social Integration

Between the start of the civil war and 1991, when the EPRDF came to power, global political conditions had changed dramatically. The Berlin Wall had fallen and the USSR was slowly dissolving. Marxist-Leninist thinking, which had constituted the main theoretical base during the struggle, had become a problematic legacy for the new government as it sought to position itself in the post–Cold War order. At the same time, to install itself firmly at the centre of the local political scene against many competing forces, the EPRDF needed strong backing from the international community. In this context the party leadership decided to publicly distance itself from its communist past, ostensibly embracing some of the principles of liberal democracy, including regular elections and a liberalized press.

These concessions, however, have to be understood in the context of a party where Marxist-Leninist ideology continued to quietly, but not less profoundly, act both as an inspiration to shape concrete policies, and as a guide for structuring the decision-making process within the party. All land in Ethiopia remained in the hands of the state, which was entitled to provide access to farmers on an equal basis. The state and the party continued to control a large proportion of shares in some of the biggest industries in the country, including in the telecommunication sector, which was kept as a monopoly, the only system that, according to Ethiopian leaders, could ensure peasants were not forgotten in the name of profit.[30]

The EPRDF sought to reconcile these contradictory tendencies, oscillating between acceptance of neo liberal rules and institutions and loyalty to the Marxist-Leninist principles that led to their success against the Derg, in the concept of revolutionary democracy. Similarly to ethnic federalism, the idea of revolutionary democracy emerged from the time of the struggle, but differently from ethnic federalism, which acted as the overarching and relatively stable discourse for re-founding the Ethiopian

---

[30] The tendency of having loyal political figures heading the most important industries in the country is particularly evident in Tigray, where the biggest industries, from tanneries to pharmaceutical factories, are clustered in a consortium known as Endowment Fund For The Rehabilitation of Tigray (EFFORT), responding directly to TPLF cadres.

nation-state, it was used as a more 'flexible and adaptable discursive tool in evolving international liberal and national contexts' (Bach, 2011, 643).

Revolutionary democracy favours a populist attitude claiming a direct connection of the vanguard party with the masses, bypassing the need to negotiate with other elites who advance competing ideas of the nation-state and of the role different groups can have within it. The concept had concrete repercussions on how priorities were set and how resources were allocated, including in the communication sector. While very little energy was invested to improve the communication channels with dissenting voices, substantial efforts were made to consolidate and reinforce the relationship with the base of political power. If the EPRDF eventually realized its hegemonic ambitions in the Gramscian sense of an internalized set of assumptions and not an imposed order (De Waal, 2012), it did so by progressively excluding interpretations of the nation-state that were in competition with its own, concurrently grounding its ideas in material realities which could be understood by the largely illiterate population.

### Including the Poor

We always said that whatever policy we decide to develop, it will always be the farmers and the peasants to implement it. So the decisions may be taken at the centre but the targets for these decisions are the farmers. So even now through technology the final targets are the farmers. It is the concept of mass mobilization. The whole idea of revolutionary democracy is to have the hegemony of ideas and views, to be the only one occupying the political space. But this has to be implemented on the ground. So technology is used to disseminate ideas but also to achieve results, otherwise people will know that what you say is just words.[31]

During the civil war Yemane Kidane's assignment was to mobilize support for the TPLF inside and outside Ethiopia. From its base in Sudan he contacted journalists and officials in ministries of foreign affairs, but also covertly conveyed leaflets to influential politicians through their Ethiopian maids. As a TPLF leader, he continued to shape state policy, especially communication and foreign policy, until 2001, when the internal split in the party forced him to leave government. Although he was not directly involved in ICT related projects, his experience in defining the TPLF and EPRDF communication strategy during and after the war, as well as his criticism of his former allies and his witty

---

[31] Interview: Yemane Kidane, Former Member of EPRDF and Officer in the Ministry of Foreign Affairs. Director, Centre for Policy Research and Dialogue, Addis Ababa, 5 June 2008.

personality, made Yemane's perspective particularly illuminating in regard to important aspects of the discourses used by the EPRDF and their influence on the re-shaping of ICTs.

As cited above, there were several key points used by the EPRDF to define and structure Ethiopian society and the party's role within it. Here I want to focus mostly on the links between mass mobilization, revolutionary democracy, and the peasantry, leaving the analysis of others, such as the importance of achieving results instead of using 'just words', for the next section.

Mass mobilization has been at the core of numerous revolutions throughout history. It refers to the need to activate large numbers to guarantee the success of a specific political project, and its nature varies according to the relationship between the mobilizing and the mobilized.[32] The Derg itself embraced mass mobilization as a key strategy first for its success and later for its survival, seeking in the masses a form of legitimation for its rule over the country (Clapham, 1990). In the case of the TPLF, the peasants were given even greater prominence and placed at the core of revolutionary efforts, not just as ideal-type referents, but also as individuals to whom the party leadership had to show its commitment (Segers et al., 2009; Young, 1997). Yemane Kidane explained how 'when we were in the bush we were sleeping with the people to show with facts what our struggle was about'.[33]

This point was further illustrated by Alfred Taban, a Southern Sudanese journalist who had been invited by the TPLF to report on their struggle:

Because of the bombings we were travelling at night. . . . We found a small town at 2 am where they said we should sleep. It was very cold, they threw us some blankets. [I said] are you going to sleep here in this cold? [They said] yes it is very late so we cannot wake up these people at this time of the night. I was shocked because my only knowledge of guerrillas was not like that. There were people that would throw away any people at any minute [at] will. Take the SPLA[34]; they wanted the best things for themselves at the expense of the citizens.[35]

---

[32] For a comprehensive review of the role of the concept of mass mobilization in revolutions see, for example, Jack Goldstone (2001).

[33] A female former fighter I interviewed in Tigray further illustrated this point with her testimony by explaining that 'during the struggle we were going house to house to talk with the women and also to help them. So at the end we were like friends. And they became interested in what we were saying'. Interview: Former TPLF Fighter, Mekele, 3 July 2008.

[34] The SPLA is the Sudanese People Liberation Front, was originally led by John Garang, and fought for the recognition of the right to self-determination of Southern Sudan.

[35] Interview: Alfred Taban, Editor in Chief of The Khartoum Monitor and BBC Correspondent in Sudan, Khartoum, Sudan, 12 April 2006. This interview was conducted with Nicole Stremlau, who has also used it in her monograph on *The press and consolidation of power in Ethiopia and Uganda* (Stremlau, 2008).

The TPLF/EPRDF's idea of mass mobilization was rooted in Leninist doctrine and heavily reliant on a direct connection between a vanguard party and the masses. The quest for 'hegemony of ideas and views' mentioned by Yemane should thus be interpreted as having the farmers as its main focus, at least during the struggle and in the initial phase of the EPRDF rule over Ethiopia. The 2005 elections, in fact, and the striking losses of the EPRDF to the opposition in many urban centres, motivated the party leadership to progressively adopt a more inclusive attitude also towards urban working and middle classes (Di Nunzio, 2014).

While the conceptualization of who were to be considered 'the masses' thus changed over time, the framing of the relationship between them and the vanguard party remained relatively stable. By claiming to have a special relationship with key constituents in Ethiopia's society, the EPRDF de facto created a way to assert its legitimacy outside of the representational model that characterizes most liberal democracies. As Nicholas Bach has convincingly remarked, however, this strategy did not develop in stark opposition with the principles of liberal democracies, but rather as a complement to them: 'The main symbols of the post-1991 regime, as relentlessly exposed by the government, are, among others, the constitution, multi-party democracy, and the electoral process, presented as founding myths of the country democratization' (Bach, 2011, 645).

Differently from China, which more visibly refused to integrate liberal institutions in its political system, the idea of revolutionary democracy emerged as a compromise that offered in principle to citizens the opportunity to express or withdraw their support at regular intervals, but that beyond the national and local elections allowed decisions taken at the centre to trickle down to the lower levels of the administration, with few or no mechanisms for challenging them. Similarly to China, however, and in accordance to what Yemane Kidane mentioned above, for this system to function and survive, tangible changes had to be delivered down to the grassroots. This motivated an increased emphasis on service delivery, and on improving the capacity of the state bureaucracy to penetrate the lives of people at the bottom of rural first and then the urban society. Technology, ICTs in particular, progressively come to play a key role in this project, keeping contact with the masses, and demonstrating commitment to them through the implementation of government plans. How this was achieved in practice will be illustrated in Chapter 6 as the design of Woredanet and Schoolnet was profoundly influenced by the necessity to replicate some of the mechanisms that had been at the centre of the mass mobilization of Tigrayan peasants at the time of the struggle with a much larger constituency.

*Excluding the Elites*

Framing the privileged relationship between the vanguard and the masses as the cornerstone of revolutionary democracy was accompanied by a complementary framing of other groups as irrelevant or as enemies of the oppressed. Below is an excerpt from an editorial published a month after the capture of Addis Ababa, which describes the members of the Workers Party of Ethiopia (WPE), the party created by the Derg, as exploiters of the innocent.

The so-called WPE is a dictatorial fascist party which had been spilling the blood of the innocents from its very foundation till its doom. On the basis of the unjustifiable expression 'priority for the comrades; the best for the comrades', WPE members used to lead an affluent life. On the other hand, the unfortunate poor were not properly paid for their labour and were even robbed of the fruits of their labour. *The Ethiopian Herald, Friday 28 June 1991*

It was not only the long-term enemy that was framed as a danger to society. Other liberation movements that had fought the Derg with agendas different from those of the EPRDF, received similar treatment.

At the present moment chauvinists living in foreign countries are doing everything to ignite the flames of war only days after the former regime, which was in the forefront of the war drama, was defeated. Only a few days ago, these anti-peace elements held a meeting in Washington and made various anti-peace decisions. We must not fail to recognize that anti-peace forces like the EPRP and MEISON undertake acts of war. These groups, being the very forces who used to murder the children of the oppressed people, have no compassion whatsoever for the oppressed. *The Ethiopian Herald, Thursday 6 June 1991*

Use of such language has continued to characterize government statements and government-sponsored media, and to be used to label different political groupings that sought to stand in opposition to the EPRDF. One of the corollaries of this exclusionary attitude was that the ideas put forward by political opponents were considered of lesser value and unworthy to be or allowed into the political debate. This attitude is well illustrated by the words of Haddush Kassu, former General Manager of the Ethiopian News Agency and one of the senior officials in the Ministry of Information. His words were a reply to a question about the censorship of oppositional blogs that started soon after the 2005 elections.

During the elections it is true that websites played a big role and people were printing articles from the Internet and using them and disseminating them. But I do not know about the relevance of these ideas, because they are just individual opinions. Some issues are controversial only for the politicians but not for the people. So we think that if people think differently they have to have the chance to express it and strengthen their way of looking at things. But if it is just about the elite agenda, the individual agenda and not the agenda of the people why we should allow them to express.[36]

As further illustrated by analysing some of the online debates that took place around the parliamentary elections in 2005, this attitude has triggered harsh responses from those portrayed as enemies who similarly employed polarized rhetoric, profoundly affecting the tone of the political debate (Skjerdal, 2011).

## Revolutionary Democracy and the EPRDF's Culture of Communication

The framework of revolutionary democracy had profound implications on the EPRDF's *culture of communication*, or how the party structured its communication with other components in society and reacted to criticism. I use the concept of culture of communication here to indicate the mix of theories and practices pursued by a group to communicate internally and externally, defining who is included and who is excluded in political communication and decision-making processes. In the case of the EPRDF, this culture progressively emerged during the struggle in the bush and continued to inform decisions and practices both during the transition in the 1990s and during the subsequent consolidation of power. In resonance with the principles of revolutionary democracy it framed the masses as the main targets in the government's communication process and emphasized that messages should be framed in a form that was possible for the target audience to understand and relate to. As illustrated below, three were its central components: an emphasis on showing results rather than making promises, a discipline ensuring that members of the government apparatus would act as messengers of ideas developed at the centre, and a disregard towards adversarial voices that refused to communicate within the framework adopted by the party/state.

### Showing by Doing

The TPLF always recognized the importance of communication in supporting its struggle. From the very beginning a variety of means were used to mobilize the local population and to make people aware of the causes for which the movement stood. Many fighters were given the task of visiting villages and explaining what the TPLF was and what its

---

[36] Interview: Haddush Kassu, Head of External Relations at the Ministry of Information and Former General Manager of the Ethiopian News Agency, Addis Ababa, 28 June 2008.

goals were. Churches and markets were used as focal points to address crowds. Leaflets in both Amharic and Tigrinya were printed in caves and secretly brought into schools and government offices. As indicated in the previous chapter, in 1979 a radio station was established to extend dissemination of the message into enemy held territory. Debretsion Gebremichael, who had been responsible for the maintenance of the radio in the bush, explained how communication was an essential element to win the war.

Communication was central to the struggle; it was the essence of the struggle for us. [...] You had really to convert people, to make them think in a different way. And unless you communicate well and deeply you cannot get to the point of converting people. It is what you communicate but it is also the design of the communication itself. This component was critical to our success.[37]

He later elaborated on what he meant with 'design of communication'.

Communication has to be not just abstract communication, just about principles. It has to be linked to the real life of people. We had to convince them through practice, showing what was practically changing in their lives and giving information that they could practically use in their life. [...] If you are talking to the peasants you have to show. The strategies that we were using in the struggle are still important and are still used now. Only the form has changed.[38]

The importance of showing and not using 'just words' was captured in many other interviews with former fighters and members of the Ethiopian government. As a female fighter who was active in mobilization during the war against the Derg explained, this strategy was called *empiricism* among the ideologist of the struggle.[39]

We were supporting empiricism. The idea to practice first rather than just disseminating ideology. We were not using theories to explain to people. We had to act first to show them. But at the same time we were thinking that practice should be led by theory. Theory was important to analyse issues. And practice should be theory driven. But you have to implement to make people understand, to explain to them.[40]

Empiricism does not operate on the principle that actions should follow words, as is generally the case when political organizations are

---

[37] Interview: Debretsion GebreMichael, Director of EICTDA, Addis Ababa, 10 June 2008.
[38] Ibid.
[39] Empiricism should not be confused with pragmatism, another of the principles guiding the operations of the fighters during the struggle. Pragmatism was embraced only by a minority of the TPLF vanguard and caused a split within the front. The idea at its core was that some key aspects of the struggle should be concealed to those who were not part of the core leadership. (Tadesse & Young, 2003)
[40] Interview: Former TPLF Fighter, Aksum, 29 June 2008.

competing for power. Rather, for the TPLF, 'actions *were* words'. They were the message. It was mostly through direct exposure to what was being done on the ground that people could be 'converted', as pointed out by Debretsion, and thus choose different courses of action. This belief continued to guide EPRDF cadres, and has strongly influenced key aspects of the re-shaping of ICTs, as will be shown when analysing the evolution of Woredanet and Schoolnet. Debretsion illustrated this relevance of empiricism in recent times.

So this is also key now, because all the strata of society have to be reached. ICTs represent an extension of that very idea. If the Prime Minister wants now to communicate with the people he can do it. So, this need to reach out to the people is still there. But now since you have a country to rule it is more difficult, you cannot gather all the people. You need the infrastructure, but communicating effectively is still an art.[41]

Similarly, Bereket Simon, explained that Woredanet was designed with the farmers as one of the main targets.

Woredanet is for different purposes. It is to strengthen the capacity of the public administration, but it is also to reach rural Ethiopia, to make sure that the farmers get the right information. Woredanet is part of the wider communication strategy we have developed. Instead of communicating with everybody, we prefer to communicate with the most advanced part of the society and let it be our messenger.[42]

Some features of Woredanet were thus optimized to emulate some of the communication mechanisms employed in the bush, but on a larger scale. Videoconferencing from the centre towards the peripheries was prioritized over Internet browsing, for example. As is further explained below, having the vanguard talking to the local political cadres was considered more important than letting them use new tools to find tailored solutions on their own.

### Internal Communication

The focus on showing results instead of just promising them was effective with the peasants during the struggle but presented a fundamental challenge: to ensure that at different levels the fighters, and subsequently the administrators, knew what these results had to be. Theory did not have to be communicated directly to the ground, but was nonetheless informing decision-making. As Yemane Kidane elaborated:

---

[41] Interview: Debretsion Gebremichael, Director of EICTDA, Addis Ababa, 10 June 2008.
[42] Interview: Bereket Simon, Advisor to the Prime Minister and former minister of Information, Addis Ababa, 24 June 2008.

When communicating in the bush we had a lot of problems in making sure that the same information could make it to the village councils without being corrupted. Because of course everybody was interpreting [it in] his own way. And these people who were leading the struggle at the grassroots level could not show that they did not know what they were fighting for and what they were doing. So even if they had not understood a message well, they had to communicate to the people what was their interpretation. And maybe this was different from the original message. [. . .] The people on the ground were the ones who had to know how to implement. But the ideology was at the centre. It was the prism through which all information was elaborated and decisions were taken.[43]

The need to ensure that a vision and the activities derived from it are known at different levels is common to many organizations. But in the case of the TPLF first and the EPRDF later on, this goal was achieved through imposing a particularly severe party discipline and recurring to ideology to exclude most forms of opposition at lower levels of both the political and the bureaucratic structure. In resonance with the principles articulated by Lenin to structure his cadre army (Bach, 2011), this form of 'democratic centralism' allowed some space for debate within the executive and central committees of the party, but once a decision had been made, criticism was considered factionalism and not tolerated, up to leading to the dismissal of those who articulated it (International Crisis Group, 2009).

This conception of internal decision making and communication profoundly influenced the ways in which ICTs came to be interpreted as the tool that could solve the leaders' long-term challenge to communicate their decisions lower down on the party and administrative structure. I earlier illustrated the importance of Woredanet in ensuring that all cadres received the same message. Amare Amsalu, CEO of the Ethiopian Telecommunication Corporation, reaffirmed this point.

When information is provided through mediators it may lose the value that the first person gave to it. But now a message that emanates from the Prime Minister can produce the same level of understanding both among officials as well as at the lowest level.[44]

Amare used the example of the Prime Minister to illustrate his point, which is similar to the example cited by Debretsion in the previous section when he noted, 'if the Prime Minister wants now to communicate

---

[43] Interview: Yemane Kidane, Former Member of EPRDF and Officer in the Ministry of Foreign Affairs. Director, Centre for Policy Research and Dialogue, Addis Ababa, 5 June 2008.

[44] Interview: Amare Amsalu, CEO, Ethiopian Telecommunication Corporation, Addis Ababa, 27 June 2008.

with the people he can do it'. These two cases are not isolated examples. Most politicians and civil servants, when asked to provide an example of how Woredanet was used, mentioned the need for the Prime Minister to communicate.[45] As will become clearer in the next chapter, this aspect guided important decisions in the design of Woredanet and Schoolnet.

### Refusal to Engage

A final aspect of the EPRDF's culture of communication is related to the relationship the TPLF/EPRDF developed with its political opponents. The vision of society advanced as part of the EPRDF's nation-building project posits a population divided between a large constituency for which the state is responsible and a minority that opposes the endeavour. Since it came to power the EPRDF has chosen not to negotiate with adversarial voices, preferring to expand its influence and presence as exemplified by ambitious projects like Woredanet and Schoolnet. The party has sought to minimize and marginalize opposition, rather than enlarge its base by incorporating new forces and perspectives. As two senior members of the EPRDF, Bereket Simon and Ahmed Hassen, Deputy Chairman of the Information & Culture Affairs Commission describe, in the initial period of EPRDF government the policy towards the opposition entailed ignoring competing ideas.

There were problems with the practical perception of what we were doing. With the new constitution there were people who were not happy with the idea of ethnic federalism. They were thinking that ethnic federalism would have endangered the unity of this country. And we had to reply to them with the practice. [...] The elites in the urban areas did not like us for the handling of the national question. So we decided that we were going to deal with this with time. Not immediately. We wanted to address this issue by showing it. And we were also busy addressing all other issues: agriculture, education, everything that was needed to rule a country. And our being busy addressing all these issues also gave the opportunity to the opposition to hammer us constantly. But we were ready to accept these hiccups. We did not have to explain. We were doing.[46]

Bereket's statement summarizes a range of issues that have been analysed so far: ethnic federalism as the core of a new discourse of the

---

[45] The interviewees were not primed but responded to generic questions. For example, they were not asked how the Prime Minister was using the system, but they were asked only to provide examples of how Woredanet was used. In some cases, such as those cited here, this question was not even asked, but the reference to the Prime Minister came spontaneously as part of the response to a different question.

[46] Interview: Bereket Simon, Advisor to the Prime Minister and former minister of Information, Addis Ababa, 24 June 2008.

nation, the dismissal of elites as inimical forces, and the importance accorded to practice rather than rhetoric. But most importantly for the present argument is observing how little relevance he attached to the engagement with other voices and the need to respond to criticism. As is typical of populist discourses, the culture of 'doing' pursued by the EPRDF was opposed to a culture of just 'talking', which oppositional forces are accused of. This point was further substantiated during an interview with Ahmed Hassen, Member of Parliament and Deputy Chairman of the Information & Culture Affairs Commission:

> We saw this initial phase as a transition period. We did not have very much hope. We hoped that a democratic process would have come through the civil society and we were hoping also through the media. But the media did not participate. They were just adversarial. And so our approach was to just ignore them. At the time of the transitional government they were attacking Meles personally but he decided just to ignore them. [...] Unfortunately there is no middle ground in Ethiopia. The culture of dialogue is not there.[47]

This confrontational environment and the lack of any desire for engagement, on both sides of the political spectrum, is one of the main factors that led to the closure of many critical newspapers, and later to the censoring of blogs. The government contributed to creating this climate but it has also been a victim of it. Its refusal to engage has polarized political debate, further radicalizing adversarial components of society that, having been framed as enemies, have become enemies in actuality.

The analysis of how the EPRDF structured its communication and reacted to criticism helps developing a broader point about *culture of communication*, as the mix of theories and practices pursued by a group to communicate internally and externally. I use this concept here to shift the focus from instrumental to more ideological aspects of communication. The predominant focus of scholarship on political communication in Western democracies, and the attention placed on studying how subsequent technological innovations have affected how parties and governments relate to citizens have led to overlook how other factors may be more relevant in different sociopolitical contexts. The strategies adopted by the EPRDF, for example, bear little trace of the professionalization of communication that has come to characterize political communication in the United States or Europe (Blumler & Kavanagh, 1999). The party, rather than specialized agencies, has maintained a leading role

---

[47] Interview: Ahmed Hassen, Deputy Chairman of the Information & Culture Affairs Commission, Addis Ababa, 13 June 2008.

in deciding the means and the languages for communicating with their constituents, and substantive messages about the role of politics in transforming society still dominate.

Similarly to the concept of political culture, which has been criticized both in political science (Lane, 1992) and in Ethiopian studies (Hagmann, 2006) for its indeterminacy and psychological reductionism, the notion of culture of communication bear the risk of essentializing social practices. But it also helps placing adequate emphasis on questions asking 'why political actors communicate the way they do?', which have been largely overlooked in favour of interrogating, for example, how a party has been successful in communicating with its constituents, or how a new techno-logical innovation has been appropriated by different contenders.

Especially in contexts where political competition is limited, ideology is likely to play a greater role and considerations about who participates in, and who is excluded from, a communication process are likely to be based more on how certain individuals are categorized according to a given framework (e.g. as rent-seekers, as vanguard, as a model farmer) rather than on calculations on the amount of support needed to pass a certain policy or on the opportunity to build a more inclusive society. Placing greater emphasis on ideological, rather than just instrumental, aspects of a communicative process thus re-opens opportunities to study not just how political actors use communication to win or maintain power, but also how they are themselves bound by the legacy of the organization they belong to, in more or less conscious ways.

## Conclusion

Ethnic federalism and revolutionary democracy have been the building blocks in the re-imagination of the Ethiopian state after the EPRDF came to power. They have served both a foundational role, offering a frame-work for different members of the Ethiopian society to think of them-selves as part of a new nation-state, and an aspirational role, informing projects that could respond to changing domestic and international conditions and defining new sets of goals for the country to achieve.

As further explained in the following chapters, at the international level the EPRDF leadership was initially reluctant to clearly spell out the features of the two discourses that were charting its nation-building project. Over time, however, ethnic federalism and revolutionary dem-ocracy provided material for the elaboration of a new discourse of Ethi-opia as a developmental state which stood more clearly as an alternative to the templates proposed by Western donors. While ethnic federalism and revolutionary democracy largely remained distant ideas for those who were not well versed in Ethiopian politics and history, the concept of the developmental state more clearly connected Ethiopia to successful examples which had emerged in opposition to liberal orthodoxy and was indicative of the greater self-confidence that the government leadership progressively gained in the international arena.

ICTs were captured in this transition, becoming both an expression and an instrument of it. While systems like Woredanet and Schoolnet initially emerged silently, as relatively unique tools for the central government to achieve its goals at a domestic level, and the defence of the national information space appeared a temporary response which would eventually succumb to international pressures, these projects and measures started to be theorized as viable alternatives for a divided country like Ethiopia to employ ICTs as instruments for development, while reducing their destabilizing potential.

# 5   Ethiopia's Developmental and Sovereign Technopolitical Regimes

*Not long ago, many of us felt that we were too poor to afford to invest seriously in ICT. We assumed that ICT was a luxury that only the rich could afford. We were convinced, and rightly so, that we should invest every penny we have on securing the next meal for our people, on putting some sort of shelter over their heads, on reducing or, as the experts in the development business would have it, alleviating absolute poverty, absolute poverty which has aptly been defined as poverty that kills. We did not believe that serious investment in ICT had anything to do with facing the challenges of poverty that kills. Now I think we know better. Now we believe we are too poor not to save everything we can and invest as much of it as possible on ICT. We recognize that while ICT may be a luxury for the rich, for us - the poor countries - it is a vital and essential tool for fighting poverty, for beating poverty that kills and ensuring our survival. That is why we are fully committed to investing as much of our time, energy, and money as possible on ICT and to its effective use in our war on poverty.*   (Meles Zenawi, Prime Minister of Ethiopia)[1]

Meles Zenawi's statement illustrates how dramatically the perception of ICTs evolved over time in Ethiopia. ICTs were initially interpreted as instruments that could do little to help a country where food security was still one of the main concerns, and would only later become, in the words of the Prime Minister, 'a vital and essential tool' for development. This chapter analyses the various steps which characterized this evolution while also addressing some key aspects concealed by the Prime Minister's words: how the investment of 'time, energy, and money' in ICTs was not simply motivated by the 'war on poverty' but, more importantly, by the desire to use technology to enact the EPRDF's political plans.

The previous two chapters examined the discourses at the core of this plan as well as those emerging around ICTs, using politics as a starting point to get at technology. This chapter and the following one move in the opposite direction, looking closely at technological artefacts to

---

[1] The Minister of Capacity Building Tefera Walwa used this quote from Meles Zenawi at e-Learning Africa, the first international conference on ICT for development, education, and training in Africa, which took place in Addis Ababa on 25–27 May 2006.

reconstruct how they have embedded specific discourses put forward by competing actors. These chapters focus on the technopolitics that emerged at the intersection between hegemonic projects and technical possibilities and on the actual technopolitical regimes that were generated from this intersection. Both chapters cover the period from 1991, when the EPRDF first seized power, to 2006, the year following the most contested election in Ethiopian history, which motivated new measures affecting both Ethiopian politics and technopolitics that will be discussed in Chapter 6.

This chapter in particular examines the steps that led to the Ethiopian government engaging more with ICTs, and how this increased engagement led to the development of two interconnected and complementary technopolitical regimes. A *developmental* technopolitical regime centred on Woredanet and Schoolnet, and a *sovereign* technopolitical regime, asserting the monopoly of the state over telecommunications and the Internet. Both regimes uniquely blended the discourses of ethnic federalism and revolutionary democracy with a commitment towards modernizing Ethiopia, and concurrently resisted the pressure that globalization was placing on the country. In discussing these technopolitical regimes, this chapter also illustrates how the process of adapting tools designed outside Ethiopia to meet local needs did not result in perfect machines that could effectively implement plans defined at the centre, but instead led to the emergence of less coherent assemblages that fell short of realizing all the aspirations expressed by the Ethiopian government.

## Fluctuations and Turning Points: Moving Towards a Developmental Regime

The process leading to the creation of a developmental technopolitical regime, with Woredanet and Schoolnet at its core, was neither linear nor smooth. On the contrary, it was characterized by a chaotic evolution, slow progress initially, and a subsequent rapid acceleration. Similar to other cases of socialization of international ideas and norms at the local level (Checkel, 1997, 2001; Keck & Sikkink, 1998), for new discourses to be effectively embraced they need to resonate with those already articulated in specific social and political environments. The fit is not always immediately apparent, and therefore must be constructed by either local or international actors, or both. In the case of Woredanet and Schoolnet this process of progressive adaptation can be divided into three different phases.

During a first phase, the discourse on ICT for development as articulated internationally emerged as mostly alien to state agents, the only ones with enough power and resources to open the path towards new applications of ICTs. In a second phase different actors, both state and non-state, progressively built the bases for a fit to be created between international and local discourses. Given the nature of the ICT agenda, this fit had to be found both at the discursive and at the material level, and required the Ethiopian government to develop an understanding of the means that could be mobilized to support its agenda. Finally, a path was opened for the creation of a new technopolitical regime, taking shape at the crossroads between the opportunities opened by the new tools and political ambitions articulated at the local level.

This *first phase* can be roughly dated to the period between 1991, when the EPRDF seized power, and the early 2000s. During this phase the government showed little inclination to embrace ICTs as advocated by international organizations and corporations. Its priority was guiding the country through a critical political transition after a long civil war and new technologies, as framed in international circles, did not appear instrumental in achieving this plan. The promotion of the private sector and of the free flow of information held very little appeal for the EPRDF. Economic growth and efficiency were certainly more interesting, but were not as crucial as political hegemony or the control of the state, which, quite predictably, did not feature in the international discourse. As a sign of this minimal interest, the centres in charge of ICTs instituted by the Derg regime were left almost untouched, in contrast to urgent efforts to re-orient other institutions, which led, for example, to the dismissal of most officers in the Ministry of Information and the Ministry of Education. As a former official of the National Computer Centre recalled: 'at the beginning they did not really care about us, we could continue to do what we were doing. Later they started asking us to do more bureaucratic work such as checking if efforts were duplicated, but we were not really affected by the change in power'.[2]

During this period the new discourse on ICTs simply fluctuated throughout different sectors of the Ethiopian society, without finding a concrete application. In the absence of a clear understanding of how technology could be used to serve the state's interests or, on the contrary, could be turned against them, the government simply acted to guarantee that no other actors would be able to seize the opportunities potentially opened by ICTs. Telecommunications continued to be a state monopoly, no private Internet Service Provider (ISP) was licensed, and even the purchase of hardware and software was complicated by a limited offer

[2] Interview: Former member of the National Computer Centre, Addis Ababa, 20 March 2008.

and by high import taxes.[3] This reactive spirit would continue to inspire the sovereign technopolitical regime, which is discussed in the second part of this chapter, minimizing the ability of actors other than the state to influence the adoption and adaptation of ICTs.

In parallel to these reactive measures, however, the new millennium witnessed the emergence of more proactive tendencies towards ICTs, opening a *second phase* that would eventually lead to the massive investments undertaken to realize projects such as Schoolnet and Woredanet. It was not one, but a series of events which conspired to produce this change, generating momentum for a new strategic approach to ICTs.

As indicated earlier, in 2001 a major split emerged in the TPLF due to the two-year long war with Eritrea, threatening the leadership of Meles Zenawi. The rift profoundly shook the party. It ended with the purge of the faction opposing Meles and led to an ambitious project of transformation to reinforce state authority (Vaughan, 2011). The institutional connections between the centre and the peripheries were strengthened, the state was reformed to act as a more active player in social and economic renewal, and ICTs were set to become a centrepiece of the new strategy. At the same time, Meles Zenawi began to more visibly assert his plan to re-position Ethiopia, both at the national and at the international level, as a developmental state. In retrospect, his project fell short of the ideal of creating a *democratic* developmental state, a concept previously theorized by Thandika Mkandawire (2001), and one Meles had publicly embraced and presented to both local and international constituencies. Some of the steps taken in the ICT sector, however, did move in the direction of reinforcing elements that characterize *traditional* developmental models, such as strengthening the bureaucracy while weakening and subordinating civil society and reinforcing the power and autonomy of the developmental elite. (De Waal, 2012; Leftwich, 1995).

This period coincided with the peak of activities on ICTs organized by the international community in Addis Ababa, forcing some key figures, including the Prime Minister, to engage more seriously with the new tools and rhetoric.[4] As previously argued, this did not mean that the discourses articulated on these occasions went unchallenged; in fact the

---

[3] All items such as personal computers, laptops, printers, etc. were subject to a 5 per cent duty and 10 per cent surtax on top of the 15 per cent VAT. Duty and surtax would only be lifted in 2008. This move was welcomed by the business sector in the country, which, however, indicated that also the VAT should be lifted in order to promote the private sector and computer literacy (Mekuria, 2008).

[4] See Chapter 3 for a list of events and training activities in which representatives of Ethiopian institutions were involved.

opposite was the case, but they offered Ethiopia's leaders the chance to reflect on which aspects of these discourses were more compatible with their plans and appreciate that, despite often being framed as a holistic package, ICTs were not a monolithic entity.

This 'unpacking' was further facilitated by international companies which, if generally interested in advocating policies stressing development and democratization, also had strong commercial interests and were eager to win large contracts in African countries, even if this meant cooperating with a government whose agenda did not resonate with the ideals these companies were publicly supporting. One of the first persons to work closely with the Ethiopian government and to illustrate how ICTs could be tailored to the country's specific needs was Noah Samara, an Ethiopian national living in the United States who, as mentioned earlier, had founded the first satellite radio network, World Space Radio.[5] After Samara, other international corporations started proposing similar or complementary ideas to respond to the requests articulated by the Ethiopian government, opening the path to a more enthusiastic appropriation of ICTs. Contracts for the implementation of both Schoolnet and Woredanet were signed with a variety of foreign partners: Cisco Systems and its South African partner Business Connexion (formerly Comparex Africa) for the provision of the networking technologies, US based Hughes Networks for the satellite connection, Japanese Panasonic for the Plasma TV screens, and Israel based VCON for most of the videoconferencing equipment.

### From Tactics to Strategy

The process of progressive accommodation with ICTs corresponded to a shift from a tactical to a strategic approach. While in the initial phase the government adopted short-term measures to resist external pressures to liberalize the sector and contain critical voices from the diaspora, in the latter it progressively managed to incorporate ICTs into its own agenda.[6] In the 1990s the EPRDF-led regime had to relate to norms and resources

---

[5] As Noah explained during a speech he delivered at the African Development Forum in 1999: 'we have embarked on a study with the Ethiopian Media Agency to put receivers in every school and attach these receivers to computers and printers. In addition to delivering the curriculum for each school, the units would address the needs of the other constituencies attached to the schools: like women, health professionals, farmers' (Samara, 1999).

[6] The resistance was further exacerbated by the experience accumulated by the Ethiopian government in the case of print media. The concessions made to donors when opening up the press led in fact to the proliferation of critical newspapers led by members of the previous regime or opposition forces (Gagliardone, 2014; Stremlau, 2011).

that were 'owned' by others (De Certeau, 1984). ICTs were closely connected to discourses that had little to do with those that had emerged in the bush and were being used to re-build the state and the nation; ICTs appeared monolithic and difficult to understand given the lack of adequate knowledge in the country. At the turn of the millennium, however, the government sought to create a space it could own and control, where it could experiment with ICTs without necessarily relating to externally imposed norms and templates. This was the space created by Woredanet and Schoolnet. Foreign companies could be brought within it to give life to projects envisioned at the top of the EPRDF leadership, responding to logics that were firmly rooted in the party's political ideology, rather than in the visions articulated by international actors.

Different accounts exist about whom within the EPRDF first proposed to embark in the realization of Woredanet and Schoolnet, but almost all of them point towards Meles Zenawi. As Myriam Said, the director of programmes and service delivery at Global Computing Solutions (GCS), the Ethiopian company that was the most involved in the realization of the project remembered:

Meles had gone to Germany and he was impressed that he was able to videoconference with other heads of state just using a good satellite. And he came back and said "Why I have to waste all this money in per diem to send my people around, when I can just put people in touch through something like this?"[7]

This account seems to emphasize the efficiency gains that Woredanet could allow, but as Myriam continued, Woredanet and Schoolnet were part of a broader effort to ensure technology could serve development efforts.

There was always a component, a technological base in any aspect of the developmental state that he [Meles] envisioned. Automating the woreda was a way of getting to know his people.[8]

From a different standpoint, the civil servants I interviewed at the Educational Media Agency and the Ministry of Education pointed instead to Noah Samara as the person who introduced ministers and technocrats to the uses of satellite communication to provide content and reach the peripheries of a large state like Ethiopia. Interestingly, as my research progressed and my questions about the origins of

---

[7] Interview: Myriam Said, Director of programmes and service delivery, Global Computing Solutions (GSC), Addis Ababa, 10 May 2013.
[8] Interview: Myriam Said, Director of programmes and service delivery, Global Computing Solutions (GSC), Addis Ababa, 10 May 2013.

Woredanet and Schoolnet became more removed in time from when the two systems were actually launched, new foundational 'myths' were added to the list. Younger engineers at Ethio-Telecom, for example, started referring to China as the inspirational force behind Woredanet and Schoolnet, and representative of donor agencies were claiming a greater role for the World Bank in first developing the idea for the two systems.

The position of Meles Zenawi within the EPRDF is likely to have made him the prime mover in initiating a project of such scope and ambition, but as this book variously explains, numerous innovations, discourses, and actors contributed to create the space for him to lead the envisioning of Woredanet and Schoolnet, connecting multiple influences within a more or less coherent assemblage. Over time, other institutions were involved to ensure this vision was widely shared and new ones were created where political will and technical expertise could be reconciled.

The Ministry of Capacity Building, headed by Tefera Walwa, was given a broad mandate to ensure technology was used in support of the on going state-building project. A national ICT committee was created with input from all the main ministries to assess the needs of different sectors, from agriculture to federal affairs. And a new institution was founded in 2003 to provide the coordination and oversight necessary to develop and manage complex projects such as Woredanet and Schoolnet, as well as other ICT projects in the country. Headed by Debretsion Gebremichael, the Ethiopian ICT Development Agency (EICTDA) became the transmission chain between the highest levels of the government and all other gears of the developmental technopolitical regime. It was a novel kind of institution in the Ethiopian landscape. Hosted in one of the newest buildings erected by the Ethiopian government, it was set to represent a new outpost of modernity. As compared to the traditional ministerial bureau, usually dated and reflecting the country's communist past, the luminous EICTDA's offices were set to incorporate the new principles of transparency and accountability. Most staff members were young graduates, among the best in the country. At the same time, like most Ethiopian institutions, it still maintained the burden of the centralized administration of power, marginalizing creative, but unaligned positions in favour of politically motivated ones.

The EICTDA, the Ministry of Capacity Building, the national ICT committee, and Ethio-Telecom, were acting as 'network organizations' (Mueller, 2010), bounded and consciously arranged to pursue a common objective. Together, they were able to communicate with the foreign companies in charge of the technical set-up of Woredanet and

Schoolnet, and ensure that the two systems, as complex as they were, could still incorporate the key aspects of the vision developed by the Ethiopian government.

### Technopolitics in Action: Embedding the Key Discourses into Artefacts

A growing understanding of how ICTs could be employed to serve its nation-building agenda and the international availability of the skills required to translate this vision into practice provided the Ethiopian government with an opportunity to turn politics into technopolitics. This enhanced dimension of political power opened up the opportunity to enact policies through the support of technological artefacts, but it also engaged politicians and engineers in complex negotiations to reconcile political aspirations with expanding technical possibilities. This section analyses the key aspects of these negotiations, focusing, in particular, on the influences exercised by ethnic federalism and revolutionary democracy on the actual development of Woredanet and Schoolnet. Through a close look at the two systems it is shown on the one hand how they were designed to structure both objects and users in ways that were instrumental to the EPRDF's national plan, and on the other hand how the material nature of ICTs often forced technocrats and politicians to revise parts of their strategies.

In order to equip the reader with all the necessary means to identify the various steps of this process of mutual influence some of the technical aspects of the two systems are briefly outlined. Fig. 5.1 illustrates the architecture upon which Woredanet and, to a certain extent, Schoolnet are based. The system is divided into three fundamental components: the satellite, represented at the top of the picture; the national data centre, on the left; and the remote sites, on the far right. Each component is described in detail below, also illustrating some key features of Schoolnet by comparing it to the very similar architecture of Woredanet.

*The Satellite.* For a country like Ethiopia, vast, landlocked, and with very little infrastructure, the use of a satellite was the most practical option to implement Woredanet and Schoolnet within a short timeframe. Hughes Network Systems provided connectivity through a C-band transponder on the Intelsat Satellite 901 in service over the Atlantic Ocean. The transponder, with a capacity of approximately 60 Mbps, had to be shared between all the services offered by the two systems. Schoolnet was allocated approximately 16 Mbps, which were used to broadcast

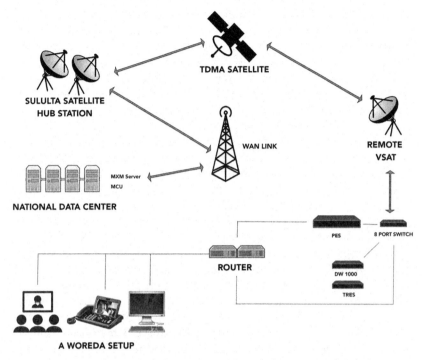

Fig. 5.1 *The Woredanet Architecture (Source: EICTDA)*

pre-recorded classes on eight channels.[9] The remaining bandwidth was used by Woredanet to provide various services: videoconferencing, emailing, voice-over- IP (VoIP), and access to the Internet. The system offered Broadband on Demand (BoD): each service was allocated a certain amount of Mbps, but each channel could be switched off to free bandwidth for the others, as was often the case.

*The National Data Centre.* Woredanet's main servers were installed in the national data centre, located in the office of the Prime

---

[9] The number of classes was later increased to 12, but this did not require augmenting the bandwidth allocated to Schoolnet on the satellite. The channels were administered through statistical multiplexing, a system which could optimally allocate bandwidth among channels. According to the system administrator in charge of the management of the bandwidth at Sululta Earth Station, 'a statistical multiplex allocates bandwidth to each channel according to the needs in a particular moment. For example, if one channel for some time has just a black screen and does not require a lot of bandwidth, extra bandwidth is freed for other channels that may have pictures or videos which require more'. Interview: System Administrator at Sululta Earth Station, 28 May 2008.

Minister. This site hosted the equipment necessary to initiate and manage videoconferencing sessions as well as to remotely control the other services provided through the satellite. The selection of the site is indicative of the strategic relevance of the system and its importance in serving a centrally defined agenda. Two sets of servers, the Media Xchange Manager (MXM) and the Multipoint Control Unit (MCU), were configured to support different videoconferencing typologies, enabling centralized communication. The three most important are detailed below.

*Broadcast* is a type of transmission whereby messages are sent from one point to all other points. It requires a stream of information to be sent only once but it does not permit any other node to interact with the source or other nodes. While it is the most centralized, it does not allow the centre to see what happens in the remote sites.

*Multipoint* transmission allows simultaneous videoconferencing between three or more remote points. It is mediated through an MCU where each party must be authenticated. The MCU receives streams of information from each node and, similarly, sends individual streams to each of them. In a situation where bandwidth is scarce, as in the case of Woredanet, only a few nodes can simultaneously participate in the same session. It is a relatively centralized system. The centre has the power to connect or disconnect parties to a specific session. It also sees what is happening in the remote sites and it is the only node that can decide whether or not to forward messages coming from one remote site to the others.

*Multicast* is a type of transmission where messages originating from each node are sent directly to all others, without the need for a central server. Multicast allows the remote sites to communicate with each other, bypassing the centre, which is required as a bridge during a multipoint session. However, similar to multipoint, multicast presents some challenges when bandwidth is scarce and multiple nodes participate in the same session. It is the most decentralized and transparent system, in theory allowing each party to join a multicast session at any time and see all other streams.

Woredanet was configured to manage each type of transmission, while Schoolnet was capable only of broadcasting messages. Also, while Woredanet content was managed at the national data centre, Schoolnet's broadcasts regularly originated from the Educational Media Agency (EMA).[10]

*The Remote Sites.* In Woredanet's architecture the remote sites are composed of regional and woreda nodes. They employ similar

---

[10] Also the national data centre could reach Schoolnet remote sites when needed.

Fig. 5.2 *A room dedicated to Woredanet videoconferencing*

equipment, with two exceptions. Regional nodes, in theory, are able to initiate a multicast session, while woreda nodes can only join an existing one. Most regional nodes are also equipped with a terrestrial connection that allows them to be connected to the Internet and use other applications on a regular basis, while woreda nodes only have access to the Internet through satellite, which provides intermittent service.[11] Apart from these differences, all remote sites are equipped with a Very Small Aperture Terminal (VSAT), a 2.4 m satellite dish connected to a router and switch, which addresses traffic to three different types of equipment: a set of PCs, two VoIP phones, and a videoconferencing system. As shown in Fig. 5.2 the front end of the videoconferencing system is constituted by a large Plasma TV screen, a video camera, and other equipment managing video and audio streams. The videoconferencing system is usually installed in the Bureau of Capacity Building in the regional and woreda offices, so it is necessary for administrators and civil servants to gather there in order to attend the videoconferencing sessions.

Schoolnet's remote sites are simpler than Woredanet's. As schools only receive broadcasted lessons they do not need videoconferencing

---

[11] For a few years also the Regional Data Centres in Gambella and Benishangul did not have a terrestrial connection.

equipment. In addition, they do not have VoIP phones and only a few enjoy an Internet connection. However, similar to Woredanet, they receive streams through a VSAT and have a 42-inch plasma television screen as a delivery mode.

As described so far, the system may simply appear to be characterized by an eclectic and complicated architecture. On the contrary, as discussed in the next section, by associating some of the components of Woredanet and Schoolnet with the specific discourses on ethnic federalism and revolutionary democracy illustrated earlier, it is possible to uncover some of the underlying motivations behind this convoluted patchwork of technology and politics.

### An Ethno-Technical Federation Tied to the Centre

The influence of the EPRDF's ethnic federalist project on the development of both Woredanet and Schoolnet can be seen in the architecture of the two systems. The promotion of a discourse reframing the domination of a single minority in the larger context of the right to the self-determination of every minority proved a challenging enterprise. This challenge often forced politicians and bureaucrats to come up with original solutions to a variety of problems, from the everyday administration of the periphery to the consolidation of power at the centre. In the case of Schoolnet and Woredanet this aspect was expressed both in the scale of the two systems and in their convoluted design. Some services, such as videoconferencing from the centre to the periphery, were privileged over others, such as the access to the Internet or the capacity to communicate horizontally among different nodes of the state apparatus.

The scale of Woredanet and Schoolnet was one of the most contentious issues dividing the Ethiopian government and the international community. Donor agencies were concerned there were no examples of systems of this kind in Africa or elsewhere in the world and were demanding to pilot them first, before full-scale implementation. It would have been more logical, for example, to start with the major towns that were easier to access and had a greater availability of skilled personnel. The government, however, was responding to a different rationale, at least publicly. As Zelalem Bekele, Chief Technical Officer at ETC, explained:

There is one principle here. When we started Woredanet and Schoolnet we went full scale and we knew it was going to be expensive but it was not unaffordable. But we had to respond to one principle in the government that is the principle of equity. You cannot derogate to that. This is something you cannot compromise.

So we had to do it for the whole country. You cannot pick up one town here and one village there and say this deserves connectivity and this not. It would be against equity.[12]

Enforcing the principles of ethnic federalism on the ground required the allocation of the same rights and resources to every ethnic group. The symbolic value of equally distributing resources among different regions was as important as their material value. It should be noted, however, that despite the EPRDF's strategy to embrace this principle publicly, they government did build a record of trialled reforms, even in key sectors such as land redistribution and public sector reform, first in the central highland regions and then in more peripheral areas (Chanie, 2009; Keller & Smith, 2005). In the case of Woredanet and Schoolnet, the need to expand state control and facilitate communication between cadres, and to enforce the type of controlled decentralization described above, represented an additional incentive to roll out the project as widely as possible.

Respecting these objectives, however, imposed serious technical hurdles, especially for Woredanet. One of the most serious constraints was imposed by the limited bandwidth available through the Hughes-managed satellite. Connecting every woreda from the outset meant catering to almost 600 centres. With only 45 Mbps allocated on the transponder to the whole Woredanet system, for every centre to be constantly connected, the bandwidth available for each individual centre would have to be reduced to an untenable speed.[13]

Paradoxically, these two problems could have cancelled each other out, at least temporarily. While almost all centres were provided with the necessary equipment to run Woredanet, the lack of skills to operate the system and address the technical problems that initially emerged reduced the operational centres to only a fraction of the total number, increasing the bandwidth available for each woreda to a level that would, indeed, allow individuals in the remote sites to browse the Internet and use email. However, it was not Internet access that was considered a priority by the central government. It was videoconferencing. And to allow videoconferencing sessions of a quality good enough for the large screens located in each remote site, the bandwidth allocated by Hughes to each Woredanet node was increased to 1 Mbps for download and

[12] Interview: Zelalem Bekele, Chief Technical Officer, Ethiopian Telecommunication Corporation, Addis Ababa, 28 May 2008.
[13] If each node had to be connected to the Internet, the connection speed would have to be around 7.5 Kbps, half the speed allowed by the first commercial dial-up modems sold on the market in the early 1990s, whose speed was 14.4 Kbps.

512 Kbps for upload. As Myriam Said, GSC's Director of programmes and service delivery, recalled 'The problem was that he [Meles] wanted the system at the quality of a football game on TV, so they had to change and tweak a lot'.[14] This dramatically reduced the number of nodes that could participate in a videoconferencing session and led to a competition for resources among such services as Internet browsing, videoconferencing, VoIP, and emailing. As individuals who managed and used Woredanet described during interviews, this problem was solved by simply switching off the channels allocated to all other services to free up enough bandwidth for central and remote sites to be 'on screen'.[15]

Additional evidence of the minimal interest in providing the periphery with a reliable Internet connection was also provided by the analysis of another aspect of the Woredanet architecture: the convoluted route that packages had to follow up and down the satellites in order to connect a remote computer with a server hosting a website. The following explanation by an international consultant details the problem.

Content from the Internet would have to travel first over satellite/fibre optic gateway from Europe, America, Asia to the ETC gateway [the teleport at Sululta] and then travel back up to a satellite (perhaps different from the first) to then be retransmitted down to the destination at a distant woreda and the user would get their desired Internet content with an extreme amount of delay. Typical roundtrip times for a single satellite hop are over 550 ms with no traffic, so a double-hop path would make interactive applications very difficult to use and websites very hard to navigate. (Haque, 2004, p. 13)

If the Internet was a priority, this complex system could have been simplified with a few changes in the architecture to reduce the two-hops to one and make the transport of Internet data faster and cheaper.[16] Videoconferencing packages, on the other hand, were not affected by

---

[14] Interview: Myriam Said, Director of programmes and service delivery, Global Computing Solutions (GSC), Addis Ababa, 10 May 2013.

[15] This aspect produced significant frustration among people using Woredanet in the remote sites. In fact, apart from when they were communicated to participate in a videoconferencing session, they did not know when they could have access to the Internet and when it would be unavailable. There was no service agreement of any kind. As an informant argued, '[N]o one in the remote sites knows when the system is going to work and for how long. From the centre, people can shut down the system without saying anything in advance, [even] just to test applications or for other reasons'. Interview: Technology officer, Local IT firm, Addis Ababa, 24 April 2008.

[16] Rather than being channelled through the teleport at Sululta, the Internet data could have been provided directly from a teleport on the Hughes or another satellite. This would have entailed equipping the remote sites with receiving infrastructure and a routing system which could allow concurrent reception and forwarding of signals from both sources (one signal from the international teleport, and the other from the 'local' teleport at Sululta).

this issue, as they only had to travel 'locally' and did not need to access data coming from outside Ethiopia. The alternative architecture that could have facilitated the browsing of websites without affecting the other services was never implemented.

The decision to favour services such as videoconferencing over the Internet were rooted in the complex plan of controlled decentralization articulated by the Ethiopian government. As Yemane Kidane summarized in a quote cited earlier, 'the people at the centre do not allow people at the woreda level to make their own mistakes. There is this obsession with control and command. So the people in the woredas, even if more trained and skilled [. . .] they are not allowed to learn from trial and error. They will always wait for instructions and will be afraid of taking responsibility'.[17] Woredanet was installed in the remote areas not to empower individuals to find solutions to their problems independently, for example, through accessing the Internet, but to offer the central power an opportunity to impart clear directions when needed, even to the most remote nodes of the state apparatus.

Similarly, the strategies that had been employed in the bush to communicate internally played an important part in favouring a service such as videoconferencing over others. This influence was noted by Haddush Kassu, the former Manager of the Ethiopian News Agency:

Face to face communication is vital to reach consensus. This is part of our way of framing communication. Woredanet comes from this attitude. The leaders of our country are here in Addis and they cannot communicate with the people all the time or travel to have face to face meetings. So Woredanet came to allow the Prime Minister and others to communicate as if they were in a face to face interaction, speaking to the people but also listening to what they have to say.[18]

The type of videoconferencing method that was chosen from those that were available represented a further illustration of how, in the minds of those who envisaged it, Woredanet had to serve the plan of progressive and controlled decentralization. Decentralization was a necessary step in the implementation of an ethnic federation, but the particular form envisaged by the EPRDF had to be controlled by the centre so as to prevent the nodes of the federal government from gaining too much independence.

---

[17] Interview: Yemane Kidane, Former Member of EPRDF and Officer in the Ministry of Foreign Affairs. Director, Centre for Policy Research and Dialogue, Addis Ababa, 5 June 2008.

[18] Interview: Haddush Kassu, Head of Research for the Ministry of Information and Former General Manager of the Ethiopian News Agency, Addis Ababa, 28 June 2008.

In resonance with this principle, multipoint communication was privileged over other videoconferencing formats Woredanet's architecture allowed. By using multipoint, all transmissions, whether between two woredas, between regions and woredas, or between the centre and regions, had to be mediated by the centre. The other nodes were not given the freedom to choose when to use the system. To participate in a videoconference, remote sites were supposed to file a request at the national data centre, but more often the national data centre would notify the administrators in the woredas to convene in front of the plasma at a specific date and time to receive a transmission.[19] As explained by a technocrat working on the Public Sector Capacity Building Program (PSCAP) reform, 'Woredanet is there to provide support for things to be done properly, and to supervise them. But still nothing can be implemented without approval from the centre. Federalism does not mean independence [...] Technology helps to keep the pieces together. Maybe in the future the regions will be strong to decide for themselves. But not now. Now it is not possible'.[20] The technical and the political were aligned to make sure that progress towards a better functioning of the peripheries of the state was gradual. The remote nodes were offered new and unprecedented opportunities, but they could be easily retracted and the nodes were always controlled at the centre. In addition, in none of the Woredanet sites I visited was there a service level agreement or a document that could explain how, when, and for how long the site would have been allowed to use the system. It was not only artefacts themselves, but also the rules developed for their operation that made the remote nodes entirely dependent on the centre to perform most kinds of actions.

The central government, however, was not completely free to dictate the conditions to the peripheral nodes of the state apparatus, as it had to work within the institutional framework it had created. This had consequences for the design and redesign of Woredanet and Schoolnet. As an ICT expert who had been deeply involved in the development of both systems, as well as in other ICT projects in the country, explained:

---

[19] An assessment commissioned by the EICTDA to an independent consultancy firm clearly illustrates this point 'BCX and VCON had designed and spec'ed the system on the basis that videoconferencing sessions would only be initiated and controlled by either the Prime Minister's office (or the National Data Centre) or by the Federal and Regional sites – remote WoredaNet sites (the vast majority) would not be able to initiate or control videoconferencing sessions, and (because of this limitation), it would thus not be possible for any remote WoredaNet sites to videoconference with each other directly' (Daedan, 2004, 54)

[20] Interview: Civil Servant, Addis Ababa, 22 May 2008.

The regions were quite assertive when they wanted to get resources. They wanted to use the rights they have been entitled of by the constitution. In the case of Woredanet, they made sure that a videoconference could be started also at the regional level, so that they could also make use of the system for their own purposes.[21]

Among the types of videoconferencing that Woredanet allowed, the solution that was privileged in the end allowed both the central and the regional governments – but not a woreda – to initiate a videoconference and communicate with the other nodes connected by the system. This is indicative of how the technical and the political had to be constantly renegotiated. Even if, with Woredanet, the central government aimed at retaining power within the ethnic federation, it still had to make concessions, some of which had repercussions for the design of the systems, when requests were made within the context of the constitutional framework the EPRDF had created when it came to power.

### Shaping Society through the Use of Technology

Some aspects of this developmental – technopolitical regime, such as its penetration in the rural areas, might appear to be a consequence of successful advocacy by international organizations to use technology for the benefit of the poor. As discussed earlier, the international community had placed significant emphasis on the opportunities offered by the new technologies to connect remote villages to resources previously available only in urban centres. A photo such as the one in Fig. 5.3, taken outside a secondary institute equipped with Schoolnet could have been taken from a report published by a UN agency or an NGO about success stories of ICT applications in remote communities. Similarly, Fig. 5.4, which reproduces a popular ETC advertisement, is an illustration of how catering to farmers was a central component of the discourse on ICTs advanced by the Ethiopian government. However, the fact that Woredanet and Schoolnet were planned to reach even the most remote areas was less dependent on voluntary alignment to a discourse articulated internationally, than on the ideological background of the EPRDF. The kind of equipment brought into schools and government offices could, and did, offer students and local administrators greater access to new training opportunities. However, this bore little resemblance to the off-ramps from information highways connecting villages to a globalized world that

---

[21] Interview with ICT expert, Addis Ababa, Ethiopia, 10 May 2013.

*Fig. 5.3 - A teacher and students in front of a VSAT terminal*

was envisaged by AISI and other initiatives seeking to create a common imagery about the role ICTs could play in development.

Commitment to the peasantry played a central role in the EPRDF's discourse on revolutionary democracy, but it was also a means of reaffirming its legitimacy and control over the territory. Woredanet and Schoolnet were designed to improve the quality of life of rural communities, but this simultaneously entailed increasing the presence of the state on the ground. The two systems sought to achieve this goal in complementary ways: by improving service delivery and by opening new communication channels directly with the grassroots. The strategy had both practical and symbolic components. The principles inspiring Woredanet were succinctly summarized in an earlier quote by Bereket Simon:

Woredanet is for different purposes. It is to strengthen the capacity of the public administration, but it is also to reach rural Ethiopia, to make sure that the farmers get the right information. Woredanet is part of the wider communication strategy we have developed. Instead of communicating with everybody, we prefer to communicate with the most advanced part of the society and let it be our messenger.[22]

---

[22] Interview: Bereket Simon, Advisor to the Prime Minister and former minister of Information, Addis Ababa, 24 June 2008.

Fig. 5.4 *ETC advertisement*

At the practical level, Woredanet had to build the capacity of the peripheral nodes of the state by training and instructing individuals, some of whom had little formal education, to enable them to provide better services. This had to benefit the whole community, but at the same time it also had to symbolize the commitment of the government to the rural population.

Local officials were expected to demonstrate the principles inspiring the Ethiopian state through their actions and become the disseminators of a wider strategy. At the lower levels of the state apparatus there was awareness and acceptance that both administrators and civil servants had to primarily serve as executors of policies that had been decided at the centre. As a woreda official explained:

This time it is possible that even the people at the grassroots level can receive the same information; they can receive the very voice of the Prime Minister. We have been using the system mostly for videoconferencing. It helps a lot to understand what the line of the government is, but also to learn new practices.[23]

The unity of the message was understood for its potential to bring the entire country together around similar principles, despite its diversity. Through Woredanet, the EPRDF leaders at the central level could reach the grassroots in a mediated way; by turning the members of the state apparatus in the peripheries into messengers of ideas and policies formulated at the centre.

Over time, Woredanet begun to be used also to send more direct messages to citizens, especially in the most remote areas. Seeking to address the challenge of providing justice in a vast and poorly connected country, Woredanet offered the basis for creating a system able to provide justice 'at a distance', and for the state apparatus to concretely show to citizens its determination to increase its presence and responsiveness on the ground. Known as TeleCourt, the system connected courts in Addis Ababa and in the regional capitals with those offices where Woredanet's Plasma TV and camera were installed, turning them in temporary courts where litigants and lawyers could be gathered. Despite the immediate reactions in some of the rural areas were of uneasiness and disbelief, as farmers who had little experience of technology were not used to see a screen 'talking' to them (Beyene, Zerai, & Gagliardone, 2015), over time TeleCourt started to be positively received. According to practicing lawyer and TeleCourt user in Debre Birhan, in the Amhara region, the new system has benefitted both ordinary citizens and the government.

There is a Woreda in north Shoa zone called Gishe Rabel. It is near Wollo. It is some 250 kms away from Debre Birhan. Think about the expense it incurs to come here from Gishe Rabel to access justice. By the way, court disputes take place between people. One person alone cannot have a dispute. He/[she] comes in with other people. All these people have to travel for 250 kilometres for justice to be served, and in the process, they lose their precious time of work. Ensuring justice in the old ways of dispensing justice involved financial losses. The government, for example, used to incur a lot of expenses in the form of allowances and other expenditures. Such expenditures are no more necessary now. This means that not only the citizens but also the government is the beneficiary of the TeleCourt system.[24]

Also ordinary citizens who have had experience of TeleCourt appear to have perceived it as a step in the right direction. A priest and a farmer in Ejere, in Oromiya region, commented:

[23] Interview: Civil servant, Awasa, Ethiopia, 27 April 2008.
[24] Interview: Yeshidinber Masresha, Debre Birhan, Ethiopia, 25 March 2014.

If one fails to kill his enemy with a stick, he'll kill him with a rifle. This happens when justice lacks in or when it falls subservient to favouritism. Such problems sometimes take place in our Woreda. The plasma court has enabled appellants to access judicial hearings at all levels and would then reduce acts of revenge.[25]

Similarly to other applications of ICTs championed by the Ethiopian government, however, also TeleCourt and its reception among citizens have to be interpreted in the context not just of a state aiming at better serving its citizens, but also seeking to increase its influence against competing systems, including those for the dispensation of justice. Although the Ethiopian constitution recognizes the legitimacy of customary law in a selected number of areas (e.g., family law), system like TeleCourt have emerged in competition with more traditional practices, offering greater incentives to resort to formal rather than informal means to resolve disputes.

### Educating the Youth, and the Masses

Compared to Woredanet, Schoolnet has emerged to serve rural communities as well as the needs of the state in a slightly different way. Schoolnet enabled students living in the countryside to access the same kind of education as those in the major towns and cities. They no longer had to rely on the weakest teachers for their education, as used to be the case.[26] This was a powerful symbol of the EPRDF's commitment to guarantee every citizen equal rights and opportunities and reduce inequalities in access to services between urban and rural residents. However, abiding by this principle also meant that for some time Schoolnet was more effective at a symbolic level rather than a practical one.

The fact that all the classes were taught in English caused serious comprehension problems for most students. In the schools I first visited in 2005 and 2006, both in towns and in remote villages, I could barely have a basic conversation in English with students who were supposed to have been trained for at least one year using English as the medium of instruction. The situation did not substantially change during my

---

[25] Interview: Temare Tewabe, Ejere, Ethiopia 8 May 2014.

[26] According to the *Education statistics annual abstract for 2006–07* (Ministry of Education, 2008), in 2006–07 there were extreme differences among regions in the number of qualified teachers, and thus the teachers possessing the necessary titles to be teaching at the secondary level. In the regions surrounding urban areas such as Addis Ababa, Dire Dawa, and Harar, more than 80 per cent of the teachers were qualified. In the peripheries the picture was dramatically different. In Gambella only 7.5 per cent of the teachers had the right titles to be teaching at the secondary level, 32.3 per cent in the Somali region and 39.7 per cent in the Southern Nations Nationalities and Peoples (SNNP) region (Ministry of Education, 2008).

subsequent visits in 2011 and 2012. When attending classes during a broadcast, I noticed that most students were trying to sketch notes on their notebooks, but had to give up after a few seconds because the teachers on the screen were too fast to follow. As confirmed in an evaluation carried out by UNDP among teachers and students, 'the speed of plasma instructions and exercises coupled with the English language difficulty of learners have impacted negatively on students' understanding of the lessons delivered' (Asefa, 2006, p. 59).[27]

Another advantage of having each student exposed to the same programming was that each of the students could be equally trained in the founding principles of the state. Civic education was among the first subjects to be included in the Schoolnet programming and, according to some of the individuals I interviewed, the way it was taught was highly problematic.[28] Below is an excerpt from one of the manuals on which the lessons were based.[29] While some of the modules for the higher grades were addressing ways to curb corruption, to respect human rights and participate in elections, other issues addressed by the civic education classes were more troubling. For example, critics of the idea of ethnic federalism would strongly challenge a statement like the one below:

The right to equality of Nations, Nationalities and Peoples includes the equal rights to full measure of self-governance [...] It guarantees the nationalities, nations and peoples' equal right to administer their own region by themselves in a democratic manner. It also creates better conditions for national unity (Engida, 2007, p. 91).

Many EPRDF cadres held a strong faith in the power of the new teaching to influence young Ethiopians. As Bereket Simon noted, in reference to Schoolnet:

In our education our cornerstones are math, science and civic and ethical education. So we can have a home-grown democracy. A country in order. Now we will have a new generation that has been trained in the principles of

---

[27] Amendments would be later introduced by EMA to respond to some of these problems (first during the school year 2007–08 and then through an overhaul of the Schoolnet content to adapt it to the new school curriculum in 2011–12), The 'real teachers', those in the classroom, started to be allocated more time for explaining what had not been clear during the broadcast.

[28] In April 2005, during one of my first visits to attend a Schoolnet broadcast in a secondary school in Addis Ababa, the teacher of civic education followed me out after the lesson and vehemently argued how what we both saw on the screen was propaganda and not educational content.

[29] I could personally attend a number of classes of civic education during my visits to Schoolnet sites throughout the country and was allowed to download most of the classes from the servers in the EMA compound.

democracy in secondary education and they will know how to contribute to the development of the country.[30]

Similarly, Haddush Kassu argued:

We can use Woredanet and Schoolnet to educate people about civics, ethics, our national flag and hymn. All the information about the nation should be strengthened through the media and new technologies.[31]

Bereket and Haddush's words acquire even more significance when located in the broader context of the role young educated Ethiopians played in the country's political transformations. As illustrated by Young (1997), many of the TPLF's early recruits during the struggle against the Derg were secondary school students. This point was further, and dramatically, illustrated by a former fighter I interviewed in Tigray:

An important school was Queen of Sheba in Adwa. But there were important schools also in Mekele. A lot of high school students joined the struggle. They were key especially at the beginning. And in Tigray the TPLF started having a lot of influence in the schools. Most of the people who joined the struggle at the time were students and many of them died as martyrs. I joined the struggle with my brothers and sisters and all of them died in it.[32]

The appreciation of the role youth can have in political mobilization persisted after the civil war, as did the strategies employed to reach out to young Ethiopians. Some of these strategies were implemented through newer means, such as the civic education programme offered by Schoolnet, while others represented a simpler extension of models that had proved successful in the past.[33]

---

[30] Interview: Bereket Simon, Advisor to the Prime Minister and former minister of Information, Addis Ababa, 24 June 2008.
[31] Interview: Haddush Kassu, Head of External Relations at the Ministry of Information and Former General Manager of the Ethiopian News Agency, Addis Ababa, 28 June 2008.
[32] Interview: Former TPLF Fighter, Aksum, 29 June 2008.
[33] An illustration of this latter tendency was offered by Solomon Inquai, an important ideologist of the TPLF and a long-serving director of the Relief Society of Tigray (REST), the NGO created by the TPLF during the war to provide humanitarian assistance to the population in Tigray and that continued to play a pivotal role in the provision of basic services in the region after 1991. His response was to a question about how the ruling party lost some key constituencies in 2005 election. 'In 2005 we lost Addis and many other towns. Since then we decided to organize youth leagues, and women leagues. Some of the members are university students or younger. We are also getting old and we need new members to replace us. Also during the struggle we had similar associations. But the reason of the election result is that we became too confident, we lost perspective. So we are trying to revive this tradition of associations, but on a wider scale. Not just for Tigray but for other regions as well'. Interview: Solomon Inquai, Former Director of the Relief Society of Tigray, Mekele, 2 July 2008.

Schoolnet, however, was not meant only to educate the youth. From the analysis of the architecture that was employed to transmit messages from EMA's headquarters in Addis Ababa towards secondary schools, it became apparent that the system was designed to target other uses, beyond the transmission of pre-recorded classes.

In contrast to the videoconferencing used by Woredanet, which was designed to be bidirectional, Schoolnet was based on static content and did not require interactivity between central and remote sites. If this had been the only use the system was designed for, employing a satellite to broadcast classes was not the most efficient mode of delivery. The provision of high quality education to both urban and rural areas, as well as the training in the principles of the state, could have been provided more easily and less expensively in different ways, for example, by saving all lessons on hard disks mounted on a local server.[34] As a young foreign consultant who visited some Schoolnet sites noted,

The first time we saw Schoolnet we were shocked. They rented a satellite to broadcast pre-recorded content. Whoever designed it was crazy. The content is static. It would have been so much cheaper to buy hard drives and install the lessons on them. A big video server would have been much cheaper.[35]

Even if Schoolnet, like Woredanet, had many weaknesses, the reason for its particular configuration was not the folly of its designers. More simply, Schoolnet was designed not only to reproduce the same educational content, but also to broadcast new messages when this was needed. When the students were not in school, the system was used as a platform for other training, including what has been described by some informants as 'political' training, based on live or recorded messages sent by the cadres in Addis Ababa to specific target audiences who were asked to gather in the school. In this sense Schoolnet complemented Woredanet. While the latter was used to reach officers in the state apparatus, the former was an instrument to communicate with larger audiences. Amare Anslau, the CEO of ETC, explained this synergy:

[34] A basic Schoolnet outlet needed at least a VSAT, a decoder, a router and a switch. Using a video-server and hard disk would have required a capacity of around 150 GB, a reasonable capacity for a hard disk even in 2004. According to EMA there were 2978 classes when the system started, and once digitized in an Audio Video Interleave (AVI) format a single class occupied around 50 MB. This system would also have allowed teachers and students to replay some lessons so as to revise key issues in the curriculum or to provide students who could not attend a class with the opportunity of catching up with the program.

[35] Interview: Consultant on ICT in Education, Addis Ababa, 24 April 2008.

Before Woredanet if the Prime Minister wanted to speak to the officials he had to call them, but now in a moment he can communicate with every woreda.[36] So this is disclosing unprecedented opportunities. The Prime Minister can address people through Schoolnet too and reach the whole country. He can also do it through Woredanet to contact every official. Now we can make sure that different people in different areas can be reached by the same message, directly.[37]

Woredanet and Schoolnet thus need to be understood not as separate programmes, but as complementary expressions of a similar need to reach the periphery of the state. They were the expression of a deep-rooted commitment towards development, providing greater education opportunities and better services. They were also tools aimed at translating this commitment into a greater political acceptance of those in power, reducing the political space available for critique and alternative.

*Internet or Intranet?*

The previous two sections have looked at how the discourses on the nation-state and society, ethnicity, and the peasantry appeared to influence the shaping of ICTs in Ethiopia and especially of Woredanet and Schoolnet. The discourses at the core of the ethnic federation motivated the decision to install the new equipment simultaneously in the key nodes of the state apparatus and the need for controlled decentralization structured communication between them. The use of ICTs to respond to the needs of rural communities was accompanied by a reinforced state presence on the ground. Through illustrating these points the two sections have also examined some aspects of what was referred to earlier as the EPRDF's culture of communication. First, the communication strategy of the EPRDF, based on showing empirical results, led the government to increase the capacity of the state to deliver basic services with the support of technology. Second, both systems, but especially Woredanet, were a response to the need to deliver the same messages from the highest to the lowest ranks of the government without intermediaries, and to have the recipients of these messages act as messengers themselves to their larger communities.

To conclude this analysis, I want to examine one final component of the government's culture of communication that has influenced the design of both Woredanet and Schoolnet, as well as the sovereign

---

[36] Here Amare refers to the fact that even Woredanet could use a broadcast type of transmission when needed. However, as compared to multi-point this type of transmission was less common.

[37] Interview: Amare Amsalu, CEO, Ethiopian Telecommunication Corporation, Addis Ababa, 27 June 2008.

technopolitical regime that is discussed in the final part of this chapter: the refusal to engage in dialogue with oppositional forces. Although both Woredanet and Schoolnet were based on the Internet Protocol and intended to deliver a variety of services, the very limited access granted to data from outside Ethiopia transformed the systems into a kind of state intranet. In the case of Woredanet, as illustrated at length above, video-conferencing was almost the only system to be employed. Email never really took off.[38] And from conversations with civil servants in woreda administrations, the possibilities of using the Internet were reduced to a minimum. Similarly, although some Schoolnet sites were supposed to receive an Internet connection, most of them did not, or only received one for a short period of time. This meant that most, if not all, information being received through the systems emanated exclusively from the centre of the state.

Woredanet and Schoolnet were essentially functioning as communication channels that were partially invisible to a large component of Ethiopian society. Woredanet allowed exclusive and routine communication between nodes of the state. Schoolnet ensured that the new generations were exposed to messages decided at the centre, without the mediation of possibly critical teachers, and it also allowed the EPRDF to reach wider constituencies discretely.[39] Use of these new channels provided the government with a strong competitive advantage over oppositional forces and prevented it from having to engage with them. As Kumlachew Dagne, a member of the association InterAfrica, who mediated the televised debates between government and opposition leaders during the campaign for the 2005 election, explained: 'During the campaign the government was having a tough time in the debates. Many opposition candidates were having more success

---

[38] An address of an officer in a woreda was designed to be: 'name@woreda.region.gov.et'.

[39] I am not implying that marginalizing teachers was one of the main reasons the system was put in place, but it is important to be aware that in the history of Ethiopia teachers have played a key role as an oppositional force. As pointed out by Markakis, in the turmoil that led to the deposition of Haile Selassie, 'The 17,500 teachers constituted more than half the country's professional stratum. [...] Their association was the only effective professional organization in existence, and it was to play a leading role in the popular movement' (Markakis & Ayele, 1986, 55). Similarly, many former TPLF fighters recognized that it was mostly in secondary schools that new recruits were convinced to join the struggle. After Schoolnet was introduced many teachers reacted negatively to their marginalization, especially the most experienced and active among them. A UN volunteer who assessed the use of Schoolnet among teachers and students noted that 'In grade 9 when they start attending the plasma lessons for the first time they do not understand but slowly they start liking it. But a lot of school deans complain that as a result of the plasma a lot of teachers are becoming passive'. Interview: UN Volunteer, Addis Ababa, 20 June 2008.

than the government leaders. As a result they cut the voices that could oppose them. And they had to rely on alternative ways to reach their goals'.[40]

In this context, Woredanet and Schoolnet assisted the government in expanding its sphere of influence through the use of technology. The EPRDF almost always refused to engage in dialogue with oppositional voices. When it attempted to do so, as indicated by Kumlachew, its culture of communication, which centred more on showing tangible results than on winning rhetorical battles, disadvantaged it in relation to the opposition. This experience reinforced the idea that the alternative strategies pursued through systems like Woredanet and Schoolnet should be strengthened in order to support the government's nation-building project and increase its legitimacy in the eyes of Ethiopia's citizens.

## The Sovereign Technopolitical Regime

The *developmental* technopolitical regime was an expression of how technology can be used to embody and proactively enact elements at the centre of a national political agenda. The *sovereign* regime emerged instead as an example of how a state can resist external pressures and assert its sovereign rights, even over a technology that is praised for its potential to erode national boundaries and in a country whose national budget heavily relies on donor funding. The state monopoly over telecommunication and Internet provision emerged as its defining feature, but similarly to the case of Woredanet and Schoolnet, elements of the discourses on ethnic federalism and revolutionary democracy intervened in shaping important aspects of it.

The strategy leading to the creation of a sovereign technopolitical regime in Ethiopia was fairly distinctive in Africa. While most countries on the continent slowly overcame their scepticism towards liberalizing the telecommunication market, only to later introduce regulatory or technical mechanisms to contain the tensions these measures introduced, the Ethiopian government decided from the very beginning to sacrifice access for control and security.[41] As explained in the following

---

[40] Interview: Kumlachew Dagne, InterAfrica, Addis Ababa, 7 June 2008. Between September 2004 and April 2005 the main parties participated in nine televised debates each covering a different issue, with some key issues such as governance or federalism and decentralization being addressed in more than one debate.

[41] The Kenyan government, for example, in the aftermath of the violence that erupted after the contested elections of 2007, introduced new measures to curb hate speech disseminated both on social media and through SMS (See for example Kagwanja & Southall, 2009)

sections, the lack of technical capabilities and skilled personnel contributed to the overall poor performance of the telecommunication system
and the limited access to services, but it was mostly ideological forces
rather than technical constraints that influenced the development of this
regime. As pointed out by Mueller (2010), in the mid-1990s states were
not prepared for the explosion of ideas and expression initiated by the
Internet. Countries such as Kenya eventually decided to bet on new
technologies, letting new spaces emerge for private operators and civil
society organizations to shape their national information societies. The
Ethiopian government, on the contrary, decided not to let anyone but
the state take advantage of ICTs until it felt ready to face the disruption
and competition ICTs would have brought, both at the economic and at
the ideational level. As Amare Amsalu, Ethiopian Telecommunication
Corporation's Chief Executive Officer, pointed out: 'We have to grow
first. Only when we will be strong enough, and we will have the capacity,
we will liberalize. Things have to be done gradually. And when we will be
ready we could go to the fight'.[42]

### Declaring One Policy, Enacting Another

In the 1990s, Ethiopia was no different from other African countries
facing the challenge of creating the infrastructural, regulatory, and human
conditions for new ICTs such as the Internet to take roots. As explained
in Chapter 2, Ethiopia had actually been one of the first countries in
Africa to introduce telephone communication, and it was the only one to
have done so outside of colonial domination. Both Emperor Haile Selassie and the military junta of the Derg continued to invest in the expansion
of the telecommunication infrastructure. Similar to other countries on the
continent, however, ongoing conflicts and the inability to create a skilled
workforce progressively weakened the ability of the national telecom
operator to provide efficient and extended access to telecommunication
services. Once in power, the EPRDF seemed inclined to open the space
for competition, a response to external demands, and a way to gain the
international support needed to rebuild a country that had suffered under
military rule and a civil war for almost twenty years. In the case of
telecommunications, however, this commitment did not find concrete
applications beyond official statements.

Ethiopian politicians had affirmed the relevance of the private sector in
developing a modern information society on multiple occasions. Meles

---

[42] Interview: Amare Amsalu, CEO, Ethiopian Telecommunications Corporation, Addis
Ababa, 27 June 2008.

Zenawi, for example, during his opening speech at the African Development Forum in 1999, when he criticized the globalization logic and reaffirmed the centrality of the state interventions in supporting growth, used encouraging words towards local private initiatives.

> On the part of Africa there is little doubt that for it to be able to take whatever opportunities there are in the global economy, it has no option but to do whatever it takes to ensure having a vibrant private sector. By this I mean, first of all, a vibrant domestic private sector. The reason for emphasizing the role of domestic private sector is neither philosophical nor political. It is merely practical. (Zenawi, 1999)

A similar rhetoric was employed in the draft ICT policy, which addressed the private sector as one of the driving forces in the creation of an Ethiopian information society. For example, the section on Private Sector Development opened by affirming, 'since the private sector plays a crucial role in accelerating the process of transforming Ethiopia into a knowledge – and information – economy and society the Government is committed to removing obstacles constraining its development' (EICTDA, 2006, p. 18). However, the provisions about the private sector either did not find a concrete application or were interpreted in a very selective fashion.

As illustrated by historians of technology who analysed similar cases, when technology emerges in critical moments in the history of a country, there is often a 'disjuncture between declared policy (policy as rhetoric) and enacted policy (policy as practice)' (Allen & Hecht, 2001, p. 18). The complex strategies pursued by politicians can be understood only by concurrently analysing what they say and how this is embodied in the technologies they directly promote or allow the space to flourish.

In Ethiopia, ICT businesses were only allowed to operate freely in areas that could produce an incremental and predictable increase in productivity and in sectors that were considered safe by the government. Continuing to follow the approach pursued by different political elites in the history of the country, newer ICTs were adopted and supported largely when they emerged as simple enhancers of tasks already defined at the centre, when they could act as sustaining, rather than disruptive, innovations (Wu, 2010). While the number of private companies operating in sectors such as sales and maintenance or in software development sharply increased over the years, no private firms were allowed to operate in the telecommunication sector (Adam, 2007; EICTDA, 2005, 2009).

The globalizing potential of ICTs and the opportunities to communicate within and beyond the national borders were perceived as a high risk component of ICTs which should be tightly controlled to prohibit oppositional forces from taking advantage of the new channels.[43] As would later become evident in cases of dramatic revolts such as those in Egypt, Tunisia, and Libya in 2011, a tight control of communication could be a matter of life or death for an authoritarian government trying to exercise control over a country and its citizens. Already in the 1990s the Ethiopian government had to face a hostile diaspora which had taken to the Internet to attack the EPRDF's national project (as will be further discussed in the next chapter) and had learned through its practice with the press what it meant to allow a plurality of voices to flourish without engaging with them. The EPRDF's initial experience with the press in fact incorporated a fatal mistake that came to define the future of political communication in Ethiopia, and was rooted in the EPRDF's culture of communication: the fact that when the new government came to power it opened the space for debate but refused to take part in the very debates it had allowed. In the ostensibly unipolar world that emerged after the fall of the Soviet Union, the pressure to respect certain 'rights' and 'freedoms' was significant and freer media represented an opportunity to boost the new government's legitimacy. Soon after coming to power the federal government created the conditions for the first private newspaper to start publishing and later spelled out their rights in the relatively progressive press law passed in 1992. As would become clear later, however, these measures were to be undermined by the EPRDF's lack of commitment to take the freedoms it had unleashed seriously, and the failure to understand what it really meant to allow a plurality of voices to compete in a post-war scenario. The result, as explained by Stremlau (2011), was disastrous. Former opponents of the EPRDF who were not allowed to compete politically launched their own newspapers to wage war against the new government, which either ignored or responded harshly to criticism, progressively poisoning the tones of the political debate, both inside and outside Ethiopia.

### A Price for the Poor and a Price for the Rich

A central element that shaped the sovereign technopolitical regime, as already mentioned, was the commitment to rural areas which, coupled with the suspicion towards urban elites, led the Ethiopian leadership to prioritize unique features of the telecommunication network, disregarding

[43] See for example the interview with Bereket Simon in Chapter 3. As he remarked, 'We studied globalization and we understood that it is a double edge sword. It creates opportunities and it also creates challenges. [...] When you implement it you also import the challenges that you have to avoid. And if you are not ready you will lose'.

successful models which had emerged elsewhere in Africa. In English-speaking countries such as South Africa, Kenya, or Nigeria, for example, ICTs had been framed as a way for local firms to provide services on the global market at competitive prices, relying on increasingly fast and widespread connections (Esselaar, Gillwald, & Stork, 2007). As Amare Amsalu, ETC's Chief Executive Officer, explained, in Ethiopia ICT policies responded to a different logic and had to be understood in the context of a divide between the peasants and the elites rooted in the EPRDF's revolutionary democratic project.

Holding telecommunications is not just about security. We need this instrument for development, so we need it for the people. Ethiopia is not like any other African country. Those countries just think that they can become rich, that the individual can become rich. But what we want is instead building in the mind of people the attachment for their land and for their country. Once you have technology you become addicted to it. So, if you allow the private they can certainly make money but what about the society? The society will not benefit from it. So the government is the one that has to make sure that things are done in the interest of the people.[44]

This commitment to rural areas and to the poor was further stressed by Bereket Simon:

The majority of Ethiopians still live in the rural areas. If you go there you do not make profit. So the private won't cover the rural areas. But if Ethiopia has to develop first it has to have the rural on board. When we will be done with this and other projects the private sector will be accepted. Look at Schoolnet. Now all the students in Ethiopia can have access to the same education. No private sector company would have done anything like that.[45]

This approach, however, led to contradictory outcomes. On the one hand, despite its commitment to the farmers, the Ethiopian government did not formulate a universal access policy that could spell out how access to basic telecommunication services to everyone would be guaranteed. Given the limited resources and expertise, the government simply did not have the means to offer widespread communication in a regime of monopoly throughout a vast country with a complex geography. In this environment a universal access policy would have been condemned to fail. At the same time, within the range of the services ETC was able to offer, including rural connectivity in selected villages equipped with phones working over a microwave communication

---

[44] Interview: Amare Amsalu, CEO, Ethiopian Telecommunication Corporation, Addis Ababa, 27 June 2008.
[45] Interview: Bereket Simon, Advisor to the Prime Minister and former minister of Information, Addis Ababa, 24 June 2008.

channel, it implemented a decisive pro-poor policy. This was reflected in the pricing ETC offered both to its fixed and mobile customers. Despite its monopolist position, ETC applied some of the lowest tariffs in Africa both for fixed-lines and for mobile communication.[46] This was counterbalanced, however, by some of the highest tariffs on the continent to call overseas (a one minute call cost Birr 11.5 in 2006, more than US$1) and one of the most expensive tariffs on the planet for accessing the Internet through broadband. In 2006, the monthly fee for a 64 kbps ADSL connection was US$200, and for a 2 Mbps line, which in the same period was normally offered in Organisation for Economic Co-operation and Development (OECD) countries for around US$20, reached almost US $5,000 (EICTDA, 2009). The policy of tariffs not only had a practical value, but also had a symbolic one, signalling to the poorest sections of society the government's commitment to keep prices low and facilitate communications for citizens within the regional and national borders, and conversely discouraging communications to and from those who had left the country.

### Technology and Ideology

The EPRDF leadership had developed solutions that were profoundly at odds with regional and international experiences, maintaining a monopoly at a time when most countries where liberalizing the market. They did this without imposing the high tariffs monopolists usually charge, but prevented any private Internet Service Provider from entering the market, a measure that not even Eritrea, Ethiopia's authoritarian and hostile neighbour, had employed (Gagliardone & Stremlau, 2011). The same solutions, however, were consistent with the discourses on the Ethiopian nation-state articulated by the EPRDF, and showed how its leadership had remained faithful to its principles, even if this had motivated often contradictory and inefficient policies. As Debretsion Gebremichael argued:

Monopoly is a crucial factor in this. It is exactly because ICTs are so important and they have the capacity to penetrate every aspect of our lives that we have to make sure that it is the state that is in charge of using and implementing them. In this phase we cannot leave it to the market. ICTs are too key for our

---

[46] Lishan Adams pointed out, using the methodology employed by the OECD to comparatively assess the cost of communication in different countries, in Africa Ethiopia was second only to Ghana in providing cheap mobile communication and had one of the lowest fixed-line tariffs on the continent, just US$0.02 per minute (Adam, 2010).

development. They are a priority. Behind the decision of leaving the monopoly in the ICTs and telecommunication market there is big philosophical thinking. It is not just because we want to make money from the use of telecoms.[47]

The hegemonic nature of this commitment, its ambition to structure the nation-state according to a plan developed by the intellectual elite within the vanguard party, though not necessarily shared by all individuals in the state apparatus, emerged even more clearly in interviews with bureaucrats and technocrats in lower positions in the government. In contrast to their politically appointed superiors, many of them relied on a less ideologically charged discourse, grounded in evidence from other markets in Africa and beyond. The opinions expressed by two civil servants cited below reflect this ambivalence between a desire to apply lessons from other countries in the continent and the awareness of government's commitment to stay the course.

I am personally not very happy with the government policy because it won't be able to provide quality service in the absence of competition. Even if you prioritize the rural, to reach 80 million people with all services in absence of competition is just impossible. The government people know it too but they are rigid. They have decided to stick to their plan.[48]

Here for example we have a monopoly of telecoms. For the Ethiopian government it is good, but even for me – I am a government official – it cannot last for long. They will have to change their policy. What they say is that Ethiopia is different from other countries like Kenya where the population is concentrated in urban areas. [...] And only a state monopoly can take care of the rural people. This may be true. But we have to find a solution. Maybe private companies will come, but it is the government that will continue to take care of rural connectivity or set rules for private companies to connect also the rural if they want to operate.[49]

These opinions, however, remained just opinions. The awareness of the contradictions the Ethiopian government got embroiled in, making a commitment to the rural population while adopting a strategy that would make it impossible to provide them with reliable telecom services, was mostly a source of frustration rather than an encouragement to change direction. The full liberalization of the market in ways that could influence, or complement, the national strategy promoted by the Ethiopian government continued to be constrained. The need to equally distribute resources among different ethnically based states to reinforce the ethnic federalist set-up prevailed even when it meant constraining the

---

[47] Interview: Debretsion Gebremichael, Director of EICTDA, Addis Ababa, 10 June 2008.
[48] Interview: Civil Servant, Addis Ababa, 29 May 2008.
[49] Interview: Civil Servant, Addis Ababa, 19 May 2008.

empowerment of private companies in ways that might eventually benefit the national economy and citizens' access to telecom services.

## Conclusion

The technopolitical regimes analysed in this chapter emerged as the result of a distinctive combination of technologies, politics, and conceptions of development. When proactively embracing ICTs to support its state and nation-building project as well as when reactively responding to pressures to liberalize and open up the market, the EPRDF placed great emphasis on ideology in making technologically relevant decisions. In this sense the EPRDF-led government has distinguished itself from other governments in the continent, but the political/ideological readings and shaping of technology should not be considered in exclusory terms (either they play a role or they don't), but in terms of degrees of influence (they can play a greater or lesser role). Ethiopia is a privileged, not a unique, site from which the processes of technological adoption and adaptation can be studied.

The Ethiopian case does not only offer an opportunity to concretely examine this abstract principle. It also helps empirically map an ongoing historical trend, which is likely to be strengthened in the future (and whose causes are further analysed in Chapter 6). The EPRDF, often influenced by Meles Zenawi's thinking, has progressively emerged as a promoter in Africa of conceptions of development that are alternative to the neo-liberal doctrines proposed by international organizations like the World Trade Organization (WTO), the International Monetary Fund (IMF), and the World Bank. These conceptions, some of which have been examined in this and in the previous chapter, have placed greater emphasis on the role of the state in development processes, reaffirming the idea of a developmental state for Africa. While some of these alternative conceptions have been long perceived as erratic and inconsistent in development circles, including the maintenance of a state monopoly on the banking and telecom sectors, there are signs they are gaining greater momentum, as indicated for example by the plan to make Ethiopia a member of the WTO even without the country liberalizing those sectors as it has been asked since it first applied for membership in 2003 (Maasho, 2013).

Ethiopia, rather than being an eccentric and isolated case, may emerge as a precursor of a larger trend, and some of the solutions it has adopted may be replicated by other developmental governments – or aspiring developmental states – on the continent. The two technopolitical regimes that have emerged in the country have been affected by numerous shortcomings and have both been technically and politically challenged, but both have provided an example of how imperfect systems may also be resilient. States like Ethiopia, but the same argument can be extended to Rwanda, will probably continue to receive donor support because of their ability to perform in technical and economic terms, and continue to be criticized for implementing the very policies that enable them to maintain the control over their societies that facilitates their efficiency. Pressures to open up and democratize will continue to be made, and they will likely continue to be ignored.

# 6    Resisting Alternative Technopolitical Regimes

---

*One of the primary characteristics of a system builder is the ability to construct or to force unity from diversity, centralization in the face of pluralism, and coherence from chaos. This construction often involves the destruction of alternative systems.*                                                                    (Hughes, 1987, p. 52)

Using ICTs to support state and nation building meant that the Ethiopian government not only had to assemble regimes which amplified the discourses at the core of its political agenda, but also that it had to resist the emergence of alternative ones that could oppose it. Since the appearance of a new discourse on ICTs and development in the 1990s, actors other than the government, both at the international and at the national level, have favoured elements of this discourse that competed with the priorities articulated by the EPRDF and sustained different sets of interests. In some cases, these alternative projects remained pure potentialities, elements of the discourse on ICTs and development included in official documents and advocated by important agents, including the World Bank, the United Nations Development Programme (UNDP), and the United Nations Economic Commission for Africa (UNECA), which found little or no application in the Ethiopian context. In other cases they were actualized in concrete artefacts and practices, leading to the emergence of technopolitical regimes that tried to oppose, complement, or 'patch' those developed by the Ethiopian government.

This chapter considers the two regimes that represented the greatest test to the solidity and endurance of the developmental and sovereign regimes created by the Ethiopian government, further illustrating how the struggle for the definition of ICTs in Ethiopia was fought both at the discursive and at the material level. It analyses how the government's active resistance to some of the uses of ICTs had to face attempts by international organizations, private companies, and opposing political groups to use new technologies in the pursuit of competing goals.

### The International Technopolitical Regime: Fighting International Politics through Technology

The implementation of Schoolnet and Woredanet alarmed members of the international community in Ethiopia. Both donor and UN agencies were critical of systems that had no precedent in the field of ICTs for development and whose scale was considered disproportionate for a poorly resourced country like Ethiopia. In addition, the unwillingness of the government to pilot the two projects first, and to provide information that could facilitate a better understanding of their scope and nature, further alienated international actors and triggered increasingly aggressive, but not necessarily effective, responses.

While the donor community had shown a commitment to ICTs in the 1990s and in the early 2000s, after Schoolnet and Woredanet became operational the majority of bilateral donors became increasingly reluctant to operate in the field of ICTs and engage in new initiatives promoted by the Ethiopian government. In contrast to what was happening on the rest of the continent, where the influence of events such as the World Summit on Information Society (WSIS) raised the profile of ICTs, donor agencies in Ethiopia seemed to grow progressively disillusioned with new technologies. During the Donor Assistance Group (DAG) monthly meetings on education which I regularly attended in Addis Ababa in 2005 and 2006, for example, it had become very difficult to place ICT issues on the agenda. Things became even more complex in the aftermath of the elections in 2005 (Abbink, 2006). The government responded harshly to the protesters who were requesting greater transparency in the electoral process, causing hundreds of deaths and the imprisonment of individuals taken from schools, universities, and even their own homes, leading many donors to reformulate their overall policies towards Ethiopia, at least temporarily.

Multilateral organizations reacted in a slightly different way to the appropriation of ICTs by the Ethiopian government, elaborating a better-articulated and more ambitious agenda. In the years following the implementation of Schoolnet and Woredanet, the UNDP and the World Bank started planning ICT projects incorporating some aspects of the ICTs for development discourse that had been resisted or excluded by the Ethiopian government. They used their leverage to encourage the emergence of a different technopolitical regime that could reduce the oddness of the developmental and sovereign regimes assembled by the Ethiopian government. By implementing more mainstream initiatives, which had been applied in other developing countries and enjoyed a greater degree of support from the international community, multilateral organizations were attempting to patch in practice what they had not been able to redress through the usual means of diplomacy and aid conditionality.


### Schoolnet vs. Schoolnet

The UNDP's project was the one in which this 'patching effort' was most evident. It consisted of the installation of computer laboratories connected to the Internet in every preparatory school (those catering for students in grades 11 and 12) already receiving broadcast content. Each lab was designed to be used by students to learn key computer skills (word processing, spreadsheet, etc.), but, more importantly, to conduct independent research using the Internet to complement the school curriculum. A total of 2,700 PCs were donated to 161 schools and each school was provided with an Internet connection initially paid for by the UNDP with the intention that the Ethiopian Telecommunication Corporation (ETC) would eventually step in and provide for it. In this case, the Internet connection was framed not as a marginal service, but as the system's defining feature: all computers were networked in a Local Area Network (LAN) and set to be connected to the Internet either through VSAT, dial-up, or ADSL. If the project managed by Educational Media Agency (EMA) in Addis Ababa was meant to reach the periphery with content defined at the centre, officially to improve the quality of education across the country, the project promoted by the UNDP was opening each school-node to the world, letting students and teachers decide which content they wanted to access.

The UNDP operated not only at the technical level, but also at the symbolic level, strategically positioning its own project in relation to the one promoted by the Ethiopian government. Similar to the Ethiopian government's project the UN's project was also called Schoolnet. The name was chosen not to frame the laboratories as an integral part of the Schoolnet system managed by EMA and by ETC, but rather to present an alternative to it. By referring to other international experiences such as Schoolnet Canada and Schoolnet South Africa, which were also based on computer laboratories connected to the Internet, the UNDP was trying to flag the use of the term promoted by the Ethiopian government as inappropriate, and reclaim the name Schoolnet for its own initiative.[1] The excerpt below, taken from an assessment by an Ethiopian

---

[1] The first Schoolnet project started in Canada in the early 1990s with the aim of wiring all secondary schools in the country to the Internet and linking students and teachers to high quality educational material tailored to the needs of students in different grades (Shade &

consultant, Gorfu Asefa, was commissioned by the UNDP to analyse the effectiveness of both Schoolnet programmes. It clearly illustrates how this strategy worked in practice.

The term SchoolNet has become part of the vocabulary of those technical personnel working in the education and telecommunications sectors two years now. The term is now extensively used by the MoE [Ministry of Education], EMA, schools and ETC in relation to pre and post-implementation activities related to the inauguration of the satellite-based educational TV program. Nonetheless, the concept of SchoolNet is understood differently by the institutions. For instance, for ETC SchoolNet means the totality of the ICT infrastructure, the VSAT terminal network, communication devices being used for the transmission of plasma lessons. From what has been gathered from students, teachers and staff of MoE/EMA working on the project, the concept of SchoolNet is associated to plasma education. On the other hand, the concept and understanding prevalent among ICT practitioners in the ICT for development circle is a bit different from the above two groups in that SchoolNet is referred as a web interface used to link learners and educators each other over the Internet and provide a framework where educational contents and resources are collectively created and used towards improving the quality of education and making the teaching-learning process interesting and responsive to problems faced in real life situations. [. . .]

For the author of this report, the SchoolNet Ethiopia Initiative is a digital connectivity initiative whose aim is to establish local area networks in schools and use the Internet to facilitate communication and interaction among students, teachers, and school administrators locally and abroad for collectively embarking on content creation and exchange of learning resources and experiences. Thus, this initiative should not be considered as a new initiative but as a call for using digital opportunities for interactive and active learning and for supplementing classroom learning resources with learning materials on the web. (Asefa, 2006, pp. 27–28)

The strategic use of the language illustrated by Asefa, referring to the project based on computer laboratories as the proper Schoolnet and to the one managed by EMA simply as 'plasma', indicating its most visible and unique feature, the 42-inch plasma TV screen, was not limited only to specialist reports as the one above, but was used in press releases and official documents produced by the UNDP and other UN agencies.[2] This had the ironic result of creating confusion among many development

---

Dechief, 2004). A similar model was later extended first to South Africa and later to other countries in the continent such as Namibia, Lesotho, Senegal, and Uganda. The Ottawa based International Development Research Centre (IDRC) played a substantial role in encouraging and funding Schoolnet systems around the African continent (Cossa & Cronjé, 2004).

[2] In many interviews with UN personnel and development workers in Addis Ababa focusing on ICT in 2006 and 2008 many confused the two projects or thought one was a component of the other.

workers who did not really understand the difference between the two projects. More importantly, this war of words was indicative of the larger political battle being fought over ICTs, including the efforts to distinguish appropriate uses from unorthodox ones, and of the ways in which both linguistic and technical aspects were mobilized to support competing projects. The government of Ethiopia was trying to promote ICT usage mostly to serve its nation-building plan, enhancing the possibilities of the centre to reach the periphery without giving peripheral nodes the capability to seek and receive information independently. On the contrary, the UNDP initiative was re-affirming the globalizing and individualistic nature of ICTs, enacting discourses articulated internationally, and allowing students and teachers to seek information independently. It stressed the role the new tools should have in facilitating the free flow of information among nations and individuals.

At the end of the 'Schoolnet conflict', however, the approach elaborated by the UNDP proved only partially successful. The UNDP's patching effort was set to produce results in the short term and it assumed that the Ethiopian government would eventually accept the new project and develop ownership of it. Acting on this assumption, few plans were made to sustain the project for a more extended period of time and to respond to the eventuality of a protracted resistance of the government to the attempts to redress its course of action. As a result, after the UNDP ceased to provide Internet connectivity, ETC did not step in as initially planned. Most of the laboratories lost their role of Internet points and instead became little more than spaces occasionally visited by students to learn some basic skills in word processing. The Ethiopian government continued to provide resources for the maintenance of the 'plasma' and to extend it to newly created secondary schools. However, it decided not to allocate any resources to increase or even to maintain the exposure of Ethiopian students to content produced outside Ethiopia.[3]


*Influencing Policy without Influencing Technology*

An analogous destiny awaited the other large initiative supported by another international organization; a project that was also aimed at

---

[3] In some cases it was the local communities that tried to mobilize resources to guarantee that the school laboratories could continue to be used as Internet points. As reported by one of the UN volunteers overseeing Schoolnet in the regions, 'In Nekempt for example, one of the towns I visited, they wanted to know about connectivity. They asked me how they could have it and they said that if the government was not going to provide it they would have found the resources for paying a connection themselves'. Interview: UN Volunteer, Addis Ababa, Ethiopia, 26 April 2008.

reinforcing an international technopolitical regime based more on openness, seeking to directly influence the sovereign technopolitical regime
created by the Ethiopian government. With a budget of more than US$
30 million, of which 25 million was granted by the World Bank, the ICT
Assisted Development (ICTAD) Project was a multi sector programme
structured to enforce aspects of the discourse on ICTs that had been
marginalized by the Ethiopian government. ICTAD advocated an
increase in Internet connectivity, more support for the private sector
and the provision of better access to market information.[4] The projects
developed to transform this vision into practice were part of a carnet of
initiatives inspired by various international experiences: telecentres
offering Internet access, business incubators, refurbishment centres,
community radios, and private Internet Service Providers (ISPs).

Despite the substantial resources available, the competition between
ICTAD and the government of Ethiopia's priorities made the implementation of the strategy developed by the World Bank slower and more
problematic than initially expected. Three years after ICTAD's incep-
tion, only a few of its objectives had been achieved. The licensing of ISPs,
agreed in the first covenant between the World Bank and the government
of Ethiopia, was achieved with great delay, and none of the licensed
companies ever started operations.[5] A similar approach was employed
for the drafting of a comprehensive ICT policy. ICTAD invested consid-
erable resources to make this process as participative and effective as
possible. Numerous events were organized in Addis Ababa to include in
the debate both the civil society and the private sector. Renowned international consultants were hired to assist in the preparation of the policy.
As a result, the consultative process was well received even by individuals

---

[4] As stated in the project document, its key areas of assistance were:

- Creating an enabling policy and a legal and regulatory framework for the growth of
  the Ethiopian ICT sector;
- Increasing connectivity and providing access to communication services throughout
  the country;
- Strengthening the institutional capacity of regulatory, advocacy, and key policy-making
  institutions;
- Establishing locally adapted ICT industry standards and data security policies;
- Fostering opportunities for women and youth as well as small and medium enter-
  prises in the ICT sector;
- Facilitating access to markets and market information for rural and urban commu-
  nities. (World Bank, 2004a, p. 1)

[5] According to the contract, the ISPs had to be licensed by September 2005, but the
licences were issued only in March 2007. However, the four companies that obtained a
licence, Millennium systems, All-In-One, Symbol Technology, and Net Computer, did
not start operations (EICTDA, 2008)

who were usually critical of the operations of the Ethiopian government. According to one of the most active civil society representatives participating in the drafting of the ICT policy:

Schoolnet and Woredanet were not debated. Someone decided it and imposed it. There was no debate around what to do with that. My guess is that they may have a hidden agenda for it. But look at the debate on ICT policy instead. That was open. They were looking around for suggestions. We debated freely, there were no restrictions.[6]

Unfortunately this inclusive experience became increasingly marred by frustration. The Ethiopian government did not keep its promise of swiftly passing the debated policy, which was approved only a few years after the consultations had taken place (the Council of Ministers passed it in July 2009) and gave little though to recommendations from civil society and the private sector. The EPRDF maintained a monopoly on telecommunication and still closely tied ICTs to government-led programmes such as the Sustainable Development and Poverty Reduction Program (SDPRP), the Plan for Accelerated and Sustainable Development to End Poverty (PASDEP), and later the Growth and Transformation Plan (GTP). In addition, as further illustrated in the following sections, the few references to applying ICTs for democratization and to the role of the private sector in building Ethiopia's information society were not translated into concrete actions.

The few successes that were achieved by ICTAD, such as the implementation of telecentres in the South-Western part of the country, the licensing of community radios and the localization of software in local languages, did not manage to seriously affect the development of ICTs in the country (EICTDA, 2008). ICTAD created new opportunities for individual communities and operated in a variety of sectors, but ultimately did not succeed in challenging the centralized use of ICTs advanced by the Ethiopian government.

In comparison with the regimes based on projects such as Schoolnet and Woredanet, and managed by EICTDA and ETC, the international technopolitical regime was less centralized and did not depend upon a unitary authority. The UNDP and the World Bank initiatives were introduced concurrently and were both aimed at using technology to enact discourses that had already been selectively refused by the EPRDF. They were not, however, implemented as part of a coordinated effort by the two institutions. This absence of coordination and the lack of

---

[6] Interview: Ahmed Hussien, Professor of Computer Science, Founder of Hilcoe (Higher Learning Center of Excellence ) College, Addis Ababa, 18 March 2008.

substantial support from other actors in the international community prevented the emerging international regime from being sustainable, and from it offering a challenge to, and possibly influencing, the ambitious plans articulated by the Ethiopian government. Returning to De Certeau (1984), it can be argued that both organizations were in a position to develop a coherent strategy, but were unable to extend it beyond the circumscribed space they owned. Their presence and role in the country was legitimate and recognized by a multiplicity of actors. The conception of ICTs they were promoting emanated directly from what, at the time, were hegemonic international discourses on the transformative power of new technologies to increase individual agency and facilitate the exchange of knowledge across borders. Both the UNDP and the World Bank could rely on a terrain from which to act. They could not, however, extend their power beyond that space. As the Schoolnet example illustrates, once the computer laboratories in schools ceased to rely exclusively on the UNDP support and connectivity had to be provided by the ETC, they were disconnected from the grid. Furthermore, the licensing of private ISPs, while agreed to in principle between the World Bank and the Ethiopian government, was prevented in reality by the latter from entering into force. The Ethiopian government was eventually able to prevent internationally promoted uses of ICTs that could threaten its political agenda from gaining traction, and to successfully magnify other aspects of new technologies that it could more easily control.

### The Failure of the Oppositional Technopolitical Regime

> Globalisation has generated new means for transnational populations to influence and for homeland governments, political parties, and social movements to seek to co-opt pressures from populations abroad. Political campaigns and strategies are in part the product of complex interactions between political and social leaders and organisations in multiple locations, with diaspora and other transnational networks serving key linking roles. These forms of cross border participation in the politics of countries of origin are increasingly important as 'political entrepreneurs' create new networks and transnational practices that are distinct from inter-state political processes.      (Lyons, 2007, p. 531)

The globalization Lyons describes, with its real and potential effects on internal politics, is what the Ethiopian government sought most actively to resist. This opposition visibly materialized in May 2006, with the blanket censorship of most of the websites and blogs hosted outside Ethiopia that were critical of the operation of the government. As illustrated below through examining three of the most popular websites blocked in Ethiopia – *Nazret*, *Ethiomedia*, and the *Ethiopian Review* – the response of the government was motivated not only by its culture of communication, which favoured dismissal over engagement, but also by the types of attacks that were launched from those online spaces that struck at the heart of the EPRDF's national discourse.


### The Free Flow of Contestation

Despite the delay in establishing the first Internet connection, the tight control over telecommunication and limited Internet penetration, the types of use of this medium developed by the diaspora as well as by the oppositional voices residing in Ethiopia, made it an effective channel for disseminating alternative discourses. This potential emerged in dramatic ways during the parliamentary elections of May 2005. By that time, the Ethiopian blogosphere was blossoming. Many bloggers had not only joined already popular platforms such as *Nazret*, *Ethiomedia*, and the *Ethiopian Review*, all populated by voices that were highly antagonistic of the EPRDF, but had started creating their own, personal, spaces. Popular bloggers such as *Enset* were influential commentators from the diaspora, while others like *Ethio-Zagol* were contributing to the online debate from Addis Ababa.

The use of the media to support political struggles was not new to Ethiopia. As discussed in Chapter 3, the TPLF had made pervasive use of the media, especially of its clandestine radio, to rally the population against the Derg. Similarly, as discussed by Markakis (1986), during the student movement and the uprising that led to demise of Haile Selassie, the distribution of clandestine publications and leaflets in the main urban centres had a central role in promoting political mobilization, especially among students.[7] There were at least two elements, however, that made communications during the 2005 elections different from these previous critical junctures in the history of the country: the increased opportunities the diaspora enjoyed to influence the political debate back in Ethiopia, and the pace at which information could flow throughout society.

---

[7] Translations from two of these leaflets provided by Markakis (1986) are indicative of how the tension among different political forces in Ethiopia is not a new phenomenon, but is grounded in a more remote past. 'Ministers and generals enrich themselves at the expense of the soldier... Ethiopia rise. Crush the government that benefits only the few', *Voice of the oppressed to the armed forces*, 17 February 1974. 'High officials and foreign capitalists are eating our flesh and sucking our blood. Next day will chew our bones. We must not keep silent. We must do something. We must rise up', *Let us strengthen our unity*, 18 February 1974.

In a move that dramatically multiplied the possibilities of diaspora voices to be heard in Ethiopia despite the limited Internet connectivity, and continuing a tendency that had already started at the end of the 1990s, many newspapers often picked up and translated opinion pieces and news published online. Eskinder Nega, who has been sentenced to jail multiple times for his critical reporting of the government, and who used to be the editor and columnist of the newspapers *Menelik*, *Asqual*, and *Satenaw*, explained how his papers served as platforms to promote awareness within Ethiopia about debates generated outside of the country:

We were publishing articles by prominent people in the diaspora. Fundamental debates were going on in websites such as Ethiomedia and the Ethiopian Review and we were translating them because we wanted to make sure they were known to the public in Ethiopia.[8]

This strategy of republishing critical pieces from the diaspora pursued by Eskinder responded to the idea of journalism as an oppositional force at a critical time in the country's history (Skjerdal, 2011). As Eskinder continued: 'The unique situation of Ethiopia forced us to be not just journalists, but activists. We were not seeking this role, but the conditions in the country forced us to do so'.[9]

This phenomenon, however, was not limited to the press. Before and after the 2005 elections, commentaries and political manifestos published online were printed and turned into leaflets. Mobile phones, especially SMS, were used to mobilize people in real time and disseminate calls for action posted in web forums in much the same way as would later be reported in the case of the revolutions that took place in Tunisia and Egypt in 2011, when new media played a significant role in circulating slogans and coordinating the protests (Wilson & Dunn, 2011), Ethiopian protesters often resorted to 'media relays', communicating information through a medium other than the one on which they had received that information from.

These interactions, between websites and newspapers, but also between mobile communication and international broadcasters such as *Voice of America* (*VOA*), made online spaces part of a wider system where oppositional voices were interconnected, maximizing the capacity to reach different audiences using a variety of platforms and languages. Most members of the Ethiopian government perceived this system as

---

[8] Interview: Eskinder Nega, Former Editor of *Menelik*, *Asqual*, and *Satenaw*, Addis Ababa, 24 May 2008.
[9] Interview: ibid.

part of a coordinated attempt to delegitimize it. As a cadre working in the communication sector retrospectively explained:

That was a period that showed how technology can also affect society negatively. [...] Short messages were used to defame people and you could not really know the source. If I send an SMS to you, then you can act as a multiplier. Also the websites were publishing a lot of factious articles. All this was making people confused. There was an uncontrolled circulation of unfiltered and unbalanced information. I think that it was a strategy of certain groups who know how to use the media. The strategy was to turn down this government and many different media were used to reach this single goal.[10]

A few days after the elections, when the government started to realize it was making greater losses than it had expected, it began to respond directly to protesters in the street, leading to numerous killings and the arrests of thousands of individuals, and also began progressively closing various communication channels, reducing their capacity to be employed, singularly or in combination, to serve the protest and disseminate alternative information and narratives. On 10 June SMSs, which had been used to mobilize people in real time in Addis Ababa and other major towns, were shut down.[11] They would be restored only two years later, on the occasion of the celebration of the Ethiopian millennium.[12] In early November 2005, some of the most vocal Ethiopian journalists, including Eskinder quoted above, who challenged the results of the election and called for more democracy, were arrested and their papers were closed down (Crawford, 2006).[13]

In May 2006, one year after the contested election, the oppositional blogs were censored including the three most popular, *Nazret*, *Ethiomedia*, and the *Ethiopian Review* (Opennet Initiative, 2007). Finally, and in this case only intermittently, radio stations broadcasting from outside Ethiopia using short waves, such as *Voice of America* and *Deutsche Welle*, were jammed.[14]

---

[10] Interview: Desta Tesfaw, Ethiopian Broadcasting Authority, Addis Ababa, 17 June 2008.

[11] In June 2005 almost everybody owning a mobile phone was receiving text messages encouraging them to participate in demonstrations, to forward messages to their friends and acquaintances, and to strike, especially if they were taxi drivers or shop owners.

[12] The first message the Ethiopian citizens received on their mobiles after a long silence was a greeting by ETC's CEO Amare Amsalu wishing them a happy new Ethiopian millennium.

[13] A full chronology of the crackdown on the media in the aftermath of the elections is offered by *Ethio-Zagol*, a famous Ethiopian blogger who used to post from within Ethiopia. His article can be found at http://seminawork.blogspot.com/2006_05_01_archive.html. Last accessed 14 April 2010.

[14] The government actively targeted foreign-based media outlets. Beginning in January, the Committee to Protect Journalists (CPJ) received reports that the broadcast signals of the

The communication system that emerged in 2005, enhancing and further interlinking networks and artefacts that had been taking shape within and beyond Ethiopia's borders, was characterized by a marked heterogeneity. It was going from long-established radio stations such as VOA that had long taken an adversarial stance towards the EPRF-led government, to blogs such as *Urael*, which *Nazret* started hosting only in 2005, quickly gaining popularity in the Ethiopian blogosphere and beyond. It lacked the coherence of a technopolitical regime and a central authority shaping its features, but, as is characteristic of technopolitical regimes, it did act towards the solution of a perceived problem. It functioned in ways that could support regime change, or at least demand greater transparency in the electoral process. It represented the result of the efforts perpetrated by actors challenging the control of the EPRDF over the nation and taking advantage of the capacity of ICTs to coalesce people residing in different locations around a common narrative. Its systemic nature is what turned the apparently insignificant number of Internet users, around twenty thousand in 2005, mobile users, numbering around four hundred thousand, and newspaper readers into a powerful wave, challenging the control of the government over its citizens, and forcing it to take more radical measures.[15]

Similar to the international technopolitical regime, this heterogeneous system of voices, technologies, and actors was enhancing aspects of the discourse on ICTs that were being opposed and resisted by the Ethiopian government. The actors at its core were challenging the use of new technologies as instruments to be used by the state to reinforce its control and legitimacy, and re-framing them as channels to connect Ethiopians outside and inside the country in an effort to find political alternatives. As a popular blogger wrote, 'The Diaspora is a political factor in the democratic struggle which is not to be underestimated. [...] In cyberspace Nazret.com and all the other publications make it impossible that we are silenced'.[16]

---

U.S. government's *Voice of America* (VOA) and the German *Deutsche Welle* were being jammed. Reacting to the reports, the spokesperson of the Mistry of Information, Zemedkun Tekle, told *VOA* that the allegations were 'utterly baseless'. The report can be consulted here www.cpj.org/2009/02/attacks-on-the-press-in-2008-ethiopia.php. Last accessed 14 April 2010.

[15] The data for Internet and mobile users are from EICTDA, which in 2005 reported the capacity of the system in Ethiopia to cater for 21,914 Internet users and for 408,134 mobile users (EICTDA, 2005)

[16] *Sickness and the nephew*, Urael on Nazret, 13 April 2006, http://nazret.com/blog/index.php?blog=13&title=sickness_and_the_nephew&more=1&c=1&tb=1&pb=1. Last accessed 12 February 2010.

In contrast to the international technopolitical regime, however, this system lacked a terrain from which to act. The actors inhabiting it could rely only on tactics, using the communicative spaces the Ethiopian government had permitted to emerge, but not on strategies, which presuppose 'a place that can be circumscribed as proper and thus serve as the basis for generating relations with an exterior distinct from it' (De Certeau, 1984, p. 34). In addition, while the individuals and groups acted against a common adversary, their objectives were divergent, often conflicting. Together, they resembled more what Milton Mueller (2010) defined as an 'associative cluster' rather than a coordinated network. They were a de facto combination of nodes lacking a single point of administration, but engaging nonetheless in sustained interactions.

An *oppositional* technopolitical regime thus remained a pure potentiality. As discussed earlier and further illustrated in the following chapter, after the elections the Ethiopian government started to progressively reclaim those areas that had allowed oppositional voices to spread and challenge its hegemony. The fact that this mix of voices, technologies, and actors did not represent a technopolitical regime does not mean that it did not represent a threat to the Ethiopian government, but that it simply did not succeed in gaining enough control, discursively and materially, of the communicative space in Ethiopia to prevail over its adversary.

The history of the use of ICTs in Ethiopia to contest government control could have been different. The mobilization in Ethiopia shared many aspects of those that were to follow in Iran in the aftermath of the 2009 elections and in North Africa in 2011 (which came to be known as the 'Arab Spring'). ICTs were central in both creating imagery for people to mobilize around and in coordinating their actions. Messages were relayed across media and attempts were made to use ICTs to raise international attention. But while the events in Iran, Tunisia, and Egypt were framed by international media and foreign commentators as spurred on, or at least profoundly shaped, by the new media, the same framework was not applied to the protests in Ethiopia in 2005.

As research on the use of ICTs during the Arab Spring has begun to show, independently from the use that was actually made of Twitter and Facebook to coordinate and mobilize, both platforms carried significant symbolic power and acted as motivators (Tufekci & Wilson, 2012; Wilson & Dunn, 2011). Social media in Tunisia and Egypt had come to be associated with the youth and with a new agenda put forward by a generation that had not been given adequate space and opportunities to shape national politics (Aouragh & Alexander, 2011). In addition, many of the claims made by the protesters were universalistic in nature, demanding better jobs, improved living conditions, political representation, and reclaiming a prosperous future that they seemed to have been excluded from. As the literature on media frames suggests (Benford & Snow, 2000; Gamson & Modigliani, 1989; Goffman, 1974; Snow & Benford, 1992; Snow, Rochford Jr, Worden, & Benford, 1986), these features offered an opportunity for international media to turn a distant conflict into an event audiences could relate with, and reinforce certain narratives while excluding others, in a mutually reinforcing cycle. While more traditional international outlets continued to rely on the established 'protest paradigm' (Harlow & Johnson, 2011), that emphasizes official sources and focuses on the spectacle of the protest, highlighting sensational details, including violence and visible drama (Chan & Lee, 1984; McLeod & Hertog, 1999), other more recent platforms, from international TV channel Al Jazeera to blogging platform Global Voices, created unprecedented opportunities for protesters to shape the narrative of the event. In the case of Egypt, once the Internet was shut down to contain the protest, Google and Twitter joined forces and created 'Speak to Tweet', a system that allowed protesters to call a phone number and have the recording of their voice available as a tweet that could be accessed by all twitter users globally (Arthur, 2011).

This type of framing and international attention was almost entirely missing in the case of the protests that followed the 2005 elections in Ethiopia. Reports in international media emphasized the violence in the streets, the number of people killed or injured and provided little information on the roots of the conflict. As for social media, in 2005 Facebook was still a platform limited to university campuses and had no presence in Africa; Twitter had yet to be launched. Bloggers, as described earlier, had risen to new prominence in Ethiopia in 2005, but almost no international media referred to online spaces to emphasize the unique aspects of the 2005 mobilizations.[17] As a result, the conflict in Ethiopia continued to remain a distant concern for international audiences, who were offered few opportunities to understand and empathize with the protesters.

This lack of opportunity was not just caused by the lack of international coverage, but also from the inability of Ethiopian bloggers to capture a more universal message that could appeal to international

---

[17] The only exception was Global Voices, where quotes from popular blogs were used to create news stories on the protest. A similar strategy was later adopted for the protests in Egypt and Tunisia in 2011, when blog posts were largely replaces by tweets and facebook posts.

audiences. As the next and final section illustrates, differently from the majority of online spaces in Tunisia and Egypt, in the case of Ethiopia most blogs had in fact largely been used to re-articulate old grievances among elites, rather than to support new discourses and agenda that could look at the country's future, rather than at its past.

### Attacking and Defending the National Narrative

Blogs and websites opposing the government in Addis Ababa were not blocked all together, but were obscured progressively during the month of May 2006. The first to condemn the filtering were Ethiopian bloggers themselves. Those operating from inside the country were able to register the online spaces that had become inaccessible on a daily basis. For example *Ethio-Zagol*, a blogger posting from Addis Ababa, wrote on 18 May 2006:

Over the last two days, all blogspots blogs [...] have been blocked in Ethiopia. Those who seek political quips from weichegud or intelligent analysis form other bloggers can't access the sites via the telecom servers. In addition, the government has blocked Ethiopian Review, cyber ethiopia, quatero and Free Our Leaders websites. My sources told me this is done by tel. [the Ethiopian Telecommunication Corporation] with the advice and help of the Chinese.[18]

This information was later confirmed by other sources inside and outside Ethiopia.[19] Defying the blocking, most bloggers residing in the country continued to update their spaces through proxies, and sent information to friends and colleagues living abroad. Websites such as the *Ethiopian review* and *Ethiomedia*, managed primarily by Ethiopians in the diaspora, continued to be adjourned as normal. Many bloggers started providing advice to their readers on how to circumvent the censorship, hoping this information could reach the

---

[18] *Government blocks bloggers*, Ethio-Zagol, 18 May 2006 http://seminawork.blogspot.com/2006/05/government-blocks-bloggers-over-last.html. Last accessed 12 February 2010.

[19] From inside Ethiopia, see for example Addis Ferengi, a French lady managing a blog from Addis Ababa hosted on the online platform nazret.com. She wrote various articles on the issue, among which are *Censorship Please forward*, Addis Ferengi on Nazret.com, 22 May 2006, (http://nazret.com/blog/index.php?blog=9&title=censorship_please_forward&more=1&c=1&tb=1&pb=1) and *All 'no-propaganda' websites are blocked now*, Addis Ferengi on Nazret.com, 28 May 2006. (http://nazret.com/blog/index.php?blog=9&title=all_no_propaganda_websites_are_blocked_n&more=1&c=1&tb=1&pb=1) Last accessed 12 February 2010.

intended targets through the websites that were still accessible, through emails or other means in the vast communicative network described above.[20] Cyber-activists operating at the international level, and advocacy organizations such as Reporters Sans Frontières (RSF) and the Committee to Protect Journalists (CPJ) also denounced this new attempt by the Ethiopian government to further curtail an already narrow space for public debate.[21]

As often happens when censorship measures are condemned by international actors and institutions, it was the simple act of blocking websites and blogs that was acknowledged while little or no mention was made of the discourses that were animating the targeted online spaces and the underlying causes that led to the censorship. Knowledge of Ethiopia's political history, and a closer examination of the articles and posts hosted on the most popular online spaces addressed to Ethiopian readers, would have shown that the filtering was just the latest incarnation of the long-term struggle between the EPRDF and other forces opposing its state and nation building plan. As the excerpts below from Ethiomedia and the Ethiopian review exemplify, the attacks waged against the Ethiopian government were not simply critical of its governance, but were directed at some of the pillars on which the national agenda was based, such as ethnic federalism which was presented as an attempt to divide rather than

---

[20] Addis Ferenji on nazret.com, for example, wrote: 'The Ethiopian government is obviously decided to silence all independent Medias [sic]. Please note that the censorship may be circumvent by using http://securebar.secure-tunnel.com and forward the information to insiders' (*Censorship Please forward*, Addis Ferengi on Nazret.com, 22 May 2006, http://nazret.com/blog/index.php?blog=9&title=censorship_ please_forward&more=1& c=1&tb=1&pb=1. Last accessed 12 February 2010). Ethio-Zagol offered a more detailed explanation on how to use these instruments: 'This blog can't be accessed in Ethiopia so the following advise may not reach its intended readers. Other websites like Ethiomedia who hasn't yet been blocked should carry the message to Ethiopian readers. Readers can use an open proxy like this which allow to circumvent the blocks. Readers should click on http://securebar.secure-tunnel.com/cgi-bin/nph-freebar .cgi/110110A and enter the address that is blocked in the displayed box. Using the proxy we can access our beloved blogs and websites even though the government has censored them' (*Government Blocks Bloggers*, Ethio-Zagol, 18 May 2006, http://seminawork .blogspot.com/2006/05/government-blocks-bloggers-over-last.html. Last accessed 12 February 2010).

[21] See, for example, Ethan Zuckerman's *Ethiopia 'pioneers' cybercensorship in sub-Saharan Africa*, www.ethanzuckerman.com/blog/2006/05/22/ethiopia-pioneers-cybercensorship-in-sub-saharan-africa/), or RSF's article: *Three more sites unaccessible, government denies being involved.* (http://en.rsf.org/spip.php?page=article&id_article=17783) and report *Dictatorships get to grips with Web 2.0* (http://en.rsf.org/spip.php?page=article&id_ article=20844). CPJ similarly denounced the censorship in a note: *Critical web sites inaccessible in Ethiopia* (http://cpj.org/2006/05/critical-web-sites-inaccessible-in-ethiopia .php). Last accessed 12 February 2010.

unite Ethiopian citizens, and revolutionary democracy, portrayed as just another form of authoritarianism.

The Meles propaganda machinery and his state apparatus are tirelessly promoting all sorts of machinations aimed at turning one Ethiopian ethnic group against another. In a police state where mismanagement, nepotism and corruption are rampant, and where the people are completely disenchanted and disgusted with the authoritarian rule of a tyrant, the illusion of stability and security would remain whimsical.[22]

Ethnic-based parcelling of the map of Ethiopia with evil design to make it convenient for cessation. This is a reckless and dangerous experiment, which should be utterly condemned not only by Ethiopians but also by all Africans suffering from tribal strife as a cancer to peace, stability and prosperity. Creation of a feudal land tenure system in which TPLF is the landlord and the peasants live in slavery in serfdom.[23]

The discourses articulated in these two posts, hosted on the *Ethiopian Review* and *Ethiomedia*, respectively, closely resemble those promoted in the 1990s by newspapers such as *Tobiya* (see Chapter 3, p. 8), further illustrating how new media were not seized upon as a way to articulate new discourses, but were largely captured by old ones. Ethnic federalism was not only attacked as a problematic strategy which would fail to hold the country together, but an 'evil design' intentionally pursued by the Tigrayan minority to subjugate other ethnic groups. Similarly, in the second excerpt, the bases of revolutionary democracy were also challenged. As previously argued, the TPLF/EPRDF had long addressed the peasants as the main beneficiaries of its policies. Reframing them as slaves serving a feudal lord, and employing imagery that was evocative of imperial Ethiopia, meant accusing the government of having simply taken the throne from previous rulers, rather than being the revolutionary force it had claimed to be.

It must be noted, however, that the heated and polemical language employed in these and similar posts was not characteristic of oppositional voices alone, but was a trait common to most of the players participating in the polarized political debate in Ethiopia. A few days before the elections, for example, the Prime Minister Meles Zenawi declared in a televised interview:

---

[22] *Deconstructing Meles Zenawi's Response to US Congress*, by Concerned Ethiopians in the United States, Ethiopian Review, 1 July 2005, www.ethiopianreview.com/2005/jul/001OpinionJuly1_2005_Re_Meles_Letter.html. Last accessed 14 February 2010.

[23] *Two successive Ethiopian despots in comparison*, by Robele Ababya, Ethiomedia, 16 August 2005, www.ethiomedia.com/fastpress/two_ethiopian_despots.html. Last accessed 14 February 2010.

I call on the people of Ethiopia to punish opposition parties who are promoting an ideology of hatred and divisiveness by denying them their votes at election on May 15. Their policies are geared toward creating hatred and rifts between ethnic groups similar to the policies of the Interahamwe when Hutu militia massacred Tutsis in Rwanda. It is a dangerous policy that leads the nation to violence and bloodshed.[24]

In the months following the elections and the unrest their uncertain result triggered, Meles' argument was often turned on its head by bloggers who used similar or greater vehemence to accuse him, not the opposition, of being the main cause of ethnic divisions. For example, a blogger writing on the Ethiopian Review pointed out how the charged discourse on ethnicity used by the Prime Minister's was also motivated by his inexperience with campaigning.

It is now clear that Meles' campaign was centred on further deepening ethnic suspicion and mistrust in to the fibre of Ethiopian politics. Lacking results to show for the 14 years of his time at the helm, the PM chose to campaign on ethnic politics platform that shamelessly dared to bring the Rwandan experience in to the Ethiopian political discourse. Meles chose this platform, not only because he lacked a record to campaign on but he also believed that ethnic politics has taken root capable of delivering votes bounty. The lesson Meles will take from this election will be the need to accelerate his divisive ethnic project. If allowed, he will come back with vengeance. Venomous ethnic division and instigation of tension among the people will be the trademark of his rule for years to come. Instability will ensue, providing Meles with the rational for his future extrajudicial measures. He will use this to impress and cajole the international community. Beware, given the chance, he will do it![25]

---

[24] Part of the speech is reported in the article *A critical look into the Ethiopian elections*, 3 June 2005, Sudan Tribune. www.sudantribune.com/spip.php?page=imprimable&id_article= 9931 Last accessed 16 February 2010. It is also referred to in (EU-EOM, 2005; Teshome, 2009)

[25] Why the result of Election 2005 matters, by Ajibew A., Ethiopian Review, 27 July 2005. See www.ethiopianreview.com/2005/jul/001OpinionJuly27_2005_Ajibew_A.htm. Last accessed 16 February 2010. A couple of other examples are reported below: 'These criminals [the EPRDF leaders] are more than capable of inflicting some atrocities, in the confusion of the time, on one or another group of Ethiopians and then blame other group(s) of Ethiopians so as to implement their "Interahamwe" dream on Ethiopia and Ethiopians. Ethiopians have to be careful not to be drawn into such traps of the criminal mafia and its head that would do anything to continue their open blunder', Call For All Ethiopians, by Girum Getinet, Ethiomedia, 3 November 2005. See www.ethiomedia .com/fastpress/call_for_all.html. Last accessed 16 February 2010. And 'The mission of the militia is to go into the Oromo and Amhara regions of Ethiopia and eliminate anyone suspected of supporting the opposition against TPLF rule. Meles and his militia commanders are carrying out this mission of search and destroy in the name of protecting Tigreyans. The true intentions of Meles are to start ethnic warfare between Tigreyans and non-Tigreyans and use this as a pretext to divide the country and the people'. The violent birth and life of Meles Zenawi may bring his downfall, by Girma

Ethiopian Review and Ethiomedia were challenging the very core of the national discourse advanced by the EPRDF, often suggesting how ethnic federalism could turn into ethnic discrimination and ethnically motivated violence.[26] These uses, however, should not justify the censoring of blogs and websites, but, together with the responses they triggered in the Ethiopian government and with the condemnation this response received internationally from organizations such as RSF and CPJ, they illustrate how local and international discourses may dramatically overlook one another. On the one hand, defending the discourse of ICTs as a globalizing force and of information as free to flow independent of frontiers sometimes required tolerating messages that leaned towards hate speech and showed little sensitivity of the complexity of the political situation in Ethiopia. On the other hand, the Ethiopian government did not seek any form of consensus on the means that could be employed to bring the debate back to more constructive dialogue and prioritized its desire to hegemonize the political scene. The government's tendency to dismiss rather than reach out to critical voices also manifested itself in this instance and in the new media, where dissent was simply removed. Ethiopia's sovereignty was affirmed in this case only at the technical, but not at the discursive level, blocking undesired spaces, while simultaneously responding to international organizations demanding that no censorship be carried out in Ethiopia.

## Conclusion

The Ethiopian government was ultimately successful in preventing the emergence of alternative technopolitical regimes that could have challenged its ability of using ICTs to support its state- and nation-building agenda. As the next chapter indicates, the initially harsh response that resulted in the censoring of blogs and imprisoning of journalists and

Bekele, Ethiomedia, 28 September 2005. See www.ethiomedia.com/fastpress/zenawi_fuels_violence.html. Last accessed 16 February 2010.

[26] Fortunately, the unfolding of the events in the aftermath of the elections proved that neither the warnings issued by the Prime Minister nor those of bloggers were justified. Violent confrontations between government opponents and police forces did erupt in Addis Ababa and other major towns, leading to killings and arbitrary imprisonments that were condemned by the international community, but they were largely motivated by politics rather than ethnicity (Aalen & Tronvoll, 2009). The government reacted disproportionally to a scenario it had not foreseen and was moved by the fear of losing control over the urban areas, while the protests were directed mostly towards institutions accused to have stolen a vote, rather than towards specific groups such as the Tigrayans. For more information, see Aalen & Tronvoll, 2009; Carter Center, 2005; EU-EOM, 2005.

bloggers would be followed by an expanded strategy seeking to legitimize these measures to both domestic and international audiences. Even the bloggers that had begun to operate in the period following the 2005 elections developed a new approach towards criticizing the government, accepting rather than openly attacking discourses on ethnic federalism, revolutionary democracy, and the developmental state and seeking to promote change and reform within, rather than beyond the framework developed by the EPRDF. As Chapter 7 illustrates, however, these attempts had to face an increasing closure from a government that, especially after the death of Meles Zenawi, grew progressively wary of any form of criticism.

# 7    ICT for Development, Human Rights, and the Changing Geopolitical Order

*All suspects are accused for their terrorist acts of conspiring, planning and instigating instability in the country. [...] In the process of their criminal activities [...] the bloggers and the journalists have participated on various trainings. They have travelled out of the country on various occasions to partake in these trainings. They have also organized the trainings in the country. In the trainings the suspects have learned how to encrypt their online communications from a software package called 'Security in a Box'.    (Charges of the federal prosecutor against bloggers of the Zone9 collective, 17 July 2014)*

In the aftermath of its failed experiment in electoral democracy in 2005, the EPRDF not only closed avenues for popular protest and forcefully consolidated power, it also began an ambitious project to progressively theorize and legitimize the measures it had adopted in the ICT sector, and in other crucial areas.[1] Up to this point, both the developmental and the sovereign technopolitical regimes had been implemented steadily but quietly. The government resisted pressures from national and international organizations and avoided publicly explaining the rationale and vision that had inspired the two regimes. Similarly, the containment of critical uses of ICTs, including the censoring of blogs and the interruption of the SMS service, received little explanation or were presented as technical glitches.

As had been the case in the past, the creation of a new space for action did not occur abruptly, but represented a further shift from a tactical to strategic approach to ICTs. Similar to what Jean Francois Bayart (2000) argued in the case of other African countries interacting with the international system, the Ethiopian government relied on extraversion to

---

[1] A notable example of this process is the Charities and Societies Proclamation which limits the ability of organizations which receive more than 10 per cent of their funds from foreign sources to engage in areas where civil society organizations have previously played an important role, such as human rights, conflict resolution and reconciliation, citizenship and community development, and justice and law enforcement services. See for example Aalen & Tronvoll (2009).

134

achieve its goals, manipulating its unequal relationship with the external environment in its own favour. The Anti-Terrorism Proclamation is the clearest example of this course of action. Passed in 2009 as a late attempt to comply with requests from the United Nations and the United States to take the fight against international terrorism to a global level, it created the legal preconditions to actually prosecute critical voices within Ethiopia (or Ethiopians in the diaspora). The quote of the charges against the Zone9 bloggers that opens this chapter is an example of how a legal provision aligning with international demands was used not to fight terrorists, but to stifle dissent. An international injunction was 'subverted from within' (De Certeau, 1984, p. 32), and used to pursue goals that were alien to it.

Differently from other cases of extraversion, however, the Ethiopian government progressively turned this relation of dependency, the necessity to seize opportunities emerging internationally to advance its own goals, into a more stable and centrally owned strategy. It capitalized on the space it had first created through extraversion and progressively expanded it even when this meant facing national contestations and international condemnations.[2] In continuity with previous phases of the national shaping of ICTs, this strategy comprised both technical and discursive elements. As this chapter illustrates, it was through its revamped collaboration with China that the Ethiopian government was able to expand access to fixed and mobile phones and to the Internet under monopoly, maintaining a control on the flow of information in the country that no other African nation had achieved before. This time, however, the discursive aspects of the government strategy also became more manifest. Declared policy (policy as rhetoric) and enacted policy (policy as practice) (Allen & Hecht, 2001) were aligned to a new degree, indicating greater confidence in pursuing an independent path in the creation of a centrally dominated national information society. In 2010 for the first time Meles Zenawi openly proclaimed his government's entitlement to protect the national information space, even if this meant jamming international broadcasters such as VOA when they were perceived to be a threat to the country's security.[3]

This chapter examines these latter transformations, and their contradictions, from two complementary perspectives. The first section illustrates

---

[2] There is a long list of articles and petitions by international NGOs, and in some cases foreign governments, condemning the abuses of the Anti-Terrorism Proclamation to stifle dissent.

[3] 'Ethiopia admits jamming VOA radio broadcasts in Amharic' http://news.bbc.co.uk/1/hi/8575749.stm. Last accessed 13 November 2014.

the consolidation and increasing assertion of the government's new course, through initiatives that exploited a changing geopolitical order in order to enhance national agendas. The second part looks at the cracks in this ambitious, but also ambiguous, strategy, indicating how the consolidation of the increasingly intertwined sovereign and developmental regimes in Ethiopia also made some of their inconsistencies more manifest.

## Consolidation through Extraversion

The consolidation of the technopolitical regimes developed in the previous decade and the resistance to the emergence of alternative ones was pursued through exploiting two apparently opposed trends that had become increasingly significant on the international stage. One was the growing interest of China in the African continent and it concurrently becoming a major international player in the telecommunications sector (Brautigam, 2009; Gagliardone, 2015; Gagliardone, Repnikova, & Stremlau, 2010; Mohan, 2013; Tan-Mullins, Mohan, & Power, 2010). Differently from Western donors, the United States in particular, which emphasized liberalization and democratization when supporting ICT programmes, China's no-strings-attached policy offered both financial and technical means for African governments to pursue their own development priorities, even when this meant increasing state control and limiting spaces for debate. The other trend was the securitization of development that had been championed by the US government in the aftermath of the 9/11 terrorist attacks and since had been progressively redefining priorities and modes of development aid. Alongside these, a third, longer-term process continued to influence the shaping of ICT policy and practice in Ethiopia; namely the commitment of the Ethiopian government to ensure that ICTs should be put at the service of development. Woredanet and Schoolnet were the first concrete example of this commitment, and in 2008 the Ethiopia Commodity Exchange (ECX) became its latest incarnation. Despite being technically disconnected from Woredanet and Schoolnet, the ECX continued to emphasize elements that had been at the core of the two previous systems, centralizing power in the hand of the state while improving efficiency and service delivery.

These three trends are examined in turn in the sections below, starting with how the Ethiopian government exploited the global antiterrorism agenda to pursue domestic goals, then analysing the role of China, and finally examining the ECX, the latest in the Ethiopian government's proactive efforts to shape the ICT sector while keeping a tight control over it.

*Terrorizing Dissent*

Ethiopia has been relatively late to enact a domestic anti-terrorism law, as compared to other countries that introduced similar legislations in the aftermath of 9/11 to comply with UN Security Council Resolution 1373, which requires states to ensure 'terrorist acts are established as serious criminal offences in domestic laws' (UN Security Council, 2001, p. 2). Coming into force only in August 2009, Ethiopia's Anti-Terrorism Proclamation was framed nonetheless as a response to the Resolution passed eight years earlier and to international pressure to combat terrorism. This decision openly contradicted a report the Ethiopian government had filed in 2002 to the Counter Terrorism Committee (CTC), the agency instituted to monitor state compliance with Resolution 1373. In its response to the CTC the Ethiopian government did acknowledge its vulnerability to terrorist attacks from organizations such as Al-Qaeda and Somalia-based Islamic group Al-Ittihad Al-Islamia, but it also clearly indicated that existing legal instruments, including the 1957 Criminal Code and the 1974 Special Penal Code, were adequate both to counter terrorism and prosecute perpetrators of terrorist attacks (Kassa, 2014).

It should be noted that since 2006 Ethiopia has fought a war in Somalia, backed by the United States, in support of Somalia's Transitional Federal Government, a war that has led to the creation of al Shabaab, a terrorist group that – paradoxically – would become one of the most serious threats to peace in the Horn of Africa (Menkhaus, 2007, 2013). It has also witnessed a number of violent episodes, including an attack by the Ogaden National Liberation Front to a Chinese-run oil field in 2007 that claimed the lives of 74 people, including 9 Chinese. However, when the Proclamation is considered not just in relation to the evolution of international and domestic terrorism, but also to other legal instruments the government has been developing during the same period and to the type of individuals who have been targeted, it acquires a different, more pernicious, meaning.

The Anti-Terrorism Proclamation shares with the Charities and Societies Proclamation (2009), the Regulation for the Re-establishment of the Information Network Security Agency (INSA, 2011) and the Telecom Fraud Offences Proclamation (2012) the common goal of extending the government 'legitimate' sphere of influence while limiting the possibility for other actors – domestic and international – to influence policy and politics in Ethiopia. The Charities and Societies Proclamation has restricted NGOs that receive more than 10 per cent of their financing from foreign sources from engaging in human rights and advocacy activities. The Telecom Fraud Offences Proclamation has re-affirmed the state monopoly over telecommunications, imposing severe sanctions for any operator trying to compete with or bypass Ethio-Telecom, and has extended the provisions of the Anti-Terrorism Proclamation to the online sphere (Article 6). Since its creation, the INSA, shaped in the guise of the US National Security Agency (NSA), has taken on the responsibility of 'protecting' the national information space, 'taking counter measures against information attacks', which the law frames as any 'attack against the national interest, constitutional order, and nation's psychology by using cyber and electromagnetic technologies and systems'.

Examining the profiles of the individuals convicted under the Anti-Terrorism Proclamation helps to further clarify the motivations behind the law and to understand how, similar to what had been experienced in other countries, including Colombia, Nepal, the Philippines, and Uganda (International Commission of Jurists, 2009), the Ethiopian government interpreted the global war against terrorism as an opportunity to pursue domestic enemies while fending off external pressure and condemnation. Out of the 33 individuals convicted under the Anti-Terrorism Proclamation between 2009 and 2014, 13 have been journalists. Some of them have been accused of planning terrorist attacks on infrastructure, telecommunications, and power lines (Woubshet Taye and Reeyot Alemu); others to support Ginbot 7, an organization led by Berhanu Nega, who in the 2005 elections had won the seat of mayor of Addis Ababa, and was included in the country's terror list soon after its establishment (Eskinder Nega, Abebe Gelaw, Fasil Yenealem, Abebe Belew); two journalists working for the newspaper Ye Musilmoch Guday were charged of plotting acts of 'terrorism, intending to advance a political, religious, or ideological cause', as part of a broader crackdown on Ethiopian Muslims (Solomon Kebede, Yusuf Getachew); two Swedish journalists who had embedded themselves with the Ogaden National Liberation Front to cover the conflict in Southern Ethiopia were also charged under the Anti-Terrorism Proclamation, and pardoned by the President after having served 450 days in prison (Johan Persson and Martin Schibbye). Some of the journalists have been charged in absentia; those who were apprehended in Ethiopia are serving sentences for up to 18 years in prison.

Numerous international organizations, including the Committee to Protect Journalists, Reporters without Borders, Amnesty International, and Human Rights Watch have accused the Ethiopian government of taking advantage of a law they label as 'deeply flawed' (Human Rights Watch, 2013) to persecute and silence critical voices. The government has responded to this criticism by re-asserting the legitimacy of its acts. Bereket Simon justified his government's decision to detain the two

Swedish journalists by labelling international pressure to free the detainees as 'a very wrong defence of foreign journalists who have been caught red-handed assisting terrorists'.[4] Similarly, in 2014 Prime Minister Hailemariam Desalegn commented on the arrest of the Zone9 bloggers (whose case is discussed in greater detail below) by alleging their links with terrorist groups. As he remarked: 'I don't think becoming a blogger makes somebody immune, if someone involves into this terrorist network that destabilizes my country'.[5]

These assertions were criticized by international pressure groups, but they also indicate how the post-9/11 agenda, primarily aimed at combating international terrorism and the possibility that instability in distant places could have repercussions 'back home', has created 'pockets of legitimacy' that can be, and have been, exploited to pursue a variety of other ends, including curbing dissent. When the Ethiopian government had to justify measures limiting freedom of expression or stifling political debate in the country, the discourse on security has been privileged over other potentially more controversial arguments. As explained in the next section, despite financial and technical support from China enabling the Ethiopian government to realize its vision of a tightly controlled national information society, the government has refrained, for example, from publicly referring to China as a model to follow in the field of media and telecommunication.

### A Quiet Partner

On 8 November 2006, Chinese telecom giant ZTE and the Ethiopian Telecommunication Corporation (ETC) signed the largest agreement in the history of telecommunications in Africa. Backed by China Development Bank, ZTE offered a loan of $1.5 billion (to which ZTE added $0.4 billion for engineering) to overhaul and expand Ethiopia's telecommunication system. The loan, to be repaid in thirteen years, was disbursed in three phases. The first phase had a particularly symbolic value. Branded 'Millennium Plan', it was expected to produce its results – laying down more than two thousands kilometres of fibre optic cable connecting Ethiopia's thirteen largest cities – by 11 September 2007, the day marking the beginning of the new millennium on the Ethiopian calendar. The second and third phases similarly focussed on infrastructure development, expanding coverage to rural areas, and building the capacity of the system to support 20 million mobile users (from the initial 1.2 million)

---

[4] Bereket Simon quoted in Davison (2012).
[5] Hailemariam Desalegn quoted in Fortin (2014).

and more than a million Internet broadband users. Resources also went towards upgrading Woredanet and Schoolnet, allowing some of the sites to progressively switch from expensive and inefficient satellite connections to terrestrial broadband.

China's support has allowed the Ethiopian government to reach goals no other African country had achieved before, dramatically expanding access in a regime of monopoly.[6] Elsewhere in Africa the liberalization of the market was what drove expansion in coverage and lowered costs. Countries that opted for a system tightly controlled by the state, such as neighbouring Eritrea, have severely lagged behind in developing information infrastructure and services. By providing capital, equipment, and the expertise, all with no strings attached in terms of policy changes (e.g., liberalizing the market), ZTE, which is partially state-owned, has not only brought the Ethiopian government out of the cul-de-sac in which it had put itself by stubbornly defending monopoly, but has also helped it realize its vision of a tightly controlled but developmentally oriented national information society.

As Amare Anslau, the CEO of the ETC at the time the project with ZTE took shape remarked in an interview in June 2008,

Holding telecommunications is not just about security. We need this instrument for development. We need it for the people. Ethiopia is not like any other African country. Those countries just think that they can become rich, the individual can become rich. But what we want is instead building in the mind of people the attachment to their land and to their country. Once you have technology you become addicted to it. So, if you allow the private they can certainly make money. But what about the society? The society will not benefit from it. So the government is the one that has to make sure that things are done in the interest of the people [. . .] You have to hold all keys in your hands otherwise change, real change, will be impossible.[7]

His words deeply resonate with those used by Debretsion Gebremichael, Ethiopia's first Minister of Information and Communication Technology and head of Ethiopia's ICT Development Agency during ZTE's expansion project, to defend the government's strategy. In the interview mentioned in Chapter 4 he in fact explained that 'behind the decision of leaving the monopoly in the ICTs and telecommunication market there is big philosophical thinking. It is not just because we want to make money from the use of telecoms'.[8]

---

[6] For a comparative analysis of China's investments in the ICT sector in Africa see (Gagliardone, 2013; Gagliardone, Repnikova, & Stremlau, 2010).

[7] Interview: Amare Amsalu, CEO, Ethiopian Telecommunication Corporation, Addis Ababa, 27 June 2008.

[8] Interview: Debretsion GebreMichael, Director of EICTDA, Addis Ababa, 10 June 2008.

As discussed throughout the book, the Ethiopian government has distinguished itself for its reliance on ideology to motivate policy decisions, but its approach has often faced resistance. Politics and technology are mutually reshaping, and technical constraints do have repercussions on political decisions, even when politicians would like it to be otherwise. Later in the chapter I will discuss the drawbacks of allowing ZTE to become the sole provider of equipment and technical expertise. Here, however, it will suffice to note how, progressively cognizant of the inability of ZTE to adequately solve the technical challenges posed by the extremely chaotic legacy infrastructure, simultaneously expanding the service while guaranteeing its efficiency, the Ethiopian government was forced to open the next expansion phase to greater competition. A competition, however, that would end up in the form of a split of the market between two Chinese companies.

On 7 June 2011, the now re-branded Ethio-Telecom issued a tender to further boost the capacity of Ethiopia's mobile phone network to 50 million subscribers by 2015, and to introduce 4G connectivity, a mobile broadband technology allowing browsing speeds of 100 Mbit per second. The tender was similarly based on a vendor financing scheme, as had previously been the case with ZTE. As Debretsion explained 'We are not investing; we are inviting companies to come with their finance'. However, in contrast to 2006, the tender was public and various companies competed. As the Wall Street Journal put it, however, 'again, financing won the day, with the two [ZTE and Huawei] pledging a total of $1.6 billion. Western equipment suppliers, such as Ericsson and Alcatel Lucent SA, couldn't match the Chinese offer'(Dalton, 2014). With the signing of two separate contracts of $800 million each with Huawei and ZTE, competition was introduced in the shape of a rivalry between two Chinese companies that have been contending for shares of the Chinese market for a long time. As a representative of Huawei in Ethiopia who requested to speak on condition of anonymity argued, 'It is normal that Huawei and ZTE compete for resources. ZTE in Ethiopia did not do a good job. It did not have enough incentives. So the government asked Huawei to come, because we have a better reputation in Africa'.[9]

Despite the different outcomes, both the first and the second deals, which together surpass $3 billion, are indicative of the different approach the Chinese government and Chinese telecoms have brought forward to enter the increasingly crowded ICT market in Africa and acquire greater influence. China has been aggressive when providing financial resources

---

[9] Interview: Representative of Huawei in Ethiopia, Addis Ababa, 9 May 2013.

to governments struggling to expand ICT infrastructure and services, and has relied on state-owned banks (China Development Bank and the Export-Import Bank of China) to offer export credit to Chinese companies willing to expand their operations abroad. Despite this increasingly outward exposure, however, the Chinese government has avoided publicly indicating its willingness to export the strategies it has adopted to develop its domestic ICT sector or indicate them as superior to those suggested by Western donors or partners. The lack of proactivity on the side of China, however, has not prevented these strategies from gaining appeal among African partners.

In a Wikileaks cable reporting a meeting between Sebhat Nega, a founder of the TPLF and one of the most influential ideologues of the Ethiopian government, and the US ambassador Donald Yamamoto, Sebhat was reported to have openly declared his admiration for China and stressed that Ethiopia 'needs the China model to inform the Ethiopian people'.[10] When I met Sebhat a few years later and asked him about his appreciation for how the Chinese government had been shaping its communication system, he first showed surprise (he was not aware his conversation had entered the public domain), but then stressed again, and even reinforced, the remark he previously made with the US ambassador. As he argued: 'The most informed society in the world is the Chinese. But we cannot reach that level. Nobody can. Everybody in the administration [in China] knows who is who and what needs to be done. And the Chinese leaders are responsive to the demands of the people'.[11]

Arguments like these are still confined to informal conversations and, while China has been publicly praised for the commitment shown towards the Ethiopian people, it has still not been hailed as a model to shape Ethiopia's information society. This may change in the near future, but the pattern that has emerged in the decade following the 2005 election, seems to indicate that the Ethiopian government has preferred to exploit the ambiguities of the dominant discourses advanced by Western donors, the United States in particular, when it needed to support unpopular decisions (e.g., the censoring of critical voices and jailing of journalists and bloggers), rather than publicly aligning with measures such as those adopted by the Chinese government to police its own information space that are still unpopular among the international community.

[10] US Embassy in Addis Ababa, Cable #09ADDISABABA149 (2009).
[11] Interview: Sebhat Nega, Founder of the TPLF and Director of the Ethiopian International Institute for Peace & Development, Addis Ababa, 11 May 2013.

## The TEDization of Ethiopia's Development

TED stands for 'Technology, Entertainment, Design' and is a global set of conferences where scientists, celebrities, politicians, and all those who have 'ideas worth spreading', the conference's slogan, are offered a stage to present their case. TED has progressively become the privileged platform for hyped discourses on the ability of innovation to change society, and a good share of TED presentations have addressed the challenges of development. In June 2007, when its international chapter, TEDGlobal, was dedicated to Africa, Ethiopian economist Eleni Gabre-Madhin was invited to present her vision for Ethiopia's (and Africa's) first commodities exchange. The question she wanted to answer, framed using the upbeat and assertive tones typical of TED conferences, was 'how can markets be developed in rural Africa to harness the power of innovation and entrepreneurship that we know exists?'

Her vision became real just a few months later. On 4 September 2007, Proclamation 551/2007 established the Ethiopia Commodity Exchange (ECX) Authority, and on 24 April 2008 the opening bell of the ECX sounded for the first time. Towards the end of 2008, after the Ethiopian government legislated that all coffee not directly exported by farmers had to be traded through the ECX, Eleni's brainchild turned into an internationally renowned institution. The ECX became the subject of documentaries presenting the Ethiopian innovation to foreign audiences, Eleni was interviewed by major media outlets catering for global audiences, and the ECX model begun to attract the attention of other African leaders willing to replicate it in their own countries.[12]

The ECX is a complex organisation. Fully owned by the Ethiopian government, but open to private operators who are willing and able to buy a membership seat, it connects a trading floor in Addis Ababa with grading centres, warehouses, and display sites all around the country. At its core, it is a marketplace for trading a wide variety of commodities, including maize, coffee, sesame, and wheat. Its mission is to 'connect all buyers and sellers in an efficient, reliable, and transparent market by harnessing innovation and technology'.[13]

ICTs have played a paramount role in making the ECX a reality. Already in the planning stages the team tasked by the Ethiopian government to realize the new project decided that an in-house suite of

---

[12] One episode of PBS's documentary series Wide Angle was dedicated to the ECX in 2009 (Wide Angle, 2009). Eleni was interviewed by the Guardian (Everitt, 2012) and Bloomberg (McGregor, 2013) and for the plan to expand the ECX model elsewhere in Africa see (Gabre-Madhin, 2012).

[13] Ethiopia Commodity Exchange, About Us. Last accessed 13 November 2014.

ICT applications had to be developed to connect all nodes of ECX and that a variety of means had to be used both to collect and disseminate information throughout the country (Gabre-Madhin, 2012). Inventories are now updated in real time through electronic receipts sent from warehouses to Addis Ababa. Thanks to the coordination allowed by the electronic system between the clearinghouse and the banks partnering with ECX, sellers can be paid on the day following the trade. Information is transmitted using a combination of technologies that can match the needs of the different actors involved in the trade. The ECX website hosts the most comprehensive set of data, while outdoor electronic ticker boards located in tens of rural towns present essential information to local farmers and traders. Prices are also broadcasted by radio and television. Mobile phones have been later added to the mix. Instant messages are sent to subscribers and a toll-free phone service has been set up for those who prefer to call in. Unsurprisingly, given the low literacy level in Ethiopia, radio broadcasts appear as the most popular channel to get updated information (Tsega, 2010), but subscribers to phone services have been rapidly rising in numbers.[14]

The ECX exemplifies a third – longer term – process that has been shaping this latter phase of the evolution of ICTs in Ethiopia, the EPRDF's determination to embrace new technology when it can act as a modernizing tool; a constructive, rather than disruptive, force that can be channelled to support centralized development processes. The ECX represents the latest instantiation of the developmental technopolitical regime Woredanet and Schoolnet first waved into life, even if it carries a significant difference. While Woredanet and Schoolnet were relatively unique systems that raised little attention beyond their direct targets (mostly administrators, citizens in the peripheries, secondary school students, and teachers) and remained largely invisible to international observers, even before its launch, the ECX has been designed to be highly public and visible to both domestic and global audiences. Framed as an example of how technology can be leveraged to help the poor, the ECX fits squarely in the hyped conception of ICT4D embodied by many initiatives launched in the United States and Europe to use technology to fight poverty, including TED. It perfectly adapted to its narrative, to the dream of technology removing middlemen and empowering the farmers to directly reap the benefits of the most recent innovations.

---

[14] In 2011, 256,000 people had a subscription to the ECX 'push' service sending out updated information by SMS and the tall free number was receiving an average of 61,000 calls per day (Gabre-Madhin, 2012).

And even if comprehensive evaluations of the ECX are missing, its numbers already chart a success story (Gabre-Madhin, 2012).[15]

Most celebratory accounts, however, overlook how the ECX's success is not only the result of an effective application of ICTs to transform value chains, but closely depends on the weight the Ethiopian government put behind the project as it is closely tied into its overarching state-building project. Similarly to Woredanet and Schoolnet, the ECX allowed expanding state control over areas that had previously been difficult to bring within the government remits. Especially in remote areas, trade in commodities used to be regulated by informal institutions, based on kin, reciprocity, and status. As one of the few systematic studies on the impact of the ECX has shown (Meijerink, Bulte, & Alemu, 2014), the ECX has progressively substituted these informal governance mechanisms. This has had the advantage of allowing traders to operate also beyond their traditional networks, but it has also eroded social capital within networks, as individuals are less likely to invest in 'social relations' with their trading partners (Meijerink et al., 2014). The ECX has centralized the power not only to grade a grain of coffee, but also the nodes and links of the complex networks that have grown around its production and sale, formalizing relationships whose quality and worthiness have been previously determined in everyday informal interactions.

## When Technopolitics Shows its Cracks

Taken together, the three processes illustrated above – the securitization of development and its exploitation to pursue internal political ends, the growing role of China in the telecommunications sector, and the pro-active investment in ICTs as a tool for modernization and development – have enabled the sovereign and developmental technopolitical regimes not only to endure and be strengthened, but also to become more visible. They have increasingly acquired the characteristic of a tactic turned strategy. Playing with the artefacts and discourses of the strong, the two regimes have created a space that has been progressively claimed as proper and legitimate and has been used to measure, include, and control foreign forces. The initial oddity of systems like Woredanet and Schoolnet and the anomaly of maintaining a monopoly over telecommunication systems have taken the shape of an alternative model.

---

[15] Figures provided by the ECX indicated that the value of its 'trades has risen by 368 per cent to reach US$1.1 billion in 2010–11. Storage operations have grown from one warehouse in Addis Ababa to 55 warehouses in 17 regional locations (Gabre-Madhin, 2012, p. 18).

As a model becomes more visible, however, so do its cracks and contradictions. Despite having shown an ability to endure what many observers would not have expected (even the WTO had to concede to the Ethiopian government determination to maintain a monopoly over telecommunication), the two systems have also progressively begun to be affected by the self-confidence turned arrogance of those who envisioned and designed them. As explained in the next two sections, this has gradually reduced the ability of the two regimes to adapt to changing circumstances, and the ambition to extend the space owned by the government has encountered resistance that can ultimately threaten the model.

### Forgetting China's Lessons

As mentioned earlier, China has notably distinguished itself from other donors for its 'no strings attached' approach to aid (Brautigam, 2009, 2011; Tan-Mullins et al., 2010). When providing support to other countries, the Chinese government has refrained from asking aid recipients to introduce policy changes or from openly suggesting they should learn from, or adopt, the strategies China has pursued for its own development. This aspect is one of the most discussed in both academic and media circles and one of the most recurrent critiques is that, as a consequence of China's approach and new line of credit, 'rogue states' may now have fewer incentives to improve their human rights and governance records, as they are less dependent on conditional aid from other donors. A less recurrent critique is that this approach may prevent important lessons China has learned from being applied and adapted elsewhere, ultimately reducing China's potential to contribute to development and possibly harming China's own long-term interests. The case of the support provided by China to Ethiopia's telecommunication sector exemplifies this point, especially when it is considered in comparison with how China has operated in other telecommunication markets in Africa.

In its own path towards development, China has demonstrated a remarkable ability to localize foreign technologies and utilize aid and foreign direct investment to strengthen its domestic market and industries (Fu, 2008; Fu, Pietrobelli, & Soete, 2011). The insistence on a no strings attached approach and the tendency to privilege turnkey projects, however, has created few opportunities for knowledge transfer and for some of the strategies China has progressively developed, often through trial and error, to be transferred to its African partners. This determination goes so far that the support to the expanding access to mobile phones and the Internet under monopoly in Ethiopia has gone against the very experience China acquired in expanding its own telecommunication system.

China's transition from a socialist regime that emphasized monopoly to an increasingly liberalized market, under internal and external pressures to reform – the latter particularly tied to the process of accessing the WTO – could have offered important lessons for Ethiopia. China's path towards liberalization was initially marred by failed attempts to open up and by power struggles between different ministries, but eventually led to the creation of the largest market of mobile and Internet users in the world (Gao & Lyytinen, 2000; Mueller, 1997; Zhang, 2002). The Chinese government began this process by first allowing limited forms of competition among companies still closely tied to central power, and then progressively opening to foreign direct investments. Rather than shaking the market with a sector reform that would have potentially led to uncontrollable transformations, smaller changes were introduced, tested, and in some cases reversed (Gao & Lyytinen, 2000).[16] This sequence of trial and error is far from a textbook approach to liberalization, but could have offered an important base from which to develop targeted measures for opening up the Ethiopian telecommunication system, also characterized by a socialist emphasis on monopoly and resistance to the changes a sudden liberalization might lead to. This point was even recognized by Chinese experts working in the telecommunication sector in Africa. As a representative of Huawei remarked:

Ethiopia should open up and allow more competition in the market if it wants to achieve its goals. Ethio-telecom, because of its poor standing, is too afraid that if anybody comes in the market all customers will go to the new company and Ethio-telecom will not survive ... Working with governments that are too centralized is frustrating because they slow things down a lot, as there is not urgency in responding to their competitors.[17]

Keeping the monopoly and entrusting all expansion projects to one company led to the creation of a poorly functioning system with little incentive to improve itself. This ultimately affected the reputation of

[16] China Unicom, the first company to enter in competition with former monopolist China Telecom, was created under a strategy defined as CCF (China-China-Foreign) by which a foreign partner of a venture invested in a joint venture, which, in turn, invested in China Unicom. As Zhang (Zhang, 2002, p. 343) remarks, 'this financing mechanism aimed to bypass the prohibition of foreign investments in telecommunications services and resolve the financing problem at the same time'. After this practice was allowed for five years, it was later sanctioned as 'irregular' by the newly created Ministry of Information and foreign investors had to draw back their investments.

[17] Interview: Representative of Huawei in Ethiopia, Addis Ababa, 09 May 2013.

ETC/Ethio-Telecom and of ZTE itself, to the point that even tightly controlled official government media in Ethiopia, including *Addis Zemen* and *The Ethiopian Herald,* have been allowed to criticize technical glitches and incompetence.[18] The contract with ZTE, because of its magnitude and unique nature – there was no competitive tender for it, in breach of ETC's own policy – came under increased scrutiny. In a 2012 report on corruption in Ethiopia, the World Bank stressed how the commitment to purchase all equipment from one supplier exposed ETC/Ethio-Telecom to the risk of overpaying for what it was getting (Plummer, 2012).[19] The Wall Street Journal warned that the poor service could ultimately harm the ability of Ethio-Telecom to generate revenues and repay its debts (Dalton, 2014). Even those working at ETC/Ethio-Telecom recognized that cooperation with ZTE came as a mixed bag. As a mid-level manager conceded,

There has not been a great transfer of knowledge. The Chinese work alone. Especially at the beginning there were many problems. The Chinese were doing everything on their own. And we realized that this was risky. They had all the privileges over the network. So over time we changed and now we are in control. And we can ask them to help us on specific things. But there is still dependency.[20]

Another ICT specialist, who has been involved in numerous government-led ICT projects in Ethiopia, summarized the relationship between the Chinese and the Ethiopian companies by suggesting that 'they are experimenting on us, but in the end we are getting the services that we need'.[21] He also noted, however, that when checks and balances are absent or too few, this experimentation may leave all parties worse off in the end. Referring to the delays in signing contracts with ZTE and Huawei after they had won the 2011 tender, he argued:

It is about politics. We are a one party system. There are internal issues and power struggles. It is more about power than about finding the right solutions for the problems that we face. Different politicians have different interests. Before with Meles there was a greater sense of urgency. If something needed to be done, it was done. He would step in and give direction. This is lacking now.[22]

---

[18] See, for example, Aregu Balleh in this undated article from *The Ethiopian Herald* www.ethpress.gov.et/herald/index.php/herald/development/4160-a-worthwhile-move-to-comfort-rather-jaded-subscribers. Last accessed 13 November 2014.

[19] Even representatives of ZTE recognized that they had to charge Ethiopia more for its network because of the large loan and long repayment period. See Dalton (2014).

[20] Interview: Manager, Ethio-Telecom, Addis Ababa, 11 January 2012.

[21] Interview: ICT expert, Addis Ababa, 30 December 2011.    [22] Interview: ibid.

Even Huawei publicly expressed frustration for the slow pace at which the Ethiopian government was making decisions (Dalton, 2014). This, however, did not lead the company to challenge the model Ethiopia had envisioned or try to steer it in different directions. Despite some of Huawei's representatives believing that competition would have actually helped the Ethiopian government in reaching its goals, these remained just personal opinions.

As suggested earlier, China's resistance to interfering in domestic affairs may ultimately backfire. Paradoxically, perhaps, Chinese companies have fared better in countries where they have been operating in a regime of tougher competition, as has been the case in China since the early 2000s. In neighbouring Kenya, Huawei has been contracted not just as part of vendor financing packages as in the case of Ethiopia; it has also won contracts with private operators because of its ability to offer good value for money (Gagliardone, 2013; Okuttah, 2012; Wahito, 2012). In Africa's largest telecom market, Nigeria, Huawei signed a US $750 million contract with the Globacom network (Aït-Hatrit, 2013). The greater scrutiny which contracts have been subject to in other countries, including Uganda, Zambia, and Algeria (Dalton, 2014; Malakata, 2012, 2013), has increasingly forced Huawei and ZTE to become more transparent and adhere to higher standards.

In Ethiopia, on the contrary, the lack of pressure to beat competitors and the limited checks and balances may lead to creating a dangerous space where no partner has incentives to improve the system to higher standards, ultimately leaving the citizens whose life the Ethiopian government has affirmed it wants to improve through ICTs, worse off than in other countries where the state has invested much less in new communication technologies.

### Undermining Ethiopia's Future

When the EPRDF first came to power it committed what could retrospectively be identified as the 'original sin' in the contemporary history of communication in Ethiopia: it opened the space for debate but refused to engage with the very debates it had allowed to bloom. As discussed earlier in Chapters 2 and 3, the liberalization of the press in the 1990s created opportunities for individuals who used to work for the previous regimes or belonged to other political movements the EPRDF had excluded from power to attack the new leaders and advance alternative political agendas. Although the criticism took on an increasingly adversarial tone, the EPRDF leadership stuck to its policy, ignoring dissenting voices and labelling them as 'anti-peace' and 'anti-constitution'.[23] This polarization and unwillingness to seeking engagement would have later poisoned also the debates emerging on the Internet, leading 'old politics' to capture 'new media'. For the EPRDF leadership it was an old generation – the one that emerged from the 1960s student movement – that had occupied both traditional and new media. As the debates that occurred around the 2005 elections indicated (See Chapter 5), the goal of some media outlets was indeed not proposing alternative policy choices, but hitting at the heart of the EPRDF's political project, reverting ethnic federalism and dismantling revolutionary democracy. For the EPRDF this 'loud minority', in the words of Bereket Simon, did not deserve to be given a space to articulate its ideas.[24]

This tension and refusal to consider the criticism emerging from oppositional outlets as legitimate, however, has progressively obfuscated the Ethiopian government's ability to appreciate the transformations in the domestic and international media scene and has undermined subsequent attempts to build a terrain where dissenting voices could meet and command reciprocal attention. The arrest of six bloggers belonging to the Zone9 collective, an informal group of young Ethiopians using social media to promote reform in the country, is the latest and one of the most dramatic incarnations of this inability of overcoming earlier mistakes. The Zone9 bloggers, most of them born in the 1980s, had distanced themselves from the forms of criticism that had been championed by the generation of the student movement, and sought to build the political debate on new bases, advocating for change and reform within, rather than beyond, the political framework the EPRDF had created for Ethiopia. Rather than asking for rewriting the constitution, they launched campaigns to #RespectTheConstitution, a hashtag first posted on twitter on 6 December 2013 asking leaders in the Ethiopian government to live up to the principles they had themselves chosen to rebuild their nation, including freedom of expression, sanctioned by Article 29. The Zone9 bloggers charted innovative ways to break the barrier that had prevented government and oppositional forces to talk to one another for decades. They championed the use of Twitter in Ethiopia to engage in conversations with prominent political figures, including with Foreign Minister Tedros Adhanom, the member of the Ethiopian government with the most active presence on social media. And differently from many other Ethiopian bloggers, the 'Zone9ers' preferred Amharic to English for

---

[23] See for example *The Ethiopian Herald*, 'Editorial', 6 June 1991, p. 7.

[24] Interview: Bereket Simon, Advisor to the Prime Minister and former minister of Information, Addis Ababa, 08 January 2012.

their posts, stressing their willingness to target Ethiopian readers and contribute to debates of domestic relevance, rather than seeking consensus among global audiences or the diaspora. And yet, ironically perhaps, when they were arrested on 25 April 2014, they were accused of 'plan [ning] to destabilise the country using social media' and of 'getting financial and intellectual support from a foreign force'.[25]

The accusations, later expanded to acts sanctioned by the Anti-Terrorism Proclamation, starkly resemble those advanced by the Iranian government against the movement that emerged after the 2009 elections in Iran (Morozov, 2012), and highlight a series of paradoxes in which the use of social media for political change has incurred in Ethiopia, but also in other closed regimes.

Firstly, while there is no empirical evidence that ICTs may lead to democratic change in closed societies (Hindman, 2008; Kalathil & Boas, 2001, 2003; Morozov, 2012), the fact that this potential is asserted – mostly by political actors in the West, civil society organizations, and mainstream media – has created incentives for those in power to limit, control, or denigrate their use. It was an email sent by the US State Department asking Twitter to postpone their website's maintenance because the Iranian youth was using the microblogging site to mobilize, which offered the opportunity to the Iranian government to accuse the United States of using new technology to destabilize the country (Morozov, 2012). Assertions about the democratic potential of ICTs in closed societies risk to act as 'self-impairing prophecies', reducing the likelihood ICTs can be actually used to produce democratic change.

A second paradox is that while journalists and bloggers like the 'Zone9ers' have shown deep commitment to use new technologies to act locally, contributing to debates of domestic relevance and disregarding foreign powers and agendas, their arrest may actually disconnect them from their grassroots supporters and push them closer to the international networks on whose behalf they have been accused to operate. The tightly controlled political environment has prevented individuals and groups in Ethiopia from openly displaying solidarity, but the arrest of the Zone9 bloggers has on the contrary sparkled an international social media campaign. Rallied by the hashtag #Free-Zone9Bloggers the campaign led to the first African-wide 'tweetathon' organized in solidarity by Nigerian and Tanzanian bloggers and legal petitions to free the bloggers addressed to the African Union and the

---

[25] These and subsequent accusations brought against the bloggers can be accessed on http://trialtrackerblog.org/press/ (Last accessed 29 September 2014).

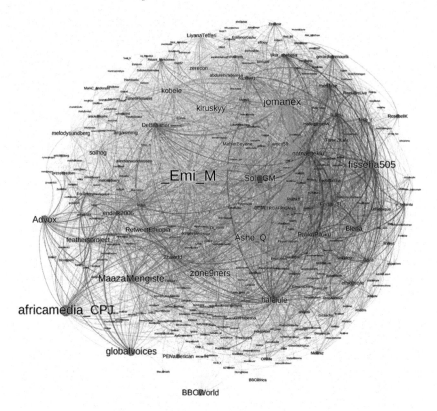

Fig. 7.1 *Relationships within the #FreeZone9Bloggers campaign*

United Nations.[26] The #FreeZone9Bloggers Twitter campaign brought together a diverse range of online communities from different parts of the world. The graph above offers an overview of the different souls of the campaign.[27]

On the left side is the global free speech activist community (formed around users such as @africamedia_CPJ, @globalvoices, @advox, and @feathersproject). On the right side are the Twitter users from the

---

[26] The tweetathon was organized on 14 May 2014 and generated 6,135 tweets per day (1,377 tweets an hour at its most active phase). Information about the tweetathon can be found at http://advocacy.globalvoicesonline.org/2014/05/12/join-the-freezone9bloggers-tweetathon-on-may-14/ (Last accessed 29 September 2014). The petition launched by the Media Law Defence Initiative can be found at www.mediadefence.org/news/mldi-petitions-au-un-free-ethiopian-bloggers (Last accessed 29 September 2014).

[27] The graph has been produced by my colleague Matti Pohjonen, who I am grateful to for his permission to re-publish it here.

diaspora (such as @fisseha505 and @Blena). And caught in the middle, are the Ethiopia-based writers (such as @halelule and @debirhaner).[28] The campaign was unprecedented for Ethiopia, with an average of 300 tweets per day using the #FreeZone9Bloggers hashtag. As some of the organizers themselves recognized, however, while it was instrumental to raising international attention, the campaign had little chances to influence the outcomes of the trial. As Befekadu Hailu, one of the Zone9 bloggers arrested in April, affirmed 'I am not saying the global support we received is not helping us. Your support is our daily bread. It is warming us like sunshine [but] they [the EPRDF] don't want take a risk. Even though they have seen our innocence regarding their fear of inciting violence after the upcoming election; they did not want to take a risk'.[29]

The arrest and trial of the Zone9 bloggers casts a dark shadow on the future of ICTs contributing to political participation in Ethiopia. Despite the bloggers' eventual release following the 2015 elections, the government showed, once again, its inability to entertain competition among different narrations of Ethiopia. In the long run, this may leave the country worse off, short of ideas about how to chart its own future. While the Ethiopian government has been relatively – and controversially – successful in prevailing over its old-time enemies, its unwillingness to engage with those individuals who have chosen to voice their criticism within the framework created by the government itself, leaves little room for reform.

## Conclusion

The Ethiopian government has shown a remarkable ability to exploit the contradictions in the agenda advanced by foreign donors in its own favour. In the ICT as well as in other sectors, it has been able to receive substantial support without necessarily subscribing to external agendas, and in some cases even openly challenging them. The government's rhetoric on the possibilities of creating developmental states in Africa

---

[28] The graph has been obtained by analysing the tweets carrying the hashtag #FreeZone9Bloggers for 30 days following the imprisonment of the Zone9 bloggers. A total of 38,487 tweets produced between 25 April 2014 and 25 May 2014 was processed through network detection algorithms in Gephi software in order to identify the enunciative agents (nodes) and the kinds of relationships around them (edges). The graph uses Degree Centrality (importance of nodes based according to links) and Modularity algorithms (community detection) to better understand the social networks behind the campaign.

[29] The Unsettling Testimony of Befekadu, http://trialtrackerblog.org/2014/08/16/the-unsettling-testimony-of-befekadu/ Last accessed 13 November 2014.

has gained traction and Ethiopia has begun to be hailed as an example even in countries with stronger democratic credentials.[30]

However, the inefficiency that characterizes Ethiopia's telecommunication system despite the enormous resources that have been poured into it, as well as the government's inability to entertain debates even with moderately critical voices indicate the risks of a strategy that has made those who developed it arrogant, and ultimately unable to interpret its vulnerabilities. The Ethiopian government has often argued that it will open up, both economically and politically, when it has established a sufficiently strong ground to ensure both stability and economic progress that will serve the country at large and not just a few individuals and foreign companies. As have years passed, however, this argument has increasingly looked like a promise that will never be fulfilled and, in the absence of some concessions, it appears that the system the EPRDF has created will ultimately lack the confidence it needs to further expand and consolidate.

---

[30] Kenya's Deputy President William Ruto mentioned Ethiopia's growth as an example to follow during in his inaugural speech on 9 April 2013. See http://allafrica.com/view/resource/main/main/id/00061068.html. Last accessed 20 December 2014.

# 8 Conclusion

The history of ICTs in Ethiopia is one of conflict, failure, and experimentation. Ethiopia has lacked human capital, centres of excellence, and local capacity. And yet, it has been able to chart radical new paths in developing its national information society, combining emerging international trends and globally available technologies in support of an ambitious plan of state and nation building.

Tracing the history of Ethiopia also allows mapping the evolutions and contradictions of 'ICT for development' in theory and practice. From a relatively cohesive and internationally recognized set of ideas about the best use of new technologies to achieve development outcomes; to a much more contested agenda, which has been resisted and re-adapted by national actors – especially governments – in order to shape profoundly different national information societies. Just as the Internet, which was initially greeted as a force that could erode national boundaries, has been progressively re-nationalized (Deibert, Palfrey, Rohozinski, & Zittrain, 2012; Mueller, 2010), the ICT for development agenda that was encouraged by the advent of the Internet seems to have fragmented, often silently, with governments and corporate actors appropriating some of its slogans, to achieve more particularistic objectives. It is not clear – yet – what exactly is going to replace it.

Some, like Google's CEO Eric Schmidt, have suggested the world is dividing into two blocs – one controlled by an alliance of democratic states, the other by sophisticated autocracies (Schmidt & Cohen, 2013). The rankings on e-readiness and freedom of the net continue to proliferate and make the news. They also serve the function of re-asserting a higher moral ground for those countries that have taken a greater role in shaping earlier stages of Internet development and diffusion (Clinton, 2010). They are of little use, however, in understanding why and how different information societies are emerging around the globe, what their main features are, and which types of conflicts lead some of these features to prevail over others. They also fail, somehow paradoxically, to take into account new transformations that are happening beyond the state.

Facebook's Free Basics (previously labelled Internet.org), for example, has adopted some of the language that has characterized ICT for development, including the need to 'bring more people online and help improve their lives' (Facebook, 2015), to create a corporate version of a walled Internet that enters into direct competition with the type of nationalized Internets many states have sought to erect and legitimize.

New approaches are needed to understand the evolution of ICTs in different parts of the globe in their own terms, and concepts such as technopolitics and technopolitical regimes can contribute to this endeavour. Rather than normatively assuming that some technologies, actors, and discourses should or will prevail over others, the idea of technopolitics offers a framework to analyse how these elements interact and clash in actuality and what outcomes they produce.

Examining technological assemblages through the notions of technopolitics and technopolitical regimes offers a less benign, but more realistic path to understanding technological evolution in context. As indicated at the beginning of this book, the idea of *regime* emphasizes the contested nature of power, the ideologies guiding the actors who drive them, and conveys the idea of a regimen, a prescription not just about technologies, policies, and practices, but also about broader visions of the sociopolitical order (Hecht, 1998, p. 18). Rather than simply theorizing a process of mutual influence between technology and politics, the framework of technopolitics offers the means to study how, and under what conditions, technology is able to re-shape politics at certain points in time or, on the contrary, it is politics to prevail.

I return to three key cases that exemplify how this type of analysis can work in practice, and conclude with an explanation of how the study of technopolitics and technopolitical regimes can serve to understand more broadly the complex ways in which ICTs, development, and politics interact.

### Ethiopia and Its Technopolitical Conflicts

The developmental and sovereign technopolitical regimes assembled by the Ethiopian government, as well as the alternative regimes that emerged to complement, patch, or oppose them, took shape as a result of progressive negotiations, both within and among different regimes. Throughout the design and implementation phases, heterogeneous entities came into contact with one another, initiating processes of transformation that were influenced by given networks of actors, technologies, and discourses, but were also influential in the redesign of those very networks. The realization of a regime was not simply the enactment of a given plan, but the progressive elaboration of responses to new opportunities and challenges, many of which were not even visible at the time the regime was imagined, but became apparent only when it started taking shape.

*Technological Frustrations and Political Demands*

The development of Schoolnet and Woredanet was neither linear nor smooth. Throughout the process that led to their design and implementation, multiple negotiations took place concurrently at different levels. Policy makers required their visions to be turned into technical features, but their aspirations were often frustrated by the inability of technocrats to fully understand whether and how this could be achieved. As an EICTDA officer recalled, '[T]he Minister of Capacity Building was asking and demanding and we had to come up with solutions to what he was asking. There was frustration after frustration'.[1] The contractors that won the bid to implement the two systems worked to fulfil the requirements published by the government in its Request for Proposal (RFP), but in ways that often took advantage of the ambiguities left unresolved by the lack of expertise within the state apparatus. This was illustrated in a report commissioned by the government to an independent evaluator in 2004 to assess how CISCO and Hughes were complying with their obligations and how some of the problems that had begun to arise could be solved:

In spite of the technology focus of the RFP, there were a number of material omissions and unclear definitions and expectations. These undoubtedly gave vendors significant leeway when interpreting the intention and meaning of the RFP, and it is thus likely that vendor submissions (although compliant to the occasionally unclear technology requirements) would not have been regarded as suitable if the technology specifications and requirements were much more clearly stated. (Daedan, 2004, p. 15)

These conflicts did not emerge exclusively as part of negotiations within and between organizations, but were affecting the interactions among technical artefacts. In order to incorporate the specific discourses on the nation, society, and communication discussed earlier, and which uniquely characterized the state and nation-building project pursued by the EPRDF, important technical features had to be modified, often radically. Artefacts designed to perform a given set of tasks, in specific environments, had to be combined and comply with new tasks in ways

[1] Interview: Civil Servant, EICTDA, Addis Ababa, 13 March 2008.

that had never been tried before. As the evaluation cited above continues, these adaptations could be highly problematic:

There is not only a real risk of the Woredanet service network becoming operationally unsustainable, but also that the project may become financially and economically unsustainable. Some of the issues that have contributed to this reality are: [...] The complexity of the HNS [Hughes Network Systems] DirecWay VSAT solution [the specific technology used to transmit data through the satellite], both in terms of the BoD [Broadband on Demand] requirement, as well as in terms of the complexity of the network design and the number of devices in the field. All this is necessitated by a requirement for a videoconferencing service which cannot ordinarily be accommodated by the HNS DirecWay VSAT platform. (Daedan, 2004, pp. 10–11)

The scenario presented in this assessment, and illustrated at length in Chapter 5, only emerged once the system started taking shape, when different actors and different artefacts started interacting among each other. Woredanet, as well as Schoolnet, did not evolve as the products of a well thought out plan, but acted as a tool 'forcing' those who had imagined them to progressively understand which features and functions they really needed. The Ethiopian leaders had to make difficult decisions, ruling some possibilities out while accepting others, thus gradually demonstrating what mattered most to them.

In this sense the evolution of a technopolitical regime can be considered the core site to study and understand how heterogeneous entities interact, the discourses that emerge as the most influential, the constraints that are the most difficult to overcome, and how power is distributed. On the one hand, the results of combining the discourses, artefacts, and actors could not have been imagined by analysing each element in isolation, or before they came into contact with one another. On the other hand, the nature of the single elements themselves became clearer as they started interacting.

### Repackaging the Internet

The trajectory of the Internet as a service offered by Woredanet exemplifies this process of ongoing reshaping. Despite the resistance towards the globalizing forces exhibited by the EPRDF, access to the Internet was initially requested as one of Woredanet's features. By the time an RFP was formulated by the Ethiopian government in 2002, browsing the web and sending emails had become standard features to be expected in any project employing ICTs to improve the efficiency of a state apparatus and its capacity to communicate with its nodes. When Woredanet started taking shape, however, the centrality of videoconferencing over other services progressively limited the bandwidth available for accessing the Internet. In addition, the architecture that was implemented made data communication within Ethiopia easier, while it strongly limited the possibilities of visiting websites hosted outside the country.[2] At a later stage, when the negative repercussions of the lack of bandwidth for videoconferencing emerged, even the thin share allocated for the Internet was used for videoconferencing sessions, effectively switching off the possibility of browsing the web. As a result, the application that, more than any other, contributed to triggering a new wave of ICT for development campaigns was progressively marginalized in order to respond to other, local, demands. There were no explicit requests to make browsing a webpage through Woredanet difficult. It was only when the Internet started interacting with other services that its relative importance for Ethiopian government became apparent. The redundancy embedded in the system as a result of conflicting global and local influences started decreasing, letting some features prevail over others. Against the assumptions of those who celebrated the transformative power of the new technology, the Internet showed little capacity of holding ground against local demands. Only some of its features survived, such as the transmission protocol it was based upon, generating new assemblages that hardly could have been predicted by analysing their constitutive discourses and artefacts in isolation.

When the developmental technopolitical regime reached greater stability, however, this did not represent the end of the negotiations that led to its realization. The balance between different discourses, artefacts, and actors was only temporary. Benefiting from the eventual implementation of the systems on the ground, the government of Ethiopia initiated new negotiations with some of the key players from a position of greater power. For example, it agreed to allow international organizations, such as the World Bank, using Woredanet to implement some of their projects.[3]

---

[2] For more detail see Chapter 4.
[3] As reported in a World Bank project document, Woredanet was perceived as an opportunity to extend the reach of The World Bank's Global Development Learning Network (GDLN), a system connecting institutions working on development issues all around the world. 'The Bank and Government teams took advantage of the Government's creation of a government network (WoredaNet) as a great opportunity to establish an interface between the Ethiopian Civil Service College' GDLN center and the Government's WoredaNet (a network of more than 600 local government sites, each equipped with video-conference equipment and local area networks). This would allow the College to reach out to about 600 local government facilities through video-conference programs, making it possible for ECSC to move toward reaching the development objectives related to the testing of electronic distance education approaches in the near future' (World Bank, 2007, p. 5)

It incorporated some of the critiques of Schoolnet in projects aimed at patching some of its problematic features. Secondary schools first in the towns of Awassa and Bahir Dar, and then in an increasing number of locations, begun to be connected to the ETC network through fibre optic cables, and equipped with video servers, which allowed teachers and students to engage interactively with the educational content. They were able to replay classes and interrupt the viewing in order to provide more time for the teacher to integrate the recorded material. Similarly, in 2008 the government lifted the taxes on hardware imports, allowing a greater amount of PCs and laptops to be sold in Ethiopia. Finally, as indicated in Chapter 7, in cooperation with the Chinese company ZTE, fibre optic was laid down in most parts of the country, allowing some Woredanet sites to switch from the expensive and unreliable VSAT connection to fibre optic and terrestrial broadband.

This further illustrates how the complexity of these interactions among competing hegemonic discourses, artefacts, and actors needs to be addressed in context. A discourse that is refused at an early stage can be accepted, at least partially, in a subsequent period after a reconfiguration of the balance with other discourses, artefacts, and actors. From a more practical point of view, it raises the important issue of timing and sequencing, and of the necessity for international actors not to push a given agenda on local stakeholders, but rather to understand which part of this agenda are the most compatible with local contexts at any given time. Accepting the evolutionary nature of technopolitical regimes can make a significant difference in planning effective interventions that are aimed at introducing new discourses and artefacts in scenarios that are different from those where they originated.

### Laws and Technology

Historical analyses of technological evolution have illustrated that when technology emerges in critical moments in the history of a country, there is often a disjuncture between declared policy – policy as rhetoric – and enacted policy – policy as practice (Allen & Hecht, 2001, p. 18). In these cases the strategies pursued by politicians are better understood by analysing policies, proclamations, and laws together with the ways in which they are embodied in technological systems, because the two realms of political action may reveal different stories. Weinberger's (2001) analysis of the Swedish military strategy during the Cold War offers a clear example of how technology quietly performed tactics that contradicted Sweden's public stance as a neutral country towards both the American and Soviet-led blocs. Swedish military technology in fact was deployed in such a way that Sweden could offer a base for American fighter jets in case of an attack, but was incompatible with the technology used by Soviet jets (Weinberger, 2001). Technology, rather than politics or diplomacy, displayed where Swedish allegiance actually rested.

Once critical moments are overcome, however, a technology is mastered and an increased understanding of how it relates to other social forces develops, declared policy and enacted policy may become aligned to a greater extent. As explained in Chapter 7, this has been the case in Ethiopia in the latter phase of the evolution of ICTs considered in this book. The Telecom Fraud Proclamation, which was drafted by the Information Network Security Agency (INSA) and was passed in 2012, represented a public and visible instantiation of the core aspects of the sovereign technopolitical regime that the Ethiopian government had initially quietly, and then increasingly assertively, developed. The proclamation introduced severe sanctions for all operators that tried to bypass Ethio-Telecom's monopolistic control over telecommunications and extended the provisions included in the Anti-Terrorism Proclamation to the digital domain. According to the law, '[W]hosoever uses or causes the use of any telecommunications networks or apparatus to disseminate any terrorizing message connected with a crime punishable under the Anti-terrorism Proclamation [...] shall be punishable with rigorous imprisonment from 3 to 8 years' (Government of Ethiopia, 2012).

By the time the law was passed a new course of action hailing security and stability as fundamental ingredients of Ethiopia's path towards development had started to be articulated more widely and visibly (Tronvoll, 2012). While the first deployment of censorship measures was disguised as a technical glitch, only a few years later Meles Zenawi declared his government's right to defend Ethiopia's sovereign information space as part of its developmental strategy. The Telecom Fraud Offences Proclamation expanded the legal foundations of this claim, regardless of the international criticism that it received.

This is another example of the recursive process characterizing the development of technopolitical regimes, their ambition towards reaching closure, defining their space as proper and resisting sanctions from the outside. Technopolitical regimes presuppose a strategic use of technology, they are the space of the powerful, and they concurrently enable power to flow through them.

## The Global Technopolitics of ICTs and Development

One of the most important lessons that can be drawn from the analysis of the Ethiopian case suggests that if researchers are overly concerned with detecting and evaluating normative processes of technological diffusion and appropriation, the complex role ICTs are actually playing in developing countries is likely to be obscured. In this book, by 'plunging' into some of the artefacts that emerged in Ethiopia as a result of the interactions and conflicts between different technologies, actors, and discourses, I sought to offer a concrete indication of how frameworks that consider the political nature of technology can better explain the transformations that are taking place in an increasingly complex and multi-polar world. These changes are not limited to ICTs, nor to Ethiopia alone. The Chinese scholar Wang Shaoguang, for example, has advanced a similar argument when reflecting on how the scholarship in the West has characterized Chinese politics. He argued that,

The analytical framework of authoritarianism from the West is completely unable to capture these deep changes in Chinese politics. In the past several decades, this label has been casually put on China from the late Qing era to the early years of the Republic, the era of warlords, Jiang Jieshi, Mao Zedong, Deng Xiaoping and Jiang Zemin. Chinese politics has made world-shaking changes during this period, but the label put on it made no change at all. (Wang in Leonard, 2008, p. 76)

Numerous leaders in Africa have been challenging the frameworks that are used to assess their progress. Ethiopia's late Prime Minister Meles Zenawi was considered one of the most vocal and articulate critics (de Waal, 2013a). Rwanda's Paul Kagame has often shown impatience towards foreign governments and organizations seeking to impose their templates (McGreal, 2013). China's increasing role in Africa has offered greater room for African leaders, both in open and closed regimes, to consider and experiment with strategies that stand in alternative to those promoted by Western donors (Brautigam, 2009).

If Africa's international politics and development belong to a contested space, the evolution of the Internet, and of ICTs more in general, has displayed remarkable parallels. As Ronald Deibert and his colleagues have convincingly argued, we have rapidly moved from a phase of relative consensus on the benefits the Internet could offer, and when concerns focussed on those cases where access to a free and unfettered Internet was denied (Deibert, Palfrey, Rohozinski, & Zittrain, 2008); to a phase where different conceptions of the Internet are battling in the open, leading to variable outcomes in different contexts (Deibert et al., 2012). The scandals revealing the indiscriminate global surveillance by the US National Security Agency have eroded the moral ground of the most powerful advocate for an open Internet (Greenwald, 2014). The impressive growth of Internet users in China under strict governmental control has offered an example of how the Internet can be deployed to support the political and economic strategies of regimes seeking to use ICTs to support development without losing their grip on power (MacKinnon, 2008; Yang, 2013). The anti-terrorism agenda has legitimated repressive measures in a broad variety of countries, including in advanced democracies (Deibert, Palfrey, Rohozinski, & Zittrain, 2010).

In this scenario, studying the evolution of ICTs through the lenses of technopolitics, which places conflict at its core, offers the opportunity to create a more grounded and realistic understanding of the struggles new technologies are producing and are subjected to. While by no means the study of technopolitics and development is meant to be limited to Africa, the continent offers an exceptional laboratory for analysis. The Internet is still taking shape in many African countries, both at the level of infrastructure and regulation; traditional and emerging global powers (i.e., United States and China) are stepping up their battle for influence on the continent; and initiatives launched by new media companies, such as Facebook's Free Basics (previously Internet.org), have shown a new determination by global corporations to enter in direct competition with governments and traditional telecommunication operators to provide connectivity also to those at the margins.

Analysing how different technopolitical regimes are emerging in Africa can thus offer important insights on the significance and direction of processes of global relevance. China, for example, has been accused to be acting as a force promoting a more authoritarian conception of the Internet globally (Cook, 2013; Farah & Mosher, 2010; Schmidt & Cohen, 2013). A comparative analysis of China's contribution to the ICT sector in different African countries, however, offers a different picture. While its contribution to shaping Ethiopia's information society somehow complies with expectations about an autocratic China seeking partnership with other closed regimes, China's support to the development of ICTs in democratic Ghana and Kenya, points in another direction. The Ghanaian government has received a concessionary loan of $180 million from China's EXIM Bank to develop its ambitious e-government project, aimed at improving service delivery also in the remote areas of the country (ACET, 2009; Gagliardone, Stremlau, & Nkrumah, 2012). In Kenya, Chinese companies and the Chinese government have provided substantial expertise and resources for the development of the country's National Optic Fibre Backbone Infrastructure (NOFBI), brining faster connectivity to both urban and rural areas and allowing a first series of e-government projects to be delivered regionally (Gagliardone, 2015; Okuttah, 2012). In neither case China appears to have advocated for adopting elements of its own model of information society, and there is no indication that Chinese influence has caused a tightening of the information space.

Paradoxically perhaps, when policies leading to greater surveillance and censorship had been considered in those countries, it was the global anti-terrorism agenda supported by the United States, rather than the need to balance between development and stability, to be invoked as a legitimizing factor (Aljazeera, 2014).

The framework of technopolitics can offer the tools to understand how these different, potentially contrasting, discursive, and technological innovations come into contact and interact at different points in time, which actors appropriate them, and leading to what outcomes. The results of studies approaching ICT and development from the perspective of technopolitics may not all contribute to the comforting narrative of a progressive and liberating role of technology that has informed much of this discipline. Technopolitics, however, can encourage a more grounded, and less techno-centric, approach towards understanding how technology and society interact, which is able to factor in, rather than leave aside, the contradictions brought by innovation and technological change.

# Bibliography

Aalen, L. (2002). *Ethnic federalism in a dominant party state: the Ethiopian experience 1991–2000*. Retrieved from http://bora.cmi.no/dspace/handle/10202/186

(2006). Ethnic federalism and self-determination for nationalities in a semi-authoritarian state: the case of Ethiopia. *International Journal on Minority and Group Rights, 13*, 243–261.

Aalen, L., & Tronvoll, K. (2009). The end of democracy? Curtailing political and civil rights in Ethiopia. *Review of African Political Economy, 36*(120), 193–207.

Abbink, J. (2006). Discomfiture of democracy? The 2005 election crisis in Ethiopia and its aftermath. *African Affairs, 105*(419), 173–199.

Abdi, J., & Deane, J. (2008). The Kenyan 2007 elections and their aftermath: the role of media and communication [Electronic Version]. Policy Briefing. Retrieved from http://downloads.bbc.co.uk/worldservice/trust/pdf/kenya_policy_briefing_08.pdf.

Abye, T. (2004). *Parcours d'Éthiopiens en France et aux Etats-Unis: De nouvelles formes de migrations*. Paris: L'Harmattan.

ACET. (2009). *Looking East. China-Africa engagements. Ghana country case study*. Retrieved from http://acetforafrica.org/wp-content/uploads/2010/08/Looking-East-China-Ghana-Case-Study-2010.pdf.

Adam, L. (2007). 2007 Ethiopia telecommunications sector performance review: a supply side analysis of policy outcomes. Retrieved from www.researchICTafrica.net.

Adam, L. (2010). Ethiopia ICT Sector Performance Review 2009/2010 (Policy Paper No. 9). Research ICT Africa.

Aït-Hatrit, S. (2013, June 12). Huawei hits the jackpot in Africa. *Africa Report*. Retrieved from www.theafricareport.com/North-Africa/huawei-hits-the-jackpot-in-africa.html.

Alexandre, L. (1989). *The voice of America: from detente to the Reagan doctrine*. New Jersey: Ablex.

Aljazeera. (2014, December 19). Kenya president signs tough "anti-terror" law. Retrieved from www.aljazeera.com/news/africa/2014/12/kenya-passes-divisive-anti-terror-law-2014121974313523159.html.

Allen, M., & Hecht, G. (2001). *Technologies of power: essays in honor of Thomas Parke Hughes and Agatha Chipley Hughes*. Cambridge: MIT Press.

Anderson, B. (1983). *Imagined communities: reflections on the origin and spread of nationalism*. London: Verso.

Aouragh, M., & Alexander, A. (2011). The Arab Spring, The Egyptian experience: sense and nonsense of the internet revolution. *International Journal of Communication*, 5, 15.

Arthur, C. (2011, February 1). Google and Twitter launch service enabling Egyptians to tweet by phone. *The Guardian*. Retrieved from www.theguardian.com/technology/2011/feb/01/google-twitter-egypt.

Asefa, G. (2006). *SchoolNet Ethiopia. Content and applications development*. Addis Ababa: United Nations Development Programme.

Assefa, T., & Tegegne, G.-E. (2007). *Decentralization in Ethiopia*. Addis Ababa: Forum for Social Studies.

Bach, J.-N. (2011). Abyotawi democracy: neither revolutionary nor democratic, a critical review of EPRDF's conception of revolutionary democracy in post-1991 Ethiopia. *Journal of Eastern African Studies*, 5(4), 641–663.

Bayart, J.-F. (2000). Africa in the world: a history of extraversion. *African Affairs*, 99(395), 217–267.

(2009). *The state in Africa* (2nd Edition). Cambridge: Polity Press.

Benford, R. D., & Snow, D. A. (2000). Framing processes and social movements: An overview and assessment. *Annual Review of Sociology*, 26(1), 611–639.

Beyene, Z., Zerai, A., & Gagliardone, I. (2015). Satellites, plasmas and law: the role of TeleCourt in changing conceptions of justice and authority in Ethiopia. *Stability: International Journal of Security and Development*, 4(1).

Bijker, W. E., Hughes, T. P., & Pinch, T. J. (1987). *The social construction of technological systems: new directions in the sociology and history of technology*. Cambridge: MIT Press.

Blumler, J. G., & Kavanagh, D. (1999). The third age of political communication: Influences and features. *Political Communication*, 16(3), 209–230.

Booth, D., & Golooba-Mutebi, F. (2012). Developmental patrimonialism? The case of Rwanda. *African Affairs*, 111(444), 379–403. http://doi.org/10.1093/afraf/ads026.

Bratton, M. (2013). Briefing: citizens and cell phones in Africa. *African Affairs*, 112(447), 304–319.

Brautigam, D. (2009). *The dragon's gift: the real story of China in Africa*. Oxford: Oxford University Press.

(2011). Aid 'with Chinese characteristics': Chinese foreign aid and development finance meet the OECD-DAC aid regime. *Journal of International Development*, 23(5), 752–764.

Bruzelius, N., Flyvbjerg, B., & Rothengatter, W. (2002). Big decisions, big risks. Improving accountability in mega projects. *Transport Policy*, 9(2), 143–154.

Callon, M. (2009). Foreword. In *The radiance of France*. Cambridge, Mass; London: MIT Press.

Carter Center. (2005). *Final statement on the Carter Center observation of the Ethiopia 2005 national elections*. Atlanta: The Carter Center.

Chanie, P. (2007). Clientelism and Ethiopia's post-1991 decentralisation. *The Journal of Modern African Studies*, 45(03), 355–384.

(2009). Disconnect between public sector management system and decentralization reforms: An empirical analysis of the Ethiopian situation. *Eastern Africa Social Science Research Review*, 25(1), 59–91.

Chan, J. M., & Lee, C.-C. (1984). The journalistic paradigm on civil protests: A case study of Hong Kong. *The News Media in National and International Conflict*, 183–202.

Checkel, J. (1997). *Ideas and international political change. Soviet/Russian behavior and the end of the cold war.* New Haven: Yale University Press.

(2001). Why comply? Social learning and European identity change. *International Organization, 55*(3), 553–588.

Clapham, C. (1990). *Transformation and continuity in revolutionary Ethiopia* (Vol. 61). Cambridge: Cambridge University Press.

(2006). Ethiopian development: the politics of emulation. *Commonwealth & Comparative Politics, 44*(1), 137–150.

Clapham, C. S. (1996). *Africa and the international system: the politics of state survival.* Cambridge: Cambridge University Press.

Clinton, H. (2010, January 21). Remarks on internet freedom [Remarks]. Retrieved March 29, 2013, from www.state.gov/secretary/rm/2010/01/135519.htm.

Collins, R., & Burns, J. (2007). *A history of Sub-Saharan Africa.* Cambridge: Cambridge University Press.

Cook, S. (2013). *The long shadow of Chinese censorship.* Washington, DC: Center for International Media Assistance.

Cossa, G., & Cronjé, J. (2004). Computers for Africa: lessons learnt from introducing computers into schools in Mozambique. *International Journal of Learning Technology 1*(1), 84–99.

Daedan. (2004). *Report to Ministry of Capacity Building and EICTDA. Evaluation of the WoredaNet implementation, the proposed VSAT Bandwidth-on-Demand solution, and proposals to the EICTDA with respect to the creation of ICT operational and support capacity.* Addis Ababa: Ministry of Capacity Building.

Dalton, M. (2014, January 7). Telecom deal by China's ZTE, Huawei in Ethiopia faces criticism. *Wall Street Journal.* Retrieved from http://online.wsj.com/news/articles/SB10001424052702303653004579212092223818288.

Davison, W. (2012, February 3). United Nations rights advocates criticise Ethiopian use of anti-terror law. Retrieved from www.bloomberg.com/news/2012-02-03/united-nations-rights-advocates-criticise-ethiopian-use-of-anti-terror-law.html.

De Certeau, M. (1984). *The practice of everyday life.* Berkeley: University of California Press.

Deibert, R., Palfrey, J., Rohozinski, R., & Zittrain, J. (2008). *Access denied: the practice and policy of global Internet filtering.* Cambridge: MIT Press.

Deibert, R., Palfrey, J., Rohozinski, R., & Zittrain, J. (2010). *Access controlled: the shaping of power, rights, and rule in cyberspace.* Cambridge: MIT Press.

(2012). *Access contested: security, identity, and resistance in Asian cyberspace.* Cambridge: MIT Press.

Deutsch, K. W. (1953). *Nationalism and social communication: An inquiry into the foundations of nationality.* Cambridge: MIT Press.

de Waal, A. (2013a). The theory and practice of Meles Zenawi. *African Affairs, 112*(446), 148–155.

(2013b). The theory and practice of Meles Zenawi: A reply to to René Lefort. *African Affairs*, *112*(448), 471–475.

Di Nunzio, M. (2014). 'Do not cross the red line': The 2010 general elections, dissent, and political mobilization in urban Ethiopia. *African Affairs*, adu029.

EICTDA. (2005). Monitoring and evaluation report on ICT laws enacted and ICT business status in major towns of Ethiopia (2005).

(2008). *Information and Communication Technology Assisted Development Project (ICTAD) mid term evaluation report*. Addis Ababa: Ethiopian ICT Development Agency.

(2009). Monitoring and evaluation report on ICT laws enacted and ICT business status in major towns of Ethiopia (2008).

Elbadawi, I., & Sambanis, N. (2000). Why are there so many civil wars in Africa? Understanding and preventing violent conflict. *Journal of African Economies*, *9*(3), 244–269.

Emmenegger, R., Keno, S., & Hagmann, T. (2011). Decentralization to the household: expansion and limits of state power in rural Oromiya. *Journal of Eastern African Studies*, *5*(4), 733–754. http://doi.org/10.1080/17531055.2011.642530.

Engida, K. A. (2007). *The new fundamental concepts of civic and ethical education for secondary school grade 9 and 10*. Addis Ababa: Aster Nega Publishing Enterprise.

EU-EOM. (2005). *Ethiopia legislative elections 2005 final report; preliminary statement on the election appeal's process, the re-run of elections and the Somali regional elections, 25 August 2005*. Brussels: European Union Election Observer Mission.

Everitt, L. (2012, December 13). How Africa's first commodity exchange revolutionised Ethiopia's economy. *The Guardian*. Retrieved from www.theguardian.com/global-development/2012/dec/13/africa-commodity-exchange-ethiopia-economy.

Facebook. (2015). Free Basics - Documentation - Facebook for Developers. Retrieved January 2, 2016, from https://developers.facebook.com/docs/internet-org.

Farah, D., & Mosher, A. (2010). *Winds from the East. How the People's Republic of China seeks to influence the media in Africa, Latin America and Southeast Asia*. Washington, DC: Center for International Media Assistance.

Featherstone, M. (1990). *Global culture: Nationalism, globalization and modernity* (Vol. 2). London: Sage.

Feenberg, A. (1991). *Critical theory of technology*. Oxford: Oxford University Press.

(1999). *Questioning technology*. London: Routledge.

Finnegan, R. (1970). *Oral literature in Africa*. Oxford: Oxford University Press.

Finnemore, M. (1993). International organizations as teachers of norms. *International Organization*, *47*(4), 565–597.

(1996). *National interests in international society*. Ithaca: Cornell University Press.

Fisher, J. (2015). Writing about Rwanda since the genocide: Knowledge, power and 'truth'. *Journal of Intervention and Statebuilding*, *9*(1), 134–145.

Flyvbjerg, B., Bruzelius, N., & Rothengatter, W. (2003). *Megaprojects and risk: An anatomy of ambition*. Cambridge: Cambridge University Press.

Fortin, J. (2014, July 18). Ethiopia: Bloggers and journalists are charged as terrorists. *The New York Times*. Retrieved from www.nytimes.com/2014/07/19/world/africa/ethiopia-bloggers-and-journalists-are-charged-as-terrorists.html.

Fu, X. (2008). Foreign direct investment, absorptive capacity and regional innovation capabilities: evidence from China. *Oxford Development Studies*, *36*(1), 89–110.

Fu, X., Pietrobelli, C., & Soete, L. (2011). The role of foreign technology and indigenous innovation in the emerging economies: Technological change and catching-up. *World Development*, *39*(7), 1204–1212.

Furzey, J. (1995). A critical examination of the social, economic, technical and policy issues, with respect to the expansion or initiation of information and communications infrastructure in Ethiopia [Electronic Version]. Empowering socio-economic development in Africa utilizing information technology.

Gabre-Madhin, E. (2012). *A market for Abdu: Creating a commodity exchange in Ethiopia*. IFPRI.

Gagliardone, I. (2013). China and the African internet: Perspectives from Kenya and Ethiopia/China y el internet africano: Perspectivas desde Kenia y Etiopía. *Index. Comunicación*, *3*(2), 67–82.

(2014). New media and the developmental state in Ethiopia. *African Affairs*, *113*(451), 279–299.

(2015). Media development with Chinese characteristics. *Global Media Journal*, *4*(2), 1–16.

Gagliardone, I., Repnikova, M., & Stremlau, N. (2010). *China in Africa: a new approach to media development?* Oxford: Oxford University Press.

Gagliardone, I., & Stremlau, N. (2011). *Digital media, conflict and diasporas in the Horn of Africa*. Open Society Foundations. Retrieved from www.alnap.org/pool/files/sf-media-report-handbook-digital-media-conflict-and-diaspora-in-the-horn-of-africa-02-20-2012-final-web.pdf.

Gagliardone, I., Stremlau, N., & Nkrumah, D. (2012). Partner, prototype or persuader? China's renewed media engagement with Ghana. *Communication, Politics & Culture*, *45*(2).

Gamson, W. A., & Modigliani, A. (1989). Media discourse and public opinion on nuclear power: A constructionist approach. *American Journal of Sociology*, 1–37.

Gao, P., & Lyytinen, K. (2000). Transformation of China's telecommunications sector: a macro perspective. *Telecommunications Policy*, *24*(8), 719–730.

Gelaye, G. (1999). Peasant poetics and state discourse in Ethiopia: Amharic oral poetry as a response to the 1996–97 Land Redistribution Policy. *Northeast African Studies*, *6*(1–2), 171–206.

Gellner, E. (2006). *Nations and nationalism*.Ithaca: Cornell University Press.

Giddens, A. (1984). *The constitution of society: outline of the theory of structuration*. Cambridge: Polity Press.

Goffman, E. (1974). *Frame analysis: An essay on the organization of experience*. Cambridge: Harvard University Press.

Goldstone, J. (2001). Toward a fourth generation of revolutionary theory. *Annual Review of Political Science, 4,* 139–187.

Government of Ethiopia. Telecom Fraud Offences Proclamation (2012).

Gramsci, A. (1975). *Quaderni dal carcere.*

Green, D. (2002). Constructivist comparative politics: foundations and framework. In D. Green (Ed.), *Constructivism and comparative politics.* London: M.E. Sharpe.

Greenwald, G. (2014). *No place to hide.* New York; London: Penguin.

Groshek, J. (2009). The democratic effects of the internet, 1994—2003 A Cross-National inquiry of 152 countries. *International Communication Gazette, 71*(3), 115–136.

Gudina, M. (2003). *Ethiopia. Competing ethnic nationalisms and the quest for democracy, 1960–2000.* Addis Ababa: Chamber Printing House.

Haas, P. (1992). Introduction: epistemic communities and internatinal policy coordination. *International Organization, 46*(1), 1–35.

Habtu, A. (2003). Ethnic federalism in Ethiopia: background, present conditions and future prospects. Retrieved from http://scholarworks.wmich.edu/ africancenter_icad_archive/57/?utm_source=scholarworks.wmich.edu% 2Fafricancenter_icad_archive%2F57&utm_medium=PDF&utm_ campaign=PDFCoverPages.

Hafkin, N. (2002). The African information society initiative: A seven-year assessment (1996–2002). *Perspectives on Global Development and Technology, 1*(2), 101–142.

Hagmann, T. (2006). Ethiopian political culture strikes back: A rejoinder to J. Abbink. *African Affairs, 105*(421), 605–612.

Harlow, S., & Johnson, T. J. (2011). The Arab spring: Overthrowing the protest paradigm? How The New York Times, Global Voices and Twitter covered the Egyptian revolution. *International Journal of Communication, 5,* 16.

Haque, S. (2004). *Draft report on rural connectivity planning and related locally sustainable technologies.* Addis Ababa: ICT – Assisted Development Project/ World Bank.

Hecht, G. (1998). *The radiance of France: nuclear power and national identity after World War II.* Cambridge: MIT Press.

(2001). Technology, politics, and national identity in France. In M. Allen & G. Hecht (Eds.), *Technologies of power: essays in honor of Thomas Parke Hughes and Agatha Chipley Hughes.* Cambridge: MIT Press.

Heeks, R. (2002). Information systems and developing countries: failure, success, and local improvisations. *The Information Society, 18,* 101–112.

Hindman, M. (2008). *The myth of digital democracy.* Princeton University Press.

Hintjens, H. (2014). As if There Were Two Rwandas: Polarized Research Agendas on Post-genocide Rwanda. *Conflict, Peace, Security and Development: Theories and Methodologies,* 133–149.

Howard, P. N. (2010). *The digital origins of dictatorship and democracy: Information technology and political Islam: Information technology and political Islam.* Oxford: Oxford University Press.

Hughes, T. P. (1983). *Networks of power: electrification in Western society, 1880–1930.* Baltimore: Johns Hopkins University Press.

(1987). The evolution of large technological systems. In W. E. Bijker, T. P. Hughes, & T. J. Pinch (Eds.), *The social construction of technological systems: new directions in the sociology and history of technology.* Cambridge: MIT Press.

Human Rights Watch. (2013). *Ethiopia: Terrorism Law Decimates Media.* Retrieved from www.hrw.org/news/2013/05/03/ethiopia-terrorism-law-decimates-media.

(2014). "They know everything we do". *Telecom and internet surveillance in Ethiopia.* Retrieved from www.hrw.org/report/2014/03/25/they-know-everything-we-do/telecom-and-internet-surveillance-ethiopia.

Hyden, G., Leslie, M., & Ogundimu, F. F. (2002). *Media and democracy in Africa.* New Brunswick: Transaction Publishers.

Ignatieff, M. (2010). *Blood and belonging: Journeys into the new nationalism.* New York: Random House.

International Commission of Jurists. (2009). *Assessing damage, urging action. Report of the eminent jurists panel on terrorism, counter-terrorism and human rights.* Geneva.

International Crisis Group. (2009). *Ethiopia: Ethnic federalism and its discontents.* International Crisis Group.

ITU. (2015). *Information society statistical profiles: Africa.*

Joergeo, B. (1988). Large technical systems: concepts and issues. In T. P. Hughes & R. Mayntz (Eds.), *The development of large technical systems,* 9–36, Köln: Campus Verlag.

Kagwanja, P., & Southall, R. (2009). Introduction: Kenya–a democracy in retreat? *Journal of Contemporary African Studies, 27*(3), 259–277.

Kahler, M. (2009). *Networked politics: agency, power, and governance.* Ithaca: Cornell University Press.

Kalathil, S., & Boas, T. C. (2001). *The internet and state control in authoritarian regimes: China, Cuba, and the counterrevolution.* Retrieved from www.carnegieendowment.org/publications/index.cfm?fa=view&id=728&prog=zgp.

(2003). *Open networks closed regimes. The impact of the internet on authoritarian rule.* (C. endowment for international peace, Ed.). Washington: Carnegie Endowement for International Peace.

Kassa, W. D. (2014). Examining some of the Raisons D'Etre for the Ethiopian anti-terrorism law. *Mizan Law Review, 7*(1). Retrieved from www.ajol.info/index.php/mlr/article/view/100534.

Kebede, T. (1994). Information technology in Ethiopia. In E. Drew & G. Foster (Eds.), *Information technology in selected countries.* Tokyo: The United Nations University.

Keck, M., & Sikkink, K. (1998). *Activists beyond borders: advocacy networks in international politics.* Ithaca: Cornell University Press.

Keller, E. J., & Smith, L. (2005). Obstacles to implementing territorial decentralization: The first decade of Ethiopian federalism. *Sustainable Peace: Power and Democracy after Civil Wars,* 265–291.

Kelsall, T. (2013). *Business, politics and the state in Africa: challenging the orthodoxies on growth and transformation.* London: Zed Books Ltd.

Klotz, A. (2002). Transnational activism and global transformations: The anti-apartheid and abolitionist experiences. *European Journal of International Relations*, 8(1), 49–76.

Kymlicka, W. (2001). *Politics in the vernacular: Nationalism, multiculturalism, and citizenship*. Oxford: Oxford University Press.

Laclau, E., & Mouffe, C. (1985). *Hegemony and socialist strategy. Towards a radical democratic politics*. London: Verso.

Lane, R. (1992). Political culture residual category or general theory? *Comparative Political Studies*, 25(3), 362–387.

Latour, B. (1992). Where are the missing masses? The sociology of a few mundane artifacts. In W. E. Bijker & J. Law (Eds.), *Shaping technology/ building society. Studies in sociotechnical change*. Cambridge: MIT Press.

(2005). *Reassembling the social: an introduction to Actor-Network-Theory*. Oxford: Oxford University Press.

Law, J., & Hassard, J. (1999). *Actor network theory and after*. Oxford: Blackwell.

Lefort, R. (2013). The theory and practice of Meles Zenawi: A response to Alex de Waal. *African Affairs*, *112*(448), 460–470.

Leftwich, A. (1995). Bringing politics back in: Towards a model of the developmental state. *The Journal of Development Studies*, *31*(3).

Leonard, M. (2008). *What does China think?* London: Fourth Estate.

Levine, D. (1965). *Wax and Gold: Tradition and Innovation in Ethiopian Culture*. Chicago: The University of Chicago Press.

Lyons, T. (2007). Conflict-generated diasporas and transnational politics in Ethiopia. *Conflict, Security & Development*, *7*(4), 529–549.

Maasho, A. (2013, July 10). Ethiopia expected to join WTO in 2015: ministry. *Reuters*. Addis Ababa. Retrieved from www.reuters.com/article/2013/07/10/ us-ethiopia-trade-idUSBRE9690BJ20130710.

MacKinnon, R. (2008). Cyber zone. *Index on Censorship*, *37*(2), 82–89.

(2012). Consent of the networked: The worldwide struggle for internet freedom. *Politique étrangère*, *50*(2).

Malakata, M. (2012, June 12). Algerian ban on ZTE, Huawei highlights corruption controversy. *ComputerWorld Zambia*. Retrieved from http:// news.idg.no/cw/art.cfm?id=D7DAD3FD-F26D-177C–2EF38733406 952D7.

(2013, September 11). Zambian terminates KSh. 18.4 billion ZTE contract over corruption allegations. *CIO*. Retrieved from www.cio.co.ke/news/top-stories/zambian-terminates-ksh.-18.4-billion-zte-contract-over-corruption-allegations.

Mansell, R., & Silverstone, R. (1996). *Communication by design: the politics of information and communication technologies*. Oxford: Oxford University Press.

Markakis, J., & Ayele, N. (1986). *Class and revolution in Ethiopia*. Trenton: Red Sea Press.

McGreal, C. (2013, May 19). Is Kagame Africa's Lincoln or a tyrant exploiting Rwanda's tragic history? *The Guardian*. Retrieved from www.theguardian .com/world/2013/may/19/kagame-africa-rwanda.

McGregor, S. (2013, April 24). Cornell Food Fight Leads Gabre-Madhin to Battle Africa Scarcity. Retrieved from www.bloomberg.com/news/2013-04-24/eleni-battles-famine-with-exchanges-born-from-cornell-food-fight.html.

McKenna, B., & Graham, P. (2000). Technocratic discourse: A primer. *Journal of Technical Writing and Communication, 30*(3), 219–247.

McLeod, D. M., & Hertog, J. K. (1999). Social control, social change and the mass media's role in the regulation of protest groups. *Mass Media, Social Control, and Social Change: A Macrosocial Perspective*, 305–330.

McVety, A. K. (2012). *Enlightened aid: US development as foreign policy in Ethiopia.* Oxford: Oxford University Press.

Meijerink, G., Bulte, E., & Alemu, D. (2014). Formal institutions and social capital in value chains: The case of the Ethiopian Commodity Exchange. *Food Policy, 49*, 1–12.

Mekuria, I. (2008, 17.02.2008). to tech enhancement. *Fortune* Government lifts computer taxes with view, pp. 1–15.

Mengisteab, K. (1997). New approaches to state building in Africa: The case of Ethiopia's ethnic-based federalism. *African Studies Review, 40*(3), 111–132.

Menkhaus, K. (2007). The crisis in Somalia: Tragedy in five acts. *African Affairs, 106*(424), 357–390.

(2013). *Somalia: State collapse and the threat of terrorism.* Routledge.

Mkandawire, T. (2001). Thinking about developmental states in Africa. *Cambridge Journal of Economics, 25*(3), 289–313.

Mohan, G. (2013). Beyond the enclave: Towards a critical political economy of China and Africa. *Development and Change, 44*(6), 1255–1272.

Morozov, E. (2012). *The net delusion: The dark side of internet freedom.* PublicAffairs. Retrieved from http://books.google.co.uk/books?hl=en&lr=& id=ctwEIggfIDEC&oi=fnd&pg=PR9&dq=The+net+delusion+:+the+ dark+side+of+internet+freedom&ots=NND2ca167Q&sig=1wYbZBpUWz 7I0Yiot7xdRTnp238.

Mueller, M. (1997). *China in the information age: Telecommunications and the dilemmas of reform.* Greenwood Publishing Group.

(2010). *Network and states. The global politics of internet governance.* Cambridge; London: MIT Press.

Negroponte, N. (1995). *Being Digital.* New York: Vintage Books.

Nelson, M. (1997). *War of the black heavens: the battles of Western broadcasting in the cold war.* Syracuse: Syracuse University Press.

Nisbet, E. C., Stoycheff, E., & Pearce, K. E. (2012). Internet use and democratic demands: A multinational, multilevel model of internet use and citizen attitudes about democracy. *Journal of Communication, 62*(2), 249–265. http://doi.org/10.1111/j.1460-2466.2012.01627.x.

Nkurunziza, J. D. (2008). Civil war and post-conflict reconstruction in Africa. In United Nations Conference on Trade and Development, Geneva.

Nulens, G., & Van Audenhove, L. (1999). An information society in Africa? An analysis of the information society policy ot the World Bank, ITU and ECA. *Gazette, 61*(6), 451–471.

Nyamnjoh, F. (2005). *Africa's media, democracy and the politics of belonging.* London: Zed books.

Okuttah. (2012, December 6). Safaricom loosens China's grip on local contracts with Sh14bn tender. Business Daily. Nairobi, Kenya. Retrieved from www.businessdailyafrica.com/Corporate-News/Safaricom-loosens-China-grip-on-local-contracts/-/539550/1638364/-/11xotu6z/-/index.html.

Opennet Initiative. (2007). Ethiopia. Retrieved from http://opennet.net/sites/ opennet.net/files/ethiopia.pdf.

Orlikowski, W. J. (1992). The duality of technology: Rethinking the concept of technology in organizations. *Organization Science, 3*(3), 398–427.

Ottaway, M. (2003). *Democracy challenged: the rise of semi-authoritarianism.* Washington: Carnegie Endowment for International Peace.

Pausewang, S., Tronvoll, K., & Aalen, L. (2002). *Ethiopia since the Derg: a decade of democratic pretension and performance.* London: Zed.

Pinch, T. J., Ashmore, M., & Mulkay, M. (1992). Technology, testing, text: clinical budgeting in the UK National Health Service. In W. E. Bijker & J. Law (Eds.), *Shaping technology/building society. Studies in sociotechnical change.* Cambridge: MIT Press.

Pippin, R. B. (1995). On the notion of technology as ideology. In A. Feenberg & A. Hannay (Eds.), *Technology and the politics of knowledge,* 43–61.

Plummer, J. (2012). *Diagnosing corruption in Ethiopia. Perceptions, realities, and the way forward for key sectors.* Washington: World Bank. Retrieved from http://econ.worldbank.org/external/default/main?pagePK=64165259& theSitePK=469372&piPK=64165421&menuPK=64166093&entityID= 000386194_20120615035122.

Pool, I. de S. (1983). *Technologies of freedom.* Cambridge: Belknap Press.

Risse-Kappen, T. (1994). Ideas do not float freely: transnational coalitions, domestic structures, and the end of the cold war. *International Organization, 48*(2), 185–214.

    (1995). *Bringing transnational relations back in: non-state actors, domestic structures and international institutions.* Cambridge: Cambridge University Press.

Samara, N. (1999). Paper presented at the African Development Forum, Addis Ababa.

Schmidt, E., & Cohen, J. (2013). *The new digital age: Reshaping the future of people, nations and business.* London: Hachette.

Schumpeter, J. (1954). *The theory of economic development.* Cambridge: Harvard University Press.

Scott, J. C. (1998). *Seeing like a state: How certain schemes to improve the human condition have failed.* Yale University Press.

Segers, K., Dessein, J., Hagberg, S., Develtere, P., Haile, M., & Deckers, J. (2009). Be like bees: the politics of mobilizing farmers for development in Tigray, Ethiopia. *African Affairs, 108*(430), 91–109.

Shade, L., & Dechief, D. (2004). Canada's Schoolnet. Wiring up schools? In A. Carr- Chellman (Ed.), *Global perspectives on e-learning: rhetoric and reality.* Thousand Oaks: Sage.

Sheckler, A. (1999). Evidence of things unseen: secrets revealed at the Voice of America [Electronic Version]. Retrieved from www.ethioembassy.org.uk/ articles/articles/may-99/Annette%20.C%20Sheckler.htm.

Skjerdal, T. S. (2011). Journalists or activists? Self-identity in the Ethiopian diaspora online community. *Journalism, 12*(6), 727–744.

Smith, A. D. (1995). *Nations and nationalism in a global era* (Vol. 83). Cambridge: Polity Press.

Smith, A. D., & Smith, A. (2003). *Nationalism and modernism*. London: Routledge.

Snow, D. A., & Benford, R. D. (1992). Master frames and cycles of protest. *Frontiers in social movement theory*, 133–155.

Snow, D. A., Rochford Jr, E. B., Worden, S. K., & Benford, R. D. (1986). Frame alignment processes, micromobilization, and movement participation. *American Sociological Review*, 464–481.

Sparks, C. (2007). *Globalization, development and the mass media*. London: Sage.

Strang, D., & Meyer, J. (1993). Institutional conditions for diffusion. *Theory and Society*, *22*, 487–511.

Stremlau, N. (2011). The press and the political restructuring of Ethiopia. *Journal of Eastern African Studies*, *5*(4), 716–732.

(2012). Somalia: Media law in the absence of a state. *International Journal of Media & Cultural Politics*, *8*(2–3), 2–3.

Stremlau, N., Blanchard, M., & Abdi Gabobe, Y. (2009). *The role of the media in the upcoming Somaliland elections: Lessons from Kenya*. London: Stanhope centre.

Suchman, L. (1994). Do categories have politics? *Computer Supported Cooperative Work (CSCW)*, *2*(3), 177–190.

Tadesse, M., & Young, J. (2003). TPLF: reform or decline? *Review of African Political Economy*, *30*(97), 389–403.

Tan-Mullins, M., Mohan, G., & Power, M. (2010). Redefining 'aid' in the China–Africa context. *Development and Change*, *41*(5), 857–881.

Tareke, G. (1991). *Ethiopia, power and protest: peasant revolts in the twentieth century*. Cambridge: Cambridge University Press.

Tegegne, G.-E. (1998). The influences of decentralization on some aspects of local and regional development planning in Ethiopia. *Eastern Africa Social Science Research Review*, *14*(1), 33–63.

Terrazas, A. M. (2007). Beyond regional circularity: the emergence of an Ethiopian Diaspora [Electronic Version]. Migration information source. Retrieved from www.migrationinformation.org/Profiles/display.cfm?ID=604.

Teshome, W. (2009). A critical look into the Ethiopian elections. *International Journal of Social Sciences*, *4*(2), 80–95.

Thompson, M. (2004). ICT, poverty and developmental discourse: a critical analysis. *The Electronic Journal on Information Systems in Developing Countries*, *20*(4), 1–25.

Toffler, A. (1980). *The third wave*. London: Collins.

Tronvoll, K. (2000). *Ethiopia: a new start? Minority Rights Group London*. Retrieved from www.refworld.org/pdfid/469cbf930.pdf.

(2012). The "new" Ethiopia: Changing discourses of democracy. In K. Tronvoll & T. Hagmann (Eds.), *Contested power in Ethiopia. Traditional autorities and multi-party elections*, 269–288. Leiden: Brill.

Truman, H. (1949). Inaugural address. Washington: Harry S. Truman Library and Museum.

Tsega, T. (2010). Ethiopian Commodity Exchange (ECX)-Connecting farmers to the market.

Tufekci, Z., & Wilson, C. (2012). Social media and the decision to participate in political protest: Observations from Tahrir Square. *Journal of Communication, 62*(2), 363–379.

Turton, D. (2006). *Ethnic federalism. The Ethiopian experience in a comparative perspective.* Oxford: James Currey.

UNDP. (2015). *MDG Report 2015. Assessing progress in Africa toward the millenium development goals.* New York.

UN Security Council. Resolution 1373 (2001).

Vaughan, S. (2003). *Ethnicity and power in Ethiopia.* Edinburgh: University of Edinburgh.

(2006). Responses to ethnic federalism in Ethiopia's Southern region. In D. Turton (Ed.), *Ethnic federalism. The Ethiopian experience in a comparative perspective.* Oxford: James Currey.

(2011). Revolutionary democratic state-building: party, state and people in the EPRDF's Ethiopia. *Journal of Eastern African Studies, 5*(4), 619–640.

Vaughan, S., & Gebremichael, M. (2011). Rethinking business and politics in Ethiopia. *Africa Power and Politics, UK Aid, Irish Aid.*

Vaughan, S., & Tronvoll, K. (2003). The culture of power in contemporary Ethiopian political life. Retrieved April 9, 2012, from www.sida.org.

von Bogdandy, A., Häußler, S., Hanschmann, F., & Utz, R. (2005). State-building, nation-building, and constitutional politics in post-conflict situations: conceptual clarifications and an appraisal of different approaches. In A. von Bogdandy & R. Wolfrum (Eds.), *Max Planck Yearbook of United Nations Law* (Vol. 9, pp. 579–613).

Wahito, M. (2012, June 28). Kenya: China to fund Kenya's fibre optic project. *Capital FM.* Nairobi, Kenya. Retrieved from http://allafrica.com/stories/201206290024.html.

Weinberger, H. (2001). The neutrality flagpole: Swedish neutrality policy and technological alliances, 1945–1970. In M. Allen & G. Hecht (Eds.), *Technologies of power: essays in honor of Thomas Parke Hughes and Agatha Chipley Hughes.* Cambridge: MIT Press.

Wide Angle. (2009). *The Market Maker.* Retrieved from www.pbs.org/wnet/wideangle/episodes/the-market-maker/introduction/5000/.

Wilson, C., & Dunn, A. (2011). Digital media in the Egyptian revolution: Descriptive analysis from the Tahrir data sets. *International Journal of Communication, 5,* 1248–1272.

Winner, L. (1980). Do artifacts have politics? *Dedalus, 109*(1), 121–136.

World Bank. (2004a). Project appraisal document on a proposed credit in the amount of SDR 17.1 million (US$ 25 million equivalent) to the Federal Democratic Republic of Ethiopia for a Information and Communication Technology Assisted Development Project.

(2004b). Project appraisal document on a proposed credit in the amount of SDR 66.9 million (US$ 100 million equivalent) to the Federal Democratic Republic of Ethiopia for a Public Sector Capacity Building Program support project.

(2007). Implementation completion and result report on a credit in the amount of US $ .55 million to the government of the Democratic Republic of Ethiopia for a distance learning LIL project. Addis Ababa: World Bank.

Wu, T. (2010). *The Master Switch. The rise and fall of information empires.* London: Atlantic Books.

Yang, G. (2013). *The power of the internet in China: Citizen activism online.* Columbia University Press.

Young, J. (1997). *Peasant revolution in Ethiopia. The Tigray People's Liberation Front, 1975–1991.* Cambridge: Cambridge University Press.

Zenawi, M. (1999). Statement by H.E. Ato Meles Zenawi, Prime Minister of the Federal Democratic Republic of Ethiopia on African Challenges and Visions for Development. In *African Development Forum.*

(2012). State and markets: neoliberal limitations and the case for a developmental state. In A. Noman, K. Botchwey, H. Stein, & J. Stiglitz (Eds.), *Good growth and governance in Africa: Rethinking development strategies.* Oxford: Oxford University Press.

Zewde, B. (2002). *Pioneers of change in Ethiopia. The reformist intellectuals of the early twentieth century.* Addis Ababa: Addis Ababa University Press.

Zhang, B. (2002). Understanding China's telecommunications policymaking and reforms: a tale of transition toward liberalization. *Telematics and Informatics, 19*(4), 331–349.

Zhao, Y. (2008). *Communication in China: Political economy, power, and conflict.* Rowman & Littlefield Publishers.

# Index